# The Making of the 20th Century

*This series of specially commissioned titles focuses attention on significant and often controversial events and themes of world history in the present century. Each book provides sufficient narrative and explanation for the newcomer to the subject while offering, for more advanced study, detailed source-references and bibliographies, together with interpretation and reassessment in the light of recent scholarship.*

*In the choice of subjects there is a balance between breadth in some spheres and detail in others; between the essentially political and matters economic or social. The series cannot be a comprehensive account of everything that has happened in the twentieth century, but it provides a guide to recent research and explains something of the times of extraordinary change and complexity in which we live. It is directed in the main to students of contemporary history and international relations, but includes titles which are of direct relevance to courses in economics, sociology, politics and geography.*

# The Making of the 20th Century

*Series Editor:* GEOFFREY WARNER

Already published

Further titles are in preparation

# Russia and the Origins of the First World War

*D. C. B. Lieven*

St Martin's Press  New York

All rights reserved. For information, write:
St. Martin's Press, Inc., 175 Fifth Avenue, New York, NY 10010
Printed in Hong Kong
First published in the United States of America in 1983
Reprinted 1984, 1987, 1989

ISBN 0–312–69608–6
ISBN 0–312–69611–6 (Pbk)

Library of Congress Cataloging in Publication Data

Lieven, D.C.B.
  Russia and the origins of the First World War.

  (Making of the twentieth century)
  Bibliography: p.
  Includes index.
  I. Soviet Union – History – 1904 – 1914.   2. World
War, 1914 – 1918 – Causes. I. Title. II. Series
DK262.L48 1983   947.08'3   82-24095
ISBN 0–312–69608–6 (Hardcover)
0–312–69611–6 (Paperback)

# Contents

For
my uncle Leonid Pavlovich

# Preface

In preparing to write this book I had the good fortune to be allowed to work in a number of archives and libraries. My thanks are owed to the staffs of: the Public Record Office in London, the Ministry of Defence of the French Republic, the Bakhmetev Archive of Columbia University, the Central State Historical Archive in Leningrad, the Archive of the October Revolution and the Lenin Library in Moscow, the Bibliothèque de Documentation International Contemporaine at Nanterre, the British Library and the libraries of the LSE and School of Slavonic Studies in London. Kay Riley read material from the Austrian archives for me and my uncle, L. P. Lieven, helped me with other German-language material.

Mr Norman Stone, Mr P.B. Reddaway and Mrs Judith Head read the text for me, as did Professor G. Warner. Mrs Marion Osborne and Mrs Carol Bartlett typed for me and my family acted collectively as proofreaders-in-chief. Ingaret Eden made final corrections.

N.B. Dates in the Julian Calendar are indicated by [O.S.]. All other dates are in the Gregorian calendar (i.e. that used by most of Europe but not by Russia before 1917).

D. C. B. LIEVEN

# Introduction

THE immediate reason for Russia's involvement in the First World War lay in the decisions taken by statesmen and generals during July 1914. No history of the origins of the war could therefore fail to pay considerable attention to the July crisis. The crisis did not, however, exist in a void. On the contrary, it was the last in a series of diplomatic conflicts which in the decade prior to 1914 had raised international tensions almost to breaking point. These conflicts cannot, however, be understood without some reference to the changing pattern of relations between the Great Powers since 1870. Thus any study of the origins of the First World War cannot ignore European diplomatic history in the period 1871–1914 and, in particular, in the decade prior to Armageddon. By using both archival sources and published Soviet material inaccessible to all but Russian-speaking specialists I hope to add something to our understanding even of this well-trodden field.

Chapters 2 and 5, together with a small section of Chapter 1, are devoted to what one might describe as the traditional field of the diplomatic origins of the war looked at from a Russian viewpoint. They focus on Russian foreign policy, only mentioning military or economic affairs when these directly impinged on Russia's handling of diplomatic problems or crises. These chapters tackle their theme chronologically.

About two-thirds of this book travels outside the realm of traditional diplomatic history. One reason why it can afford to do so is that the English-speaking reader can already find a number of excellent works which will provide him with detailed descriptions of the diplomatic crises of 1904–14. Nevertheless, the main reason for devoting so much space to a study of themes outside the usual range of diplomatic history is that these elements often underlay and explained the manoeuvrings of the European chancelleries. This is to some extent self-evident. Thus frequent use of terms such as 'Great Power Politics' or the 'Balance of Power' suggests that the key to pre-war international relations was power. This meant both economic and military potential, together with the willingness to use them in the pursuit of governmental policies. To a great extent a state's power both defined the role it sought to play in international affairs and determined its ability to sustain this role. For a study of Russia and the origins of the First World War it is therefore crucial to establish where Russia stood in the hierarchy of Great Powers, how able her armed forces were to back diplomatic policies by force, and to what extent the Empire's rivals did or did not respect and fear Russian power. In addition, European relations in the period 1870–1914 were in part merely the product of shifts in the power of the various major states. Between 1815 and 1870 the four leading continental states, Russia, Prussia, Austria and France, were of roughly similar weight. Britain, which the industrial revolution had raised to a position of pre-eminence in Europe, used its might to assert its sovereignty over the seas and sought to maintain a rough balance between the continental nations. The unification and economic development of Germany unbalanced the continental equilibrium. It led inevitably to the growth of German interests and ambitions in areas previously regarded as sacrosanct by other powers. It also caused these powers to look to a defence of their security and interests against their over-mighty and potentially dangerous rival. It would only be partly wrong to write the history of international relations before 1914 as if it were the product not of human will but of the movement of impersonal factors of power.

Geography and geopolitics also help explain states' policies. Britain's role in international affairs was, for instance, conditioned by the fact that she was an island whose wealth and security depended on maritime communications. This not merely influenced the British government's conceptions about national interests, it also created traditional popular instincts about Britain's role in world affairs which exercised real constraints on British foreign policy. Unlike Britain, Russia was a continental power, unprotected by a moat or a navy from the immediate consequences of shifts in the European balance of power. She was a vast multi-national empire faced after 1905 with Great Power rivals on her western and eastern frontiers and fearful of anti-Russian movements among the minority races which she had in the past conquered. The greatest threat to vital Russian interests would lie in an invasion by land from the west into European Russia and the Ukraine, where most of the Empire's population and economic wealth was concentrated. Another key Russian interest was the defence of the trade routes out of the Black Sea on which the

Empire's economic development increasingly depended. Geography and geopolitics help explain not just Russian views about national interests but also European conceptions about international relations. The idea of the balance of power, which as we shall see played a crucial role in the Russian government's thinking about international relations, was a peculiar product of European history in the previous two centuries. In this period a number of states of roughly equal power had emerged and a consensus had to some extent developed among them that they all had an interest in not allowing any one of their number to become over-mighty. European diplomats were thus deeply influenced by a notion which had for instance, little relevance to the Americas or South-East Asia, where traditionally a single power exercised a dominant influence over vast areas of the globe.

If economic, military, geographical and geopolitical factors are of vital interest to anyone studying the origins of the First World War, so too are the societies and political systems of the European Powers. States' goals and the manner in which they were pursued were greatly influenced by the nature of the group or groups which held political power within them. Though none of Europe's rulers before 1914 were pacifists, some were distinctly less apt to glorify the use of force in the pursuit of a state's goals than were others. Moreover, within the various ruling groups there were often great differences of opinion as regards both national interests and the best means to pursue them. Finally, though all Europe's rulers were to some extent constrained by the views of at least certain sections of their societies, both the degree to which this was true and the precise nature of these constraints differed from one state to another. One aim of this book is to provide a Russian perspective on the all-European problem of the relationship of external and internal policy. Another aim is to see to what extent the Russian system of government influenced the goals and methods of the state's foreign policy in the decade prior to 1914.

If one studies Russian views on relations with Germany in the pre-war years two dominant tendencies emerge. One stressed that the best way to keep the Germans peaceful and reasonable was to deter them from aggression by a display of Russian power and Anglo-Franco-Russian unity. The other believed that the growth of German power made inevitable a challenge to one or other of Europe's major states, which had between them come to control much of the earth's territory and resources. They urged that Russian efforts should be directed at turning Germany westwards towards a struggle with

Britain for maritime supremacy. Russian foreign policy combined elements of both tendencies, though by 1914 deterrence was very much to the fore. Deterrence, however, failed. France and Russia were not strong enough to deter Berlin from war since the Germans could reasonably hope to defeat both of them. At the same time, the Franco-Russian policy of deterrence, embodied in huge armaments programmes, did help persuade the Germans that unless they struck quickly their ambitions might in a few years' time be unrealisable given their enemies' potential might. If the Franco-Russian policy of deterrence failed, so too, however, did the pursuit of semi-appeasement of the British Foreign Secretary, Edward Grey. This merely convinced Berlin that London might stand aside in a continental conflict, increased the uncertainty of international relations and encouraged the Germans to adopt risky policies.

Chapter 1 of this book sets out Russia's position in the hierarchy of the Great Powers and illustrates the constraints which geography and economics, together with the nature and ideology of the Old Régime, put on Russian foreign policy. Chapter 2 looks at Russia's part in the diplomatic history of the First World War's origins. Chapter 3 establishes which individuals and groups played important roles in Russian foreign and defence policy. Chapter 4 studies the views and nature of these key actors. Here, for instance, one will find the arguments of the two 'tendencies' referred to in the previous paragraph. The sections on P. N. Durnovo and Prince G. N. Trubetskoy, who put the case for 'deflecting' or deterring Germany with the greatest clarity and force, go to the root of Russia's dilemma in the pre-war years and are the most important pages in this book. Finally, Chapter 5 deals with the crisis of July 1914 and the outbreak of war.

# 1 Russia as a Great Power

THE birth, life and death of the Russian Empire were all linked closely to its struggle to acquire and retain the status of a European Great Power. Tsar Peter the Great's proclamation as Emperor of all the Russias on 22 October 1721 (O.S.), the first birthday of the Empire, followed three weeks after the signing of the Treaty of Nystadt which had established Russia as a European power by confirming her replacement of Sweden as the dominant force in the Eastern Baltic. Peter's successors strained every muscle to maintain this position and it is significant that the most fundamental political changes carried out in Russia between Peter's death and 1905, the so-called Great Reforms of Alexander II, followed directly after Russia's humiliation in the Crimean War and were designed above all else to secure her position amongst the leading European powers by modernising the social, economic and administrative structure of the Empire. When on the outbreak of the First World War Nicholas II's manifesto to his people spoke of the overriding need to 'protect the honour, dignity and safety of Russia and its position among the Great Powers' it was therefore asserting fundamental and traditional principles of the Imperial state.[1]

As one would expect, these traditions were reflected in the values and attitudes of those who governed Russia in the reign of Nicholas II. The Russian nobility had always been above all a service class, ultimately deriving not merely its lands and fortunes but also its status and its self-esteem from service to the autocratic state. At least until 1861 this service had almost always been military and the knowledge that the eighteenth century alliance between autocracy and gentry, best embodied in the service of noble officers in the armies of the autocratic state, had by 1814 raised a hitherto weak and little respected country to a position of pre-eminence in continental Europe was a cause of lasting pride to the Russian nobility. The great territorial gains of the eighteenth century, which laid the basis for Russia's future political and military might were of course in themselves a cause for self-congratulation but their impact was all the greater because they gave Russia for the first time the right to enter that club of European nations which was for more than two centuries regarded as having a monopoly of all that was most progressive and civilised on earth. Few members of the Empire's nineteenth or early twentieth century ruling class would have denied A.P. Izvol'sky's comment that to 'decline to the level of a second class power' and 'become an Asiatic state... would be a major catastrophe for Russia'.[2]

To understand the mentality of Russia's ruling élite one needs a certain sense of its members' background and upbringings. The most important factor to bear in mind here is the extent to which this élite was still dominated in Nicholas II's reign by members of old gentry families and permeated by a military ethos. The best cross-section of this governing élite is provided by the 215 men who were appointed to the State Council, Imperial Russia's most prestigious political institution, between 1894 and 1914.[3] The Council itself before 1905 acted as the highest advisory body to the monarch on questions of legislation, after that date being transformed into the upper house of the new bicameral legislature, but for our purposes the key point to remember is that its appointed members included all the Empire's leading statesmen, together with its most senior officials, diplomats, military officers and judges; in addition, a small number of conservative professors and leading spokesmen for the landowning gentry were appointed to the Council between 1894 and 1914. Eighty-one of these 215 men, including many top civil officials, had been educated at military schools: moreover, as we shall see, the élite civilian boarding schools which were attended by a large proportion of the other 134 did not lag far behind the cadet corps in their celebration of the Russian state's past glories. One out of every three of the 215 members of the Council belonged to families already noble before 1600, while most of the other two-thirds of the group came from well-established landowning or service backgrounds. Not just metaphorically but also literally these men were the heirs of Suvorov and Kutuzov, (Russia's two leading military heroes of the late eighteenth and early nineteenth centuries) nine members of the Council actually being descended in the direct male line from generals prominent in the wars against revolutionary and Napoleonic France. Such an élite was bound to be acutely conscious of its traditions and disinclined to play second fiddle on the world stage. A.N. Naumov, for instance, was an intelligent, politically experienced and well-balanced member of the Council, yet, watching the centenary parade on the battlefield at Borodino, he could not restrain himself from demanding of the Foreign Minister S.D. Sazonov, whether such a spectacle of power and pride was compatible with the restrained, even in his view pusillanimous, role adopted by Russian diplomacy in the Balkan crisis of 1912.[4] If Naumov here spoke for the ruling élite's heart, the comment of the former Minister of the Interior, P.N. Durnovo, that 'in my eyes all so-called cultural needs retire into second place before the urgent necessities on which depend the very existence of Russia as a great power' could well be taken as the motto of the régime which governed Imperial Russia.[5]

By 1914 maintaining Russia's position as a leading European power was, however, more difficult than it had been at most times during the previous two centuries. This was not, of course, because the basic rules of international relations had changed over this period. In early twentieth century Europe as before no international body and no dominant superpower existed which could effectively have limited the freedom of action of the continent's sovereign states. As a result, each of these states was fated, to a greater or lesser extent, to live in a permanent situation of nervous insecurity about the aggressive intentions and military potential of its neighbours. The only reliable constraints on a state's aggressive plans were its rulers' sense of their own self-interest and the fear and jealousy aroused in all the remaining states by any act of successful aggression committed by one of them. If all states, and especially the smaller ones, looked to this balance of power, fear and jealousy as a safeguard of their own independence it was nevertheless true that for a Great Power formidable armaments were a necessity. These alone would give a state the right to be regarded as one of the arbiters of Europe's fate and would provide it with an automatic seat in those occasional congresses and conferences between representatives of the continent's most powerful countries which were the nearest pre-war Europe came to having an international government.

If the rules of international relations had not changed much in the 200 year life of the Russian Empire nor, to a remarkable extent, had membership of the Great Power Club. France, Prussia/Germany, Austria, Russia and Britain remained the leading actors in Europe as they had been in 1763. Italy had replaced Spain as an honorary Great Power. It is of course true that the growth of the world's economy and communications network had resulted in the

expansion of the European powers overseas but in general this merely meant that the old struggle between the European states to control
areas and resources had now been extended to a wider geographical
area. Of the non-European countries only the United States and
Japan had really begun to force on the European powers an awareness of their existence and their interests. By 1914 Russia was conscious of the potential power of the United States in the Pacific but
the United States' lack of either means or will to back its policies by
force meant that for the moment the Russians paid much less attention to American plans for the future of the Asian continent than they
did to those of Japan. After the latter's dramatic victory over Russia
in the war of 1904–5 the Japanese were a force with which Petersburg
of course had to reckon very seriously.

Even so, it was the shift in the balance of power within Europe
which represented the major threat to Russian interests. The pre-
eminent position among the continental powers which Russia held
in 1815 had in the course of the following century been undermined
by the late development of the Russian economy in relation to
those of the central and western European states. Russia's relative
economic backwardness, which had crippled her war effort in
1854–5, became even more dangerous when there occurred in 1871
what Peter Saburov described as 'the most important event of the
second half of the last century... the transformation of Prussia into
the powerful German Empire.' The rapid economic development
of Germany after 1870 increased the threat to Russia's relative
standing among the Powers and, potentially, to her security. The
basic change in Russia's position caused by the events of 1870–1 is
reflected with crude accuracy by the 20 per cent jump in defence
expenditure between 1866–70 and 1871–5.[6]

Of course, in the period 1855–1914 the Russian economy did not
stand still. Nor was the Russian government unaware of the dangers
of economic backwardness. Immediately after the end of the Crimean
War the state encouraged the rapid development of the railway system, an essential basis for both economic and military modernisation.
Russia's railways, 720 miles long in 1857, had by 1913 grown to 48 600
miles. Even so, in 1910 European Russia had less than one-tenth the
length of railway per square kilometre of Britain or Germany.[7] Especially during Serge Witte's tenure as Minister of Finance in the 1890s
rapid industrial development became a, if not the, major priority of
the Imperial state, in large part precisely because Witte was deter-

mined that Russia should not become, like Persia or China, a mere agrarian colony of the developed industrial states of Central and Western Europe.[8] In the three decades before 1914 Russian industrial production grew at a considerably faster rate than that of any other European power. Nevertheless, though on the eve of the war Russia was approaching or surpassing French levels of iron, steel, coal or cotton goods production she was still in general far behind either Britain or Germany. In 1912, for instance, Russian coal production was 13 per cent of Germany's, that of pig iron 23 per cent and of steel 26 per cent, though the number of spinning spindles in the Russian Empire was drawing near the German level.[9] Only in potential resources, both human and natural, did Russia compare favourably with the Germans but the problems of creating the social and economic infrastructure and generating the skills and the capital which would make possible the mobilisation of this potential were considerable. Education was a key factor in the whole complicated process of modernisation and it is a mark of Russia's overall progress that, despite the great problems of creating an adequate network of schools to cover this vast and sparsely-populated land, between 1895 and 1911 the number of elementary schools trebled, by 1912 approximately 57 per cent of Russia's school-age population attending educational institutions. Nevertheless, at that moment Russia had 1.2 schoolteachers per 1000 population, Italy 2.2, Japan 2.8, Austria-Hungary 3.2, France 4.0, Great Britain 4.4, and the United States 5.7.[10] In 1913 Russia's rate of overall literacy was approximately 30 per cent and, according to Olga Crisp, 'this was a much lower rate than for mid-eighteenth century England'. [11]

In some ways Russia's position in the years prior to 1914 mirrors that of Britain in the 1930s. Both empires faced the problems of defending far-flung territories with an economic base that was, in relation to that of potential enemies, not as strong as it had once been. Russian territory was, it is true, a compact mass, not a group of possessions scattered across the globe whose defence depended on British ability to monopolise control of the seas, but the extent of the Russian Empire greatly reduced the advantage of its rulers' possession of interior lines. Although before 1905 the Russians to some extent had themselves to blame for arousing Japanese enmity, the growth of a powerful Japan was in any event bound to threaten the security of Russia's Far Eastern possessions. In 1912 the population of all Siberia was less than ten million, that of Japan more than five times greater. Since Russia had no shipbuilding capacity in the Far East, to challenge Japanese domination of the Pacific required the despatch of Baltic squadrons on a 17,000 mile journey to Vladivostock. Even army units from Central Russia faced a 6000 mile journey to the Maritime Province in the east. When after 1905 it was decided that military considerations necessitated the double-tracking of the Trans-Siberian railway, the construction of the Amur railway and the increase of the carrying capacity on certain other strategic railways, the Ministry of Communications requested 1500 million rubles over a five year period to fulfil these tasks. This sum has to be compared with the 36.2 million and 53.5 million that the central government spent on agriculture and justice respectively in 1906.[12] In June 1909 the Russian Minister of War, V.A. Sukhomlinov, told the French Military Attaché that in the event of a German-Japanese alliance Russia's ability to play an active role in Europe would be drastically reduced[13] but Russian fears in the Far East were not confined to Japan. Some highly intelligent and influential Russians, of whom Prince S.N. Trubetskoy and M.O. Menshikov were the best known, were already becoming terrified by the potential threat to Russia's half-empty Asian possessions from the huge Chinese population, as well as by what they saw as alarming indications of a restoration of China's unity and military power.[14] Sazonov was himself not free from such fears, warning Berlin in 1912 that although a stable and united China might suit European commercial circles, Russia and 'China were coterminous over an immense length of frontier and it was not to her interest that China should become a strong military power'.[15]

The fact that the western and southern borderlands of the Empire were populated overwhelmingly by non-Russians also presented problems to Petersburg. The 1897 census revealed that Great Russians made up just under 45 per cent of the Imperial population and that they were concentrated in the central regions of European Russia. As nationalist ideas spread across Europe from west to east fears grew in Petersburg about a threat to Imperial unity, especially if the minorities' disaffection were to be encouraged in time of war by foreign enemies. Partly for this reason and partly in response to Russian nationalist sentiment the government began in the second half of the nineteenth century to enforce the spread of Russian language, culture, and religion into some of the non-Russian areas in part at the expense of the local ethnic majorities but also to undermine the position of Swedish, German and Polish minorities which had traditionally dominated Finland, the Baltic Provinces and Belorussia respectively. This policy of russification led to widespread anger, which was reflected in fierce disturbances in the non-Russian areas in 1905. By 1914 Petersburg had good reason to fear trouble in Finland and Poland in the event of war. The Russian ruling group was divided as regards how seriously it viewed the Ukrainian nationalist threat[16] but Vienna's support for the Ukrainian movement was causing increasing alarm and resentment in Petersburg.[17] Defeat by Japan had made many Russians exaggeratedly pessimistic about their Empire's weakness and the growing threat of Asian nationalism. This was reflected in the somewhat panic-ridden fears of some Russians about the Panislamic movement.[18] Nevertheless, there was some reason for fear, for Petersburg exercised power but little influence over the Empire's large Moslem population which, in the Caucasus, showed serious signs of unrest between 1905 and 1914. This helps explain Sazonov's great concern about the activities of 'Young Turk' agents both in the Caucasus and in Afghanistan, the latter of which he saw as a potential base for a Panislamic movement in Central Asia.[19] It also provides a reason for Petersburg's determination to maintain impressive military forces in border areas both to overawe the local population and to deter neighbouring states from any efforts to exploit the disaffection of Russia's ethnic minorities.

As regards the security of Russia's Asiatic borders one difficulty lay in the government's inability to control the regions beyond its frontiers by indirect economic penetration. Such control, quite apart from the profits it might bring to Russian industry, was desirable in order to check either the growth of any rival power's hold on these areas or the development of political or religious movements which might exert a dangerous influence on the indigenous population in Russia's borderlands, which was very often of the same race or religion as its neighbours beyond the frontier. Because of Russian industry's insufficient capital and competitiveness, in order to ensure indirect control the Russian government often had to invest large sums either as subsidies to Russian businessmen or in directly financed state projects, a policy that was pursued by Witte as Minister of Finance. When in the financial crisis brought on by the Japanese War the régime was forced to recognise that the continuation of this policy was beyond its means, the only alternative course, one subsequently pursued in both Manchuria and Persia, was often to use political power in areas beyond the frontiers in order in one way or another to create artificial barriers against foreign enterprise behind which Russian capitalists could operate with better chances of success. Not surprisingly, however, this policy did not endear Russia to other European powers and fear of antagonising Berlin forced Russia in 1910 –1911 virtually to abandon this line in Persia and to consent to the construction of railways which would open the Persian market to powerful German competition.[20]

Thus even as regards the security of her Central Asian and Caucasian frontiers Russia's problems were directly linked to the backwardness of the Empire's economy in comparison to that of Central and Western Europe. In discussing the link between backwardness and Great Power status a certain caution is, however, required if only to offset the great exaggeration of Russia's weakness often made by Soviet historians in the Stalinist era. Growing rapidly in economic and military potential, even in 1914 Russia was considerably stronger than Austria or Italy and roughly on a par with France. As Prince G.N. Trubetskoy stated, however, Russian resources did not match her military commitments,[21] especially as the latter were interpreted by Russia's pessimistic generals and ambitious admirals. In its effort to meet these commitments the state at times came close to bankrupting the treasury and undermining the Russian economy, which helps explain the pressure from within the government for international agreement on the limitation of armaments. The strain of defence expenditure on the economy is best illustrated in statistical terms. In 1913 the government consumed 10.3 per cent of Russia's net national product; in Italy, the next most backward of the Great Powers, the average figure between 1901 and 1910 was 4.4 per cent.[22] On the eve of the war in France the local authorities spent 28 per cent of the overall governmental budget, in Prussia 39 per cent and in England 46 per cent. The Russian figure was 15 per cent which becomes all the more striking when one realises that it was the local government budget which bore the major burden of promoting primary education and rural development.[23] In the first thirteen years of this century the rapid expansion of the Russian economy resulted in a 93 per cent increase in the state budget, central government expenditure on agriculture and education almost quadrupling. Even so, the army still received five times more than education in 1913 while the spiralling naval budget was even now greater than that of the agricultural and judicial departments combined. Despite the rapid economic expansion of recent years Russia's per capita income in 1913, $57, was still only 27 per cent of England's but 50 per cent more of the average Russian's income was appropriated by the state for current defence expenditure.[25] Because of the relative lack of private capital in Russia and because large sums were required to develop an adequate social and economic infrastructure in this vast and backward land the Russian government ought to have been investing far more than its European rivals in roads, hospitals, schools and other services. The overwhelming burdens of defence meant that in fact it was investing much less.

This represented not just a major strain on the Russian population but also a direct threat to that military potential which high defence expenditure was supposed to ensure. If small educational budgets, for instance, owed much to the armed forces' prior claims on the exchequer, intelligent Russian and foreign observers were well aware that the low levels of literacy and initiative in the ranks of the Russian army had a pernicious effect on the latter's efficiency.[26] Unproductive military expenditure retarded Russia's economic development, yet the backwardness of the Russian economy meant that Petersburg got much worse value for the money it spent on defence than did its European rivals. In 1912, for instance, the British reckoned that warships built in Russia cost 60 per cent more per ton than in the UK.[27] Only economic development could free the Russian treasury from its dependence on indirect taxes, foreign loans and state monopolies and create a flexible fiscal system capable of sustaining the strains of a European war.[28] To achieve this development and lessen the pressure on the consumer for domestic capital accumulation the Russian government encouraged foreign investment. Without massive Western, and in particular French, purchase of Russian state bonds it would have been impossible for Petersburg to sustain both high levels of defence expenditure and a massive railway construction programme based on the subsidised production of Russia's nascent industries. Though necessary and successful, the import of foreign capital did, however, have some unwelcome side effects on Russian foreign policy. Defence of Russia's international credit and of the gold standard depended on the maintenance of a favourable trade balance, which in turn rested ever more squarely on huge exports of grain though the Dardanelles.[29] This greatly increased Rusia's vulnerability to political instability or change at Constantinople. Moreover, although the relationship between the French creditor and the Russian debtor was by no means as wholly weighted in the former's favour as some have imagined, Paris was able, especially in 1905–6, to derive certain political and military advantages from its loans to Russia.

The strategic, economic and demographic factors already mentioned provide a necessary but by no means sufficient explanation of either Russia's potential or her performance as a Great Power between 1854 and 1914. Administrative and political considerations were also very important. Of course, all these factors were closely intertwined. Economic and financial weakness was, for instance, a major reason for the state's inability to create a civil administration capable of controlling, influencing and transforming the life of the ordinary subject. In the villages where in 1914 more than four out of every five Russians still lived, even the most basic function of any political authority, namely the preservation of law and order, was carried out by the peasants themselves rather than by the state. Indeed in an Empire of over 100 million peasants there were before 1903 not even 10,000 rural state policemen.[30] Since the organisation, operations and personnel of central government and their impact on foreign policy will be discussed in chapter 3 they can be passed over in silence here. It should, however, be stressed that in the major tests of Russia's potential as a Great Power in the half century before 1905, namely the wars of 1854–6, 1877–8 and 1904–5, administrative and military bungling was a factor of very great importance.

Of the many elements that limited the power of the early twentieth-century Russian state bureaucratic inefficiency was probably the most traditional. The growing internal political conflict was much more novel and at least as important. In the half-century before 1914, in Russia as elsewhere, traditional religious, patriarchal and local loyalties which had for long underpinned society were increasingly dissolving under the joint impact of the ideas of the Enlightenment and French Revolution, transmitted through modern systems of mass education and communications and the great social transformation brought about by the development of industry and capitalism. Faced by these potentially disintegrative forces the rulers of many of Europe's nation states found nationalism to be a powerful ideology with which to hold together their societies and attract loyalty to themselves. In a multi-national empire, however, the result of appeals to Russian national feeling were bound to be much more equivocal. Even if, as was almost always true with the Imperial ruling élite, one could convince oneself that Ukrainians and Belorussians were merely

Russians speaking a local dialect one was still left with one-third of the population for whom Russian nationalism was at best of limited interest and at worst a threat to their own culture, language and traditions.

Still more serious was the fact that throughout the last six decades of its existence the Imperial régime was faced by the indifference, hostility and in many cases implacable hatred of part of even ethnically Russian educated society. From the 1860s Russian internal politics had always some of the characteristics of a war, with officialdom on one side, revolutionaries on the other and attempts to find some peaceful evolutionary path of political development always failing in the crossfire of the two rival armies. Russian conservatives for long comforted themselves by the knowledge that oppositional elements within Russian educated society constituted but a tiny fraction of the total population and this was, of course, quite true. Christopher Read believes that at the beginning of the twentieth century the number of educated Russians opposed to the basic principles underlying the existing Russian social, political and economic order, a group usually and usefully defined by the term intelligentsia, was not more than 50,000 out of a population of over 130 million.[31] Nevertheless, the intelligentsia's influence was far greater than a mere counting of heads might suggest, for in many ways it set the tone and defined the content of social debate in late nineteenth and early twentieth century Russia.

The intelligentsia's overriding concern with moral, socio-economic and internal political issues left it with little time for questions of foreign policy or defence. Count Nostitz, the Russian Military Attaché in Paris, wrote in 1912 that whereas in the rest of Europe there existed a considerable body of semi-popular literature on the armed forces, military planning and the nature of a future war there was virtually no market for this in Russia.[32] In any event, hatred for a régime held responsible for the poverty, inequality and lack of freedom in Russian society led much of the intelligentsia to deny any legitimacy to the state's foreign and defence policy. Captain Langlois, one of the French army's leading experts on Russia, wrote in 1913 that 'Russian youth, unfortunately supported or even incited by its teachers, adopts anti-military and even anti-patriotic sentiments which we can scarcely imagine'.[33] Of course, the degree of hostility to the state and its army differed. Its most extreme form in nineteenth and twentieth century Russia was found originally in the anarchism of

Bakunin and Kropotkin and, subsequently, in Bolshevism. The latter's policy in the First World War that Tsarism's defeat was the supreme interest of the Russian and international working class was derived from a marxist belief that the proletariat had no motherland, nevertheless its social and psychological roots lay in part in the fierce hatred for the Imperial state of many members of the nineteenth century intelligentsia.

Many Russian socialists were not internationalist in the Bolshevik sense. On the contrary, the agrarian socialist and revolutionary tradition was thoroughly national in its idealisation of the Russian peasant and his collectivist instincts. Nevertheless, the hatred of most Russian socialists, marxist or otherwise, for the Imperial state was considerable. P.A. Lavrov spoke for the whole socialist movement when he stated that

> the history of the Russian state is the history of the systematic economic looting, intellectual oppression and moral corruption of our country. Every progressive thing that has been done in Russia has been done against the state, and everything that has come from that source has been harmful to society.[34]

The demand in the Socialist Revolutionary Party Programme of 1906 for the abolition of the Imperial army and its replacement by a militia was the logical corollary of such a view.

Although after 1906 one branch of Russian liberalism began to seek reconciliation with the state and the patriotic tradition, right up to 1914 many liberals regarded the armed forces and Russian nationalism with deep ambivalence because of the close connection of both with the autocratic régime. In addition, not merely did the Russian citizen traditionally feel little responsibility for the policies of a government over which he exercised scant control, there was also a strong current even in nineteenth century conservative political thought which stressed that the bureaucratic state and its headquarters in Petersburg were an alien and Germanic creation on Russian soil. It is only within the context of the traditional sense of the 'foreignness' of the state, the Germanic tendencies of its rulers, that some of the wilder rumours about 'dark forces' and treason so current in 1914–17 could have taken root.

Peter Kenez writes that:

turn-of-the-century Russian culture was peculiarly inhospitable
to military values and virtues. At the time when a substantial part
of English, French and German educated public opinion was seized
by nationalism and gladly identified with the nationalist-
colonialist exploits of their governments – carried out, of course, by
the army, the Russian intelligentsia had different concerns. Russian literature had no Kipling, and Russia's best historians had
other interests than the glorification of military conquest. When
Treitschke was writing about blood and iron, Klyuchevsky was
analysing the origin of serfdom in Russia.[35]

Kenez's main concern is with the isolation of the Russian officer
corps from society and the effects of this isolation on its attitudes,
composition and intellectual calibre. The alienation of much of educated society from the state weakened the latter in other crucial respects as well, however. For the modernisation of Russian society the
régime had to rely on the collaboration of professional educated elements, of whom primary schoolteachers were an excellent example.
The power that these teachers possessed through their ability, in part,
to shape the consciousness of their newly literate peasant pupils was
considerable and, because of the teachers' political views, aroused
great fear in the eyes of the authorities and Russian conservatives.[36]
Such fear was justified. In the first All-Russian Congress of Teachers
in December 1913, 40 per cent of the delegates were uncommitted to
any party; of the remaining 60 per cent, some three-quarters were
revolutionary socialists, 10 per cent were on the right, 12 per cent were
liberals or radical-liberals and only 2 per cent belonged to the Octobrist (right-centre) party.[37] No doubt many of these teachers were
similar to the one encountered by Bernard Pares in Tver Province
who was filling his library with marxist works, was encouraging his
charges to raze the estates of the local gentry and was teaching them
about Nicholas the Last.[38] If the Prussian schoolteacher can be described as the architect of Sadowa and Sedan the Russian's role was
somewhat different. It may well be that *sub specie aeternitatis* the values
taught by the Russian teacher were of greater worth but in terms of
building up a self-confident, patriotic, militaristic youth convinced of
the virtues of its country's rulers they clearly left something to be
desired.

Of course, the increasing hatred of the regime and social order
among Russian peasants and workers was encouraged but by no

means solely caused by the propaganda of revolutionary elements. The traditional bases of peasant loyalty and conservatism were being undermined by the development of that secular, literate and materialist culture which the whole process of modernisation encouraged. Much of the urban working class was still closely linked to the countryside both mentally and by the property rights and family connections which tied them to the villages. Nevertheless, urban workers were by 1914 far more literate than the village population, more easily organised and much more susceptible to revolutionary propaganda. Subjected to the usual sufferings of European nineteenth century proletariats in the early phase of industrialisation, the Russian working class was also, however, living in an age when fully developed socialist doctrines now offered an alternative to liberalism and in a country where an important section of the educated classes was committed both to socialism and to the overthrow of the existing order by force. The Russian working class cut its teeth in 1903–6 and, although temporarily cowed by the repression of the 1905 Revolution, its militancy was growing sharply in the years before 1914. By 1914 the Bolsheviks held two-thirds of the seats allocated to workers in the Russian Duma and controlled most trade unions and other labour organisations. In that year there were 5.4 times more strikes in Russia than in France, 3.6 times more than in Britain and 2.8 times more than in Germany, almost all these strikes coming before the outbreak of war which, indeed, followed shortly after the suppression of fierce rioting in Petersburg.[39]

If the government had little doubt about the possible danger to state security from the proletariat in time of war, peasant attitudes in 1914 were less easily gauged. The widespread agrarian disturbances of 1905–6 had been repressed and the countryside was largely quiet in the years preceding 1914. Even though by that year the gentry and middle classes only held about one-tenth of Russia's arable land there were, however, no grounds for belief in the disappearance of that peasant commitment to the expropriation of the estates and larger farms which the elections to the first two Dumas had revealed in 1906–7. As Prince E.N. Trubetskoy wrote in 1915, in the years before the war the threat of further agrarian riots, the increasing moral nihilism of peasant youth, the growing evidence of hooliganism, drunkenness, and declining religious faith, all these aroused fears among the upper classes about the impending disintegration of rural society. No one could know for certain whether, if war should come,

its discipline and purpose would result in a resurgence of that traditionally stubborn and courageous peasant patriotism which both before and since has rescued Russia's rulers in moments of invasion and
crisis.[40]

If, as a contributor to *Novoye Vremya* correctly wrote in February
1914, 'in the final resort the external strength of a state is concealed in
its internal closeness to the people'[41] then it is clear that the external
weakness of the Russian state was both cause and effect of the suspicion, incomprehension and hatred which divided it from much of
Russian society. Russia's defeat in the Japanese War, for instance,
owed much to military incompetence but in fact by the late spring of
1905 the Russian army in the Far East had every chance of defeating
the outnumbered and overstretched Japanese forces, while Japan's
finances were even less capable than Russia's of sustaining many
more months of war. The Special Conference at Tsarskoye Selo on 24
May 1905 (O.S.) which decided to end the conflict did so because of
the threat of internal revolution not of external defeat or financial
crisis.[42]

At the same time, however, the régime's failures in war and diplomacy between 1854 and 1914 represented a dire threat to internal
stability in Russia. As a number of former ministers and high officials
pointed out to Nicholas II in 1905, the periods of greatest political
turbulence in their lifetime had come after Russia's failure in her last
three major wars.[43] In part this was because for an élite which in-
vested so much of its pride and prestige in foreign and defence policy
defeat in these spheres was quite likely to lead to a loss of self-
confidence and even to a questioning of fundamental aspects of the
existing political system. As the events of 1904–5 showed, however,
attempts at reform and liberalisation conducted from a position of
weakness might merely lead to the growth of opposition and serious
danger of revolution. It is important to realise that it was essential for
the survival of the Imperial régime both that it be considered invinc-
ible and that it be feared by its subjects. In the naively honest way that
partly distinguished it from later authoritarian régimes the Imperial
state did not hide this fact. The Fundamental Laws of the Empire
spoke of obedience to the crown being based in part on fear, while the
national anthem glorified the might and power of the Russian
monarch. As one of the régime's most intelligent defenders in the
reign of Nicholas II, L.A. Tikhomirov, wrote to P.A. Stolypin, so long
as the Emperor's subjects felt that opposition to the state was both

futile and dangerous they would take its existence as 'given' and tailor their political objectives to forms and limits it considered acceptable. Given time this attitude would become habitual and the state could on this basis achieve compromises even with hostile groups such as the proletariat. Should it, however, seem that the régime was weak and amenable to pressure then both the number of those willing actively to oppose the state and the radicalism of their programmes would increase tremendously.[44] It hardly needs to be added that defeat in war or even diplomacy, especially against so little regarded a foe as the Japanese, inspired not respect or fear for the régime but rather contempt, an emotion that the crown could not afford to see develop among its subjects.

Russia's lack of success in war and diplomacy in the six decades before 1914 sapped the country's moral strength. The triumphs of Britain and Germany in the military, diplomatic and economic spheres put these countries by 1914 in the front rank of the world's leading nations and enabled Englishmen or Germans to feel a foot taller than the rest of mankind. This was a source of national pride, self-confidence and unity. It helped reconcile the worker to the state and the Bavarian or Scotsman to rule from Berlin or London. One manifestation of the patriotic militarism evident in German and British society was the enthusiastic training of volunteer, reserve and auxiliary military cadres. The nearest Russia came to the British OTC or Territorials were her schoolboy 'funnies' (*poteshniye*), whose emergence after 1906 reflected the increasingly nationalist sentiment existing in some elements of educated society. The *poteshniye*'s enthusiasm for patriotism and military drilling won them the strong support of Nicholas II but they were not taken seriously by the military authorities and had a very small overall impact on Russian youth.[45] In assessing the mood of Russian society it is also worth noting that the shooting, sporting and other paramilitary organisations so prevalent in the contemporary Soviet Union barely existed in Imperial Russia.[46] The Moscow student 'ashamed' in 1911 to be seen by Captain Wavell 'in the uniform of the worst army in the world'[47] had few counterparts in Britain or Germany and the widespread evasion of military service by young men from the educated classes in 1914–17 must be seen as a reflection of pre-war Russians' lack of that self-confident, often arrogant belief in their own society, its values and its government which was very strong in the German and British upper and middle classes.[48] Equally important, the peasant reservist whom

Sergeant Oskin remembers departing to war in August 1914 convinced that 'the Germans will lick us good' was the product of a society that had been 'licked good' by Westerners, not to mention Japanese, for many decades.[49] That was one reason why, even in the patriotic euphoria that followed the outbreak of war, *Novoye Vremya*'s leading columnist, Menshikov, had to 'allow that there isn't nowadays among the masses that faith, that capacity to catch fire, that there was in the days of Suvorov and Napoleon'.[50]

Of course, to give a retrospective assessment of Russia's potential as a Great Power is not by any means to prove that Russia's rulers were aware of their empire's weaknesses or that they necessarily acted in the light of such awareness. Much of this book will attempt to show to what extent this was actually the case in the period 1905–14. One generalisation that can, however, be made with confidence for the whole period 1856–1914 is that Russia's performance in the three major wars during these years was bad enough to show most of her political leaders the wisdom of moderation in foreign policy. In the light of the Crimean War it would have taken a hardened optimist to deny the Grand Duke Konstantin Nikolayevich's statement that 'we cannot deceive ourselves any longer... we are both weaker and poorer than the first-class powers, and furthermore poorer not only in material but also in mental resources, especially in matters of administration'.[51] If patriotic opinion found it satisfactory to hold Bismarck and Peter Shuvalov to blame for Russia's diplomatic defeat at the Congress of Berlin after the Turkish War, K.P. Pobedonostsev, a key adviser to the last two Romanov emperors, was too realistic to enjoy such illusions. Having seen the tremendous strains even war with the Ottomans imposed on Russia and the sombre light which it threw on the prestige and efficiency of her ruling circles in the future he was to be very wary about advocating adventure in the field of foreign policy.[52] Still more shattering was Russia's defeat by Japan. Even General A.A. Kireyev, an optimist and a Panslav to the hilt, confessed in his diary in 1909 that 'we have become a second-rate power' and feared that he was living amidst the disintegration of Russia's moral forces, internal unity and capacity or will to fulfil her role in history.[53]

A publicist and a courtier, closely connected to many of the Romanovs, Kireyev in many ways personified those forces in Russia which were most likely to drag the empire into a European war. Less well-known than his fellow generals, M.D. Skobelev, M.G. Chernyayev and R.A. Fadeyev, Kireyev was nevertheless a leading figure in late nineteenth and early twentieth century Panslav and nationalist circles and his diaries are of considerable interest. As one would expect of a senior officer in late Victorian Europe, Kireyev had no qualms about what subsequent generations would condemn as imperialism. As he wrote in 1900, 'of course we, like any powerful nation, strive to expand our territory, our "legitimate" moral, economic and political influence. This is in the order of things'.[54] Kireyev had the officer-patriot's intense concern about Russia's standing in Europe and his hypersensitivity to questions of honour and prestige. He looked back wistfully to the era when Nicholas I's Empire stood first among the European powers and where Russian prestige or honour was at stake was capable of risking the state's life with something approaching the degree of irrational courage with which he would no doubt have been willing to sacrifice his own. The collapse of Russia in March 1909 before German and Austrian pressure to recognise the annexation of Bosnia-Hercegovina is the lowest point in Kireyev's diaries. 'Shame! Shame!', he wrote. 'It would be better to die!'[55]

In the 1880s and 1890s Kireyev fulminated against Russian diplomacy, which in his view was too timid and failed to appreciate and use the Empire's true strength. His exaggerated estimate of the latter owed much to Kireyev's dim understanding of economic and social matters. In his comparisons between Russia and the Western states, at least until the shock of the 1905 Revolution, he followed the line of the early Slavophils. Like Alexis Khomyakov and Ivan Kireyevsky, Kireyev believed that no society could survive unless it was based on an overriding ethical principle. For him Orthodox Christianity provided this principle in Russia and linked Tsar and people with bonds of true faith, trust and sentiment. He contrasted Russia's internal cohesion in a naive and Slavophil way with the egoistical, materialist and increasingly pluralist principles which underlay Western society and, in his view, doomed it to collapse. Kireyev was convinced that as the heir of Orthodox Byzantium and as the major Slav state Russia's destiny lay unequivocally in the Balkans. To withdraw from the struggle to unite and lead the Orthodox and Slav cause was to deny Russia's destiny and thus call into question the principles on which the Russian 'church-state' and Russian society rested.[56]

Here, of course, Kireyev was emphasising a number of themes central to the history of Russian nationalism. Since the fifteenth century the Russian state had regarded itself as the Third Rome, the only surviving independent bearer of the Orthodox ideal and therefore the natural leader of the Orthodox community. Slavophilism, Russia's variation on the pan-European theme of Romantic nationalism, developed in the reign of Nicholas I a whole set of religious, philosophical, ethical, social and political conceptions, which were linked to the assertion of the uniqueness and spiritual superiority of the Russian people in comparison to the nations of Western Europe. With the death of the earlier and more philosophically inclined Slavophils and, still more, after the shock of Russia's defeat in the Crimean War the Slavophil 'cause' tended to become ever more entwined with a concern about questions of foreign policy and the assertion of Russia's role as a Great Power. The bible of this 'Panslav' corruption of earlier Slavophil theories was N.Y. Danilevsky's *Russia and Europe*, first published in 1869, which saw Russia's destiny as lying in the creation and leadership of a great Slav federation which, standing as a bulwark against an alien Western civilisation, would ultimately surpass it. In addition to the Orthodox and Slavophil elements in the development of Russian nationalism it is also, however, important to bear in mind the history of Russian involvement in the Balkans in the eighteenth and nineteenth centuries. In this period Russia had for many reasons been the major enemy of the Ottomans and therefore a potential ally for their Christian subjects. Although the Russian state and the Balkan Christians used and misused each other over the centuries, the decisive role played by the Russian army in the liberation of the Peninsula is indisputable and stood in contrast to the pro-Ottoman tendencies prevalent in Vienna and London. Memories about the armies of P.A. Rumyantsev, A.V. Suvorov, M.I. Kutuzov, I. Diebitsch, Y.V. Gurko and M.D. Skobelev added to Orthodox and Slavophil ideals an historically based patriotic emotion often connected with memories of personal suffering or effort. One of Kireyev's brothers had, for instance, been killed in action against the Turks. Especially when combined with the soldierly principles and optimistic judgements about Russian power of a Kireyev, the mix of ideals and memories which led Russia to assert her claim to pre-eminence in the Balkans was a powerful and potentially dangerous brew.

Those who held ministerial posts between 1855 and 1905 were, however, very seldom as sanguine as Kireyev about Russia's potential. P.A. Valuyev, one of Alexander II's most trusted advisers, wrote in 1876 that the Foreign Minister, Prince A.M. Gorchakov, had told him 'that we are a great, powerless country. True. There is nothing more fortunate than knowing that truth. One can always dress up finely but one needs to know that one is dressing up'.[57] Gorchakov's successors in the Foreign Ministry, N.K. Giers, Lobanov-Rostovsky and V.N. Lambsdorff, were no less realistic or cautious than their predecessor. The Ministry of Finance, too well aware of Russia's economic and financial weakness to suffer from delusions of power, was also a permanent force for moderation in foreign policy. In the opposing camp it is true that there were generally to be found some aggressively-minded generals and a number of figures, usually outside the official government, who advocated a more determined and nationalist foreign policy. The importance of such figures was greatly increased by the fact that ultimately the autocrat decided questions of foreign policy and in so doing might well be swayed by an exaggerated concern for prestige, an overestimate of Russian power or simple inexperience and naivety. Giers was almost as horrified by Alexander III's discussions with M.N. Katkov as Lambsdorff was later to be by Nicholas II's trust in A.M. Bezobrazov. In general, however, at least in Europe, the Russian government acted with restraint in the period 1856 to 1905. Even in 1877–8 when state interests and rational moderation went temporarily overboard under Panslav pressure, the Empire's rulers nevertheless in the end did not attempt to flout the realities of power and retreated before Anglo-Austrian opposition before it was too late. Nor, despite his anger, did Alexander III set Europe by the ears by invading Bulgaria in 1886–7. No doubt an awareness of weakness rather than an overdose of virtue explains Russian moderation between 1856 and 1905. Still, at least, in Valuyev's words, Russia's rulers knew they were dressing up.

In the period 1871–1905 the most significant move in Russian foreign policy was the cementing of the Franco-Russian alliance by the agreements and ceremonial visits which occurred between 1891 and 1894. The alliance was in many ways a logical consequence of the war of 1870–1. The sudden establishment in the centre of Europe of a unified and militarily formidable German Empire was bound to arouse fears in Russia. In the last five years Germany had after all attacked and in a matter of weeks routed the armies of the other two truly Great Powers on the European continent. Whatever the warm relations between Russia and Germany's rulers in 1871, personalities and political sympathies changed whereas overwhelming German power not just remained but grew ever more formidable. It is therefore not surprising that many Russians desired France's restoration to

Great Power status so that she might, if need be, act as a diplomatic or even military counterweight to Germany.

Of course had full trust existed between Petersburg and Berlin this desire would have been unnecessary. Such trust was, however, scarcely the hallmark of relations between the nineteenth century Great Powers. In addition, though it is true that so long as William I and Alexander II were alive Russo-German enmity was unlikely, there existed in Russian society a tradition of considerable resentment against Germans, which was owed above all to the size and prosperity of the German community in Russia and the successful careers in the armed forces and civil service of so many of its representatives. Events in Europe in the 1870s and 1880s increased this resentment. Failure to have their way in the Balkans both in 1878 and in 1885–7 was blamed on Bismarck by many Russians. The accusation was unfair but it owed something to the Chancellor's reputation for omnipotence and more to Russians' understandable, if misdirected, rage about the successes of Austria, Russia's rival and Germany's ally, in the Balkan Peninsula. It was galling in the extreme that the Habsburg Monarchy, the great opponent of the liberation of the Slav peoples from Ottoman rule, by 1887 not merely occupied Bosnia-Hercegovina but also indirectly dominated Serbia through her client, King Milan, and in addition had the satisfaction of seeing a Catholic and pro-Austrian prince on the Bulgarian throne. Meanwhile Russia, which had sacrificed much for the liberation of Bulgaria and independence of the Serbs in 1877–8, now had to be satisfied with the friendship of Nicholas of Montenegro. The fact that the Russians were largely themselves to blame for their predicament did nothing to decrease their desire to pin the responsibility elsewhere.

Bismarck's efforts in 1887 to cool Russian ardour by applying financial pressure merely had the effect of throwing Russian securities on to the French market, while the spread of protectionism in Eastern Europe resulted in conflict and even a tariff war between Germany and Russia. As D. Geyer rightly insists, however, it would be a fundamental error to stress financial or economic reasons for Russia's diplomatic shift from Germany to France;[58] the evidence available does not support such a claim and it is, for instance, significant that I.A. Vyshnegradsky, Russia's Minister of Finance, was an opponent of the French alliance.[59] Far more important as regards the origins of the alliance was the insecurity felt in Petersburg after Bismarck's removal in 1890, an insecurity greatly increased by the wavering but in general unfriendly course being steered by William II. The Germans' refusal to renew the Reinsurance Treaty and their unwillingness to grant even Giers' request for a more or less platonic written declaration of friendship was almost bound to undermine the Foreign Minister's stand against a French alliance and to make Russia's rulers feel their isolation. Given the existence of the Triple Alliance, of the Mediterranean agreements which bound Britain to Austria and Italy and of the feelers which seemed to be passing between London and Berlin it is not surprising that Petersburg looked to Paris for support. The fact that the French had by 1891–3 made themselves worthwhile allies by restoring their armed forces, that the Republic, even if not individual ministries, was now more or less stable and that Giers was by 1891 more convinced than in the past of the essential moderation of France's leaders all helped make the alliance possible from the Russian point of view.

How important was the Franco-Russian alliance and what were its aims? Above all the alliance committed Russia to the defence of the European balance of power in the face of Germany's increasing might. Should Berlin seek to turn France into a German satellite by the use or threat of force Russia would intervene. Russia thus denied Germany a free hand in Western Europe, just as the Dual Alliance of 1879 had signified Berlin's refusal to accept any Russian threat to the independence or existence of the Habsburg Monarchy. Though defensive, the alliance with France had its dangers for Petersburg. Between 1890 and 1914 Germany was very much the most powerful state in continental Europe and might well be drawn irresistibly towards an assertion of this might in its foreign policy. Russia was now committed to the defence not just of its own interests but also to those of its ally against any German desire to exercise its muscles. The logic of the Franco-Russian alliance was therefore that Germany should use its growing strength away from Europe and from France and Russia's colonial possessions. In addition, the alliance somewhat reduced the flexibility of Russian policy. Henceforth Paris watched with a jealously possessive eye its ally's relations with Berlin. Moreover, if conceivably France and Russia could have maintained an implicit commitment to each other's independence even without a formal alliance, once the latter was signed it was almost impossible to abandon it without sending shockwaves through all the European chancelleries, announcing Russia's lack of interest in the balance of power and thereby maybe encouraging Germany to aggression. Nevertheless, the effects of the alliance can be exaggerated. The key underlying factor in Russian foreign policy between 1890 and 1914 was that Petersburg sufficiently distrusted Berlin not to allow it to increase its supremacy in Europe further by eliminating France from the Great Power league. The alliance was the result not the cause of this suspicion. The events of 1894 to 1905 moreover showed that although the alliance may have increased the self-confidence of Petersburg and Paris it did not inspire either to aggression. The Russians showed no inclination to fight for French interests in Alsace or Africa, nor France for Russian ones in the Balkans or at the Straits (a shorthand for the city of Constantinople, the Bosphorus and the Dardanelles). If, as we shall see, in the three years prior to 1914 Paris did begin to view German action even outside its own sphere of interest as an overall threat to the balance of power and French security the chief blame for this must lie on Germany's own unnecessarily clumsy and aggressive diplomacy. Those Russians who believed that only alliance with France could effectively deter Germany from aggressiveness saw Berlin's forward policy in the period 1905–14 as being caused above all by the weakness of the Franco-Russian alliance as a result of Russia's defeat and revolution in 1905. Other Russians on the contrary argued that Berlin was only attempting to assert the power it undoubtedly possessed. They wished not to attempt the dangerous and maybe impossible task of checking German expansionism but rather its diversion into areas where Russian interests would not be crucially affected. This conflict of views will be a major theme in the remaining chapters of this book.

# 2 Russian Foreign Policy 1905-1914

DEFEAT by Japan coupled with the revolutionary disturbances of 1905–6 exposed the weakness of the Russian state. Aware of this weakness, those who directed Russian foreign policy sought to guarantee to Russia peace and security in order to preserve her from both external and internal shocks. The cornerstone of Russian foreign policy in the early twentieth century was the French alliance, designed above all to protect the two countries' status and interests in the face of the growing power of Germany. In the course of the Russo-Japanese War, however, this alliance came under heavy strain. The Russian government's attention was centred on the Far East, its main foe being the Anglo-Japanese alliance. Britain was seen by the Russians as having incited Japan to war, provided her with the means to fight and as having acted during the conflict in a thoroughly unneutral manner. The Dogger Bank Incident brought the British and Russian Empires close to war in October 1904. Meanwhile France, Russia's ally, was in 1903–4 growing ever closer to Britain, moving from an amicable solution of colonial squabbles towards a general understanding with London on European and world affairs. The Germans did their best to exploit this potential split in the Franco-Russian alliance and to win the Russian Empire over to their side. In October 1904 and July 1905 Berlin proposed a Russo-German alliance which Paris would be encouraged or coerced into joining and which would have Britain as its target. In July 1905 the Treaty of Bjorkoe seemed to crown German efforts with success. Unfortunately for German hopes, however, Lambsdorff, Witte and the Grand Duke Nicholas Nikolayevich succeeded in persuading Nicholas II both that the new treaty was incompatible with the French alliance and that Russian interests demanded that the latter be preserved. The events of 1905–6 indeed showed that although the Russian government greatly desired good relations between the three leading continental powers, if forced to make a choice it would opt for Paris rather than Berlin.

For this there were many reasons. Weakened by war and revolution and unable even to fulfil the requirements of the Franco-Russian military convention of 1894, Russia was in no position to twist its ally's arm by attempting to push Paris towards reconciliation with Berlin. War and revolution had brought the Russian financial system close to collapse and unless large foreign loans were forthcoming the Imperial government would be forced to declare its bankruptcy to the world by abandoning the gold standard and failing in its obligations towards Russia's foreign creditors. Though the French government's attitude to Russian appeals for loans was bound to be influenced by fears for French investors should Russian finances collapse, nevertheless in the autumn of 1905 Paris was determined that Russia should pay a diplomatic price for French financial aid. That price was the strong support given by Russia to its ally in the Algeciras conference, which was made insultingly clear to Berlin when *Le Temps* published Lambsdorff's instructions to Russia's representative at the conference in March 1906.[1] In the following month despite his own strong anti-British feelings General F.F. Palitsyn, the chief of the Russian General Staff, proved amenable to the French desire to drop the clauses in the Franco-Russian military agreement of 1900 which related to a future war with Britain.[2] It is true that whereas one can document the relationship between Russia's financial plight and her attitude at Algeciras, one cannot prove that the Chief of the General Staff's willingness to accede to French wishes was directly linked to the huge loan which was being concluded at the very moment of Palitsyn's conversations with his French counterparts. Nevertheless, so great was Russia's financial need and so strong the Imperial government's determination not to meet the newly convoked and radical First Duma in a state of bankruptcy that it would be stretching credulity to imagine that such considerations did not affect the Russian stance in the military conversations of April 1906. The events of 1905–6 confirm therefore that France's superiority to Germany in financial power, caused by a unique combination of high French saving and low domestic industrial investment, was a factor in keeping Russia loyal to the French alliance in this period.

It was, however, by no means the only or the most important factor. As we have seen, geopolitical, military and diplomatic considerations lay behind the conclusion of the Franco-Russian alliance in 1892–4 and these had lost none of their weight in 1905–6. On the contrary; if Germany was more powerful than her neighbours in 1894 the same was still truer a decade later, especially of course after Russia's collapse in the Japanese War. Moreover, in the first half of William II's reign German policy had become more ambitious and less predictable than had hitherto been the case, which inevitably affected Russian attitudes towards the Second Reich. As Count Osten-Sacken, Nicholas II's Ambassador in Berlin, wrote in May 1906, German ambitions in Asia and the Moslem world had 'for the first time' made the German Empire 'a possible adversary' of Russia's well-established interests in these areas.[3] Of course, Russia could seek security in a close alliance with Berlin, hoping that her German ally would treat Russian interests with consideration and would direct her ambitions into areas to which Russia was indifferent. Such a policy would, however, have required dropping Russia's commitment to the European balance of power which was, as we will show, central to much of Russian diplomats' thinking about international relations. It would also have required great confidence in Berlin's restraint and in the Germans' good intentions towards Russia. It is, however, clear that those who directed Russian foreign policy in 1904–6 neither trusted William II nor were prepared to accept the risks entailed in abandoning support for the balance of power and accepting German military preponderance in Europe. Count V.N. Lambsdorff, for instance, in October 1905 denounced William II's 'crude attempt' at Bjorkoe to cause trouble between Petersburg and Paris which in the Foreign Minister's view betrayed the German Emperor's usual 'lack of scruple'. He did not doubt that William II would use the Russian Emperor's signature on any compromising documents 'to bring about disclosures in Paris and London which would be harmful for Russia', forcing her into isolation and dependence on Berlin. The latter was unacceptable to Lambsdorff, who wrote that 'from many years of experience I have drawn the conviction that to be genuinely on good terms with Germany the alliance with France is necessary. Otherwise we will lose our independence, "and I know nothing more burdensome than the German yoke" '. As he had written a year before, if an isolated Russia found herself in alliance with her more powerful German neighbour 'the latter would of course...not lose the opportunity to make her feel the whole difficulty and price of these bonds of iron'.[4]

Given the existence of the Entente Cordiale a Russian government wishing to maintain the French alliance had, however, to improve its relations with London. Otherwise Paris would find itself in an impossible position, torn between the rival claims of its two diplomatic 'friends'. Moreover, as Count A.K. Benckendorff the Russian Ambassador in London wrote in October 1906 it was not just Petersburg's links with Paris but also its relations with Tokio which depended on an Anglo-Russian understanding.[5] This was a matter of great importance to the Russians. In 1905–6 Russia's good relations with the Central Powers seemed to ensure her security in Europe. In the Far East on the other hand her situation appeared precarious. The Treaty of Portsmouth had been very unpopular with Japanese public opinion, which considered Japan to have been ill-rewarded for her victories over Russia. Now firmly established on the Asian mainland, Japan was building up her armed forces at speed.[6] Meanwhile Russia's army was in disarray, her navy at the bottom of the ocean and the imposing aura of her might which had protected her possessions before 1905 in shreds. Japanese aggression would, however, require large foreign loans, the obvious markets for which were in Paris and London. In addition, Tokio would hardly risk taking on the Russians unless, as in 1904, its rear was protected against European intervention by the friendly support of its British ally. As Izvol'sky stated in both April and August 1907, an understanding with Britain was therefore important if relations between Petersburg and Tokio were to be guaranteed against further shocks.[7]

For a government anxious to ensure Russia peace and security agreement with Britain was also of course valuable in itself. Anglo-Russian rivalry had been a constant factor in European relations in the nineteenth century and although the two Empires had only once come into direct armed conflict their hostility had led to a number of crises and wars between surrogates. Although the Anglo-Russian agreement of 31 August 1907 did not remove all grounds for misunderstanding between the two powers, serious conflicts erupting in particular as regards Persia, it did nevertherless restrain mutual suspicions to an extent sufficient to allow a limited collaboration in European questions from 1908–14. Russia's defeat in 1905 was the essential backdrop to the agreement, simultaneously reducing both her ambitions in Asia and British fears of Russian power. On the whole, the British gained most from the agreement. Russia's consent not to have direct relations with the Afghan authorities caused considerable difficulties for the Imperial authorities in Central Asia when questions of irrigation, pest control and refugees emerged, something which the British Foreign Office itself admitted.[8] Although the Russian sphere of influence in northern Persia was larger, more populous and richer than Britain's zone in the south, this reflected the Russian

Empire's greater weight in Persian affairs before 1907 as well indeed as Petersburg's far superior ability to bring direct military pressure to bear on its Persian neighbour. The willingness of the Russian government to accept a division into spheres of influence was itself a retreat from Petersburg's conviction in 1905 that it could through its influence in Tehran indirectly control the whole of Persia;[9] moreover, when not merely Russia's commercial interests but also the stability of her border regions were endangered by Persian anarchy in 1907–14 Russia's ability to counter this anarchy by military means was constrained by a regard for British susceptibilities. Nor did the Russians fully reap the rewards at the Straits which many of them hoped to gain from agreement with Britain in Asia. When in October 1908 Izvol'sky attempted to cash the somewhat vague promises of support given in 1907 he discovered that the British government was not willing to accept his claim that the Straits be opened in peacetime to the warships of the Black Sea's riparian powers, insisting instead that free passage should be granted to all. Given the fact that Russia's interest in free passage was far greater than Britain's this seemingly even-handed attitude was somewhat bogus and unhelpful.

The ultimate result of the Anglo-Russian agreement of August 1907 was that Britain and Russia were able to unite first diplomatically and then militarily to counter German efforts to dominate the continent of Europe but this was very far from being Izvol'sky's original intention. The Foreign Minister hoped to ensure peace for Russia by coming to agreements with the neighbouring powers, Britain and Japan in Asia, Germany and Austria in Europe, to ensure the avoidance of serious conflict. He was well aware that Germany might look with a jaundiced eye on any agreement between Britain and Russia, stating in February 1907 that such an agreement would only benefit Russia if it did not arouse German resentment.[10] Throughout the long-drawn-out negotiations with London Izvol'sky went out of his way to placate Berlin and ensure that German interests were in no way affected by the Anglo-Russian agreement.[11] Concern for German feeling led him to refuse to guarantee the *status quo* in the Persian Gulf, to negotiations with Berlin about the Baghdad railway and German interests in Central Persia and in October 1907 to the signing of an agreement with Germany about the *status quo* in the Baltic. The latter agreement, kept secret from London and Paris, was designed to show the Germans that Russia by no means belonged to a united bloc opposed to their interests but on the contrary was willing to negotiate separately with its neighbour whenever their mutual advantage required joint action.[12]

Although Izvol'sky's policy did not seem before 1908 to have aroused serious German resentment it was unfortunately to fail.[13] As Nicolson wrote in January 1908, Izvol'sky's attempt to balance between the Anglo-French and German-Austrian blocs and to maintain good relations with all the powers was a policy which 'would require some skill and adroitness to pursue for any length of time, and it is doubtful if it will be found a feasible one'.[14] The level of hostility between the Powers meant that Izvol'sky's balancing act was regarded with suspicion on all sides, each power bloc attempting to use his conciliatory efforts to compromise Russia in the eyes of the other. Just as Vienna complained that London viewed Austrian policy only through the distorted prism of its suspicion of Germany, so Russian observers came to realise that Berlin's obsession with its conflict with London led it to misread Russian intentions.[15] German attitudes towards foreign policy in the period 1906–9 were in any event influenced by the sense that the Empire's overwhelming preponderance of military and economic power on the continent did not seem to be resulting in diplomatic successes. On the contrary, defeated at the Algeciras Conference in 1906, Germany had also seen the influence it had so carefully built up in Constantinople seemingly destroyed overnight by the Young Turk revolution. While the German monarch was making himself the laughing-stock of Europe by the *Daily Telegraph* interview, his British uncle's machinations seemed to be uniting the other major powers by a series of agreements designed, so it was felt, to check the legitimate growth of German influence in the world. The desire strongly to support Germany's sole reliable ally, to assert German power and to show the disadvantages of uniting against it all help explain Berlin's strategy in the Balkan crisis of 1908–9, as also does a not wholly unjustified German resentment that their refusal to exploit Russia's weakness in 1904–5 had neither led to better diplomatic relations between the two empires nor spared Germany from the malicious and ignorant outpourings of the Russian press.

The Balkan crisis of 1908–9 was scarcely unexpected, the *status quo* in the Peninsula being extremely fragile. As Izvol'sky warned his fellow ministers in January 1908, in the Balkans 'events do not depend on us' and Russia could have a crisis imposed on it against its will at any time.[16] The policy inherited by Izvol'sky was that of co-operation with Vienna to support the *status quo*, a course enshrined in the 1897 Russo-Austrian agreement. When disturbances in Macedonia seemed likely in 1903 to undermine the peace of the Balkans Russia and Austria agreed at Murzsteg to support a programme of reforms which would satisfy the grievances of the Macedonian people and thus, it was piously hoped, ensure tranquillity in the peninsula. Izvol'sky was a supporter of the Austro-Russian understanding and greeted Aehrenthal's appointment as Foreign Minister in October 1906 as a joyful sign that Vienna was still committed to the *entente*.[17] The events of the next two years were, however, to disillusion not only him but also Prince L. P. Urusov, the Russian Ambassador in Vienna and a strong advocate of a close understanding between the two courts. Even in May 1907 Urusov warned that Aehrenthal lacked the sympathy shown by his predecessor, Goluchowski, for the *entente* with Petersburg.[18] In part this was because the balance of power between Russia and Austria had shifted strongly, if temporarily, in the latter's favour between 1897 and 1908, especially given the determined support Berlin was willing to offer for Vienna's policies by the latter date. Whereas in 1903–6 Russian internal weakness had been mirrored in Austria, the solution to the crisis between Vienna and Budapest left the Ballhausplatz freer to pursue a more daring foreign policy. In Viennese eyes such a policy was of special use since it would show both the other powers and Austria's own people that the Monarchy was still capable of acting independently and with energy in the pursuit of its interests. [19] Russian suspicions of Aehrenthal were confirmed when in January 1908 he failed to warn Petersburg in advance of his plans for Austrian railway building in the Sandjak of Novibazar, the Russians being convinced, mistakenly as it transpired, that he had wrung the concession for this construction from the Sultan by promising to go slow on Macedonian reforms. As a result, Izvol'sky sought to work more closely with London to keep the reforms alive but he did not abandon his support for Russo-Austrian collaboration in the Balkans. In reply to an earlier Austrain note Izvol'sky stated on 2 July 1908 that although the preservation of the *status quo* remained his hope and changes in the Treaty of Berlin would require the consent of all the powers, nevertheless prior Austro-Russian agreement on joint action should the Ottoman Empire collapse was desirable. With a lack of caution, derived both from hunger for a diplomatic triumph and over–confidence in his own skill, Izvol'sky stated in writing that a Russo-Austrian agreement in this event could entail the Habsburgs' annexing Bosnia, Hercegovina and the Sandjak, while Russia secured its interests at the Straits.[20]

At his famous meeting with Aehrenthal at Buchlau in mid-September 1908 Izvol'sky learned that Austria intended definitely to annex Bosnia and Hercegovina and deduced that Vienna would move in about three weeks' time.[21] This placed the Russian Foreign Minister in an extremely difficult position. The annexation by Austria of two Slav provinces liberated by Russian efforts in 1877 was bound to cause indignation in his own country. Even Nicholas II, who was no Panslav and understood the realities behind the annexation crisis, stated that Austria's absorption of the two provinces 'sickens one's feelings'.[22] Given Vienna's determination to act, however, Russian protests would certainly prove fruitless and possibly dangerous. Russia was unfit for war, moreover it would have been madness to unleash a European conflict as a result of the annexation of two provinces already in practice under Austrian rule. Since the Central Powers knew well that Russian protests would never be backed by deeds, opposition to Austrian policy would lead nowhere but to Russia's humiliation and her exposure as a toothless power. To avoid such humiliation Izvol'sky was prepared to go along with Vienna's schemes. He argued rightly that in annexing the provinces and evacuating her garrisons from the Sandjak Vienna was gaining paper and losing real advantages. In his telegrams of 17 September he stressed that he had in addition secured Aehrenthal's agreement to certain compensations for Montenegro, Serbia and Bulgaria as well as Austrian support for Russian interests at the Straits.[23] In his letter to N.V. Charykov of 24 September Izvol'sky wrote that he had warned Aehrenthal of the 'possibility and even inevitability' of the decree of annexation being followed by a European conference to review the Treaty of Berlin. He hoped that in this conference Russia would not merely derive advantages at the Straits but also gain prestige for her support for the interests of the smaller Slav states. While agreement with Vienna on the annexation would avoid the dangers of Austro-Russian confrontation, Izvol'sky felt that Austrian interests would suffer from her violation of treaty rights and from the alarm that her aggressive move would cause within the Balkans.[24]

Events were to show, however, that Izvol'sky's views were optimistic. On arrival in London the Foreign Minister found the British to be opposed to his plans for the Straits. Worse still, Austria's declaration to the powers stressed that Izvol'sky had given his unconditional consent to annexation, conveniently ignoring the reservations and stipulations which the Russians, so they claimed, had attached to their agreement.[25] Aehrenthal flatly opposed Izvol'sky's plans for the discussion of all the changes in the Berlin Treaty at a congress, thus presenting Europe with the annexation as a *fait accompli*, while threatening the Russian Foreign Minister with the publication of secret documents revealing Izvol'sky's consent to the annexation both of the two provinces and of the Sandjak. In addition, when Stolypin was informed of the terms of Izvol'sky's agreement with Aehrenthal the Premier was furious and, backed by the Council of Ministers, threatened to resign unless Russia refused to accept the annexation of Slav land by a Germanic power and opposed Austrian schemes at any European congress.[26] Stolypin was himself considerably more pro-Slav in sympathy than either Nicholas II or Izvol'sky but his opposition to the deal made at Buchlau also owed much to a well-justified presentiment about the indignation this agreement would cause in the Duma and the press. For Izvol'sky, himself very much in favour of working with public opinion, the extent of the latter's fury came as a surprise and helped cause him to change his policy. Since it would be 'exceptionally difficult' to ignore public feeling in this matter, the Foreign Minister accepted that 'the practical path' of agreement with Vienna 'is closed to us'.[27] The only possible option therefore was to work with the other powers to ensure the convocation of a conference to consider changes in the Treaty of Berlin. This was, however, to commit Russia to a policy almost doomed to failure. The key to the annexation crisis was that Austria was prepared to fight in defence of what seemed to her an essential interest and that Germany was willing to support her. Since neither Russia, Britain nor France were prepared to back their opposition to Austria's move by force the crisis could only end one way, especially after Vienna had secured Ottoman consent to annexation by a healthy financial indemnity. In the last week of February 1909 Vienna presented notes in Belgrade and Petersburg demanding recognition of the annexation and making it clear that failure to comply would result in the invasion of Serbia. Russian attempts to secure some dignity from the rout through Berlin's mediation merely resulted in a fierce German note of 21 March which demanded immediate, unconditional and unequivocal acceptance of Austrian claims.[28]

By ignoring the good diplomatic rule that defeated enemies should be given a golden bridge across which to retire with honour Kiderlen-Wächter secured a temporary triumph at the expense of considerable longer-term damage to Russia's relations with the Central Powers. Fear of an Austrian invasion of Serbia led Russia's rulers to capitulate in the face of German pressure but the major lesson they drew from the crisis was that if similar humiliation were to be avoided in the future both the Russian armed forces and the Empire's links with London and Paris would have to be strengthened. German behaviour in March 1909 was also to exert a real influence over the way in which the Russian government handled the crisis of July 1914. In 1914 Austria again threatened unilateral action against Serbia and on 29 July Germany again intervened in Petersburg to demand that the Russians cease their military preparations and thus capitulate to Austrian pressure. Sazonov's furious refusal of Pourtales' demand both reflected the extent to which Russian ruling circles had felt their previous humiliation in March 1909 and showed their determination not to knuckle under to German threats a second time.[29] A further effect of the crisis of 1908–9 was to add some body to the often superficial and platonic feelings of sympathy which many Russians felt towards the Slavs. The crude and bullying tactics used by Germany and Austria in both Belgrade and Petersburg did to some extent reflect that Germanic racial arrogance towards the Slavs, many traces of which are to be found in the Central Powers' diplomatic correspondence.[30] Of course, in regarding the culturally and economically more backward peoples who surrounded them as 'lesser breeds' the Germans were by no means unique among the pre-war 'imperial races', a fact that the brown and black skins of most of the British, American, and French subject peoples should not be allowed to obscure. One might even argue that the Germans and Austrians were unfortunate in that their 'lesser breeds' had a Slav great power willing up to a point to protect them. In the context of this book, the important point to grasp, however, is that in international crises the sometimes irrational strength of the pro-Slav sentiment not just of Russian public opinion but also on occasion of members of the government owed something to an instinctive sense that Germanic arrogance towards the Slavs entailed an implicit denial of the Russian people's own dignity and of their equality with the other leading races of Europe. The effects of this racial instinct cannot be quantified and should not be exaggerated but they certainly did have some influence on Russian policy in the crises that led to the outbreak of the First World War.

For all its resentment at German actions in March 1909 the Russian government, however, remained committed to good relations with its western neighbour, which it knew well to be crucial for European peace. After appointment as Foreign Minister in September 1910 Sazonov's first foreign visit was to Potsdam, where his negotiations with Bethmann-Hollweg brought about an atmosphere of greater trust between the two governments and showed that the Russians were willing to make considerable concessions to Germany in order to secure good relations. From the Russian point of view the main gain from Potsdam was Berlin's promise not to support any aggressive Austrian moves in the Balkans. In return the Russians promised, to the dismay of their French and British allies, to drop their opposition to the Baghdad railway and to link it with the Persian centres of population by themselves constructing a line from Tehran to Khanikhin. This promise, together with the Russians' subsequent commitment to a tight schedule for the construction of the Tehran-Khanikhin line, represented a major concession which was sure to result in Russian goods being driven out of some Persian markets by superior German competition. The risks of attempting to block legitimate German demands for access to the Persian market were, however, recognised in Petersburg which, bowing to the inevitability of conceding German claims, comforted itself by the fact that in return Berlin had promised neither to build railways in any area bordering on Russia's Caucasian districts nor to seek large-scale economic concessions in Russia's northern zone of influence in Persia. In the eighteen months following Potsdam Russo-German relations improved considerably, becoming much warmer than Berlin's links with London or Paris. Russian restraint during the Agadir crisis was appreciated by the Germans and Petersburg certainly urged compromise on Paris, Izvol'sky warning Caillaux in August 1911 that the Franco-Russian alliance was 'purely defensive' and could not be invoked automatically to cover an aggressive French stance towards German claims in Morocco.[31] The amicable meeting between the Russian and German Emperors at Baltic Port in June 1912 represented the high-point in the pre-war relations between the two empires before Balkan complications began the downward spiral which led to the crisis of July 1914.

The underlying cause of these complications was the conflict that existed between the territorial *status quo* in Central and South-Eastern Europe and the growing nationalist sentiment of the local populations. It is important to do justice to both sides in this conflict which, in its broad outlines, was similar to many which exist today in the Third World. On the one hand, the growth of popular nationalism in the Balkans reflected the development of modernising and democratic forces in the Peninsula and was further justified by the oppression to which many of the smaller peoples were subjected not just in the Ottoman domains but also in the Hungarian and, to a much lesser extent, Austrian halves of the Habsburg Monarchy. On the other hand, the collapse of the territorial *status quo* was bound to cause chaos and conflict. The nationalism of the formerly 'second-class' peoples was no less chauvinistic and often at least as inclined to persecute rival races as had been that of the previous 'master nations'. In addition, as the Second Balkan War was to show, the ambitions of the various Balkan peoples were in sharp conflict. So long as the question of Constantinople was not raised the disintegration of the Ottoman Empire in Europe might perhaps lead to nothing worse than wars between the Balkan states but the same could scarcely be true of the collapse of the Habsburg Monarchy. The latter would not merely bring on a direct confrontation between German and Slav nationalism in Central Europe, it would also have immense implications for the continent's balance of power in which all the leading states took a close interest.

In its Balkan policy Petersburg had two options. It could seek agreement with Vienna to maintain the *status quo* or even ideally to regulate and control the latter's adaptation to changing circumstances. On the other hand, it could attempt to build up support in the Peninsula against Russia's old Habsburg rival. The effect of the annexation crisis and of the somewhat unscrupulous methods employed by Aehrenthal was to push Russian policy very strongly in the latter direction. Reflecting on the events of 1908–9 even Prince N. Kudashev, the fair-minded and intelligent Counsellor in Vienna, wrote in September 1912 that Austro-Russian suspicion was 'such a deep feeling and on our side so well founded that for the moment one could not even talk about a return to Austro-Russian friendship, which was so skilfully made use of by Austria in the past'.[32] Suspicion of Austrian methods was in 1909–14 combined with an obsession about the Monarchy's expansionist ambitions in the Peninsula. Though exaggerated and one-sided this obsession did, however, reflect Russian knowledge of the existence of influential aggressive circles in Vienna and Petersburg's fear that these circles would gain control in the event of Francis Joseph's death or the Ottoman

Empire's collapse, both of which appeared likely in the near future.

In the years prior to 1914 Austro-Russian co-operation was unfortunately both crucial for European peace and very difficult to maintain. Old suspicions exacerbated by the Bosnian crisis stood in the way of agreement between the two empires, as did racial sensitivities. Russia's historical role as liberator of the Balkans was difficult to square with Austria's determination to control adjacent territories in which irredentist movements could be based. Pragmatic and realistic considerations also impeded the old German desire to divide the Peninsula between Russian and Austrian spheres of interest, assigning Constantinople to the former and the Western Balkans to the latter. Vienna believed that Constantinople was of such strategic and moral importance that its possession by Russia would allow the latter an unacceptable predominance in the Near East. Petersburg believed on the contrary that possession of the Straits and the city was in itself insufficient and might indeed prove more of a hindrance than an asset. N. de Basily, the deputy chief of Sazonov's Chancellery, stressed in November 1914 the tremendous cost in both manpower and money which the adequate garrisoning and fortification of the Straits area would demand[33] and two years earlier A.A. Lieven, the Chief of the Naval General Staff, had insisted that secure possession of this region required the domination of its hinterland both in the Balkans and Asia Minor,[34] thus ruling out the abandonment into Austrian hands of the many hundreds of thousands of excellent Serb and Bulgar troops which Russia wished to have on its side in any future conflict with the Central Powers.

Whatever conflicts divided the rival empires before 1914 it should, however, have been clear to their rulers that the overriding interest both of the two dynasties and of the overwhelming majority of their peasant subjects lay in the avoidance of war and the smoothing over of all causes of tension in the Balkans. Unless checked, Austro-Russian rivalry was almost sure to lead to war in the period 1909–14. For a start, the two empires' competition was bound to be exacerbated by the fact that internal weakness meant that neither régime could afford to suffer major blows to its prestige in its foreign policy. In addition, in Austro-Russian collaboration lay the only hope of preserving any order in the Balkans. Rivalry between the two empires would be exploited by the Balkan states for their own ends, moreover fear that, unless humoured, their Balkan clients would go over to the enemy camp greatly weakened Austrian or Russian ability to impose restraint in times of crisis. Thus obsession with the Austrian threat led Petersburg to countenance the thoroughly risky Serb-Bulgar Treaty of February 1912 and restrained it from using all possible means to impose its desire for peace in Sofia and Belgrade in the summer of 1912. Unfortunately, the sharper the conflicts between the two Empires became, the less willing grew their rulers to risk the alienation of Balkan clients by demands for restraint, since in a European war the military support of these clients was reckoned in both Vienna and Petersburg to be of crucial importance. A further element in Balkan instability lay in the insecurity of the Balkan governments themselves and in their vulnerability to internal nationalist pressures which often had strong support in the states' own officer corps and in secret terrorist organisations such as IMRO or the Black Hand, both of which were closely linked with their national armies. In the particular case of Russo-Serb relations the effects of Petersburg's difficulties in imposing restraint in Belgrade and of the Serbian government's own problems in controlling the army were exacerbated by the personality of N.V. Hartwig, Russia's representative in Serbia in the prewar years.

Hartwig saw his role in Belgrade as being to secure the maximum possible Russo-Serb solidarity in order to ensure effective united action in what he saw as the inevitable future conflict with Vienna. His success in binding Belgrade to Petersburg was undoubted. The British mission in Serbia reported that whereas when Hartwig arrived in the wake of the Bosnian crisis Russian prestige was at a low ebb, his popularity was such by early 1912 as to ensure that his 'opinion is unquestionably taken on most matters of foreign policy'.[35] A year later G.H. Barclay, the British Minister, wrote that thanks to Hartwig 'Serbia is, practically speaking, a Russian province' and that he had never known the Serb government to act 'against the directions of the Russian Minister'.[36] Nicolson commented on hearing of Hartwig's death that 'he was a faithful and active supporter of Russian policy. His Serbian policy was, as far as Russian interests were concerned, distinctly a success'.[37]

Few of Russia's leading diplomats would have agreed with this generous assessment. A.P. Izvol'sky,[38] N.N. Shebeko,[39] A.A. Savinsky,[40] A.V. Neklyudov[41] and N.N. Giers[42] all in their time denounced the dangers of Hartwig's 'incurable Austrophobia' and of his disloyalty to overall Russian foreign policy. Benckendorff's complaints about Hartwig's actions in Tehran revealed many of the defects the latter was later to display in Belgrade. These included an exaggerated distrust of the machinations of Russia's rivals, in this case Britain, coupled with an incautious and uncritical acceptance of the views of the anti-British local elements by whom he surrounded himself.[43] In Belgrade, Hartwig's interpretation of the Balkan crisis was entirely one-sided and the Russian Minister seems to have been blind to the risks entailed in the policies he supported or the incautious statements he so often made. Unlike Neklyudov or Neratov, in October 1911 Hartwig was willing to accept a Serb-Bulgar treaty without any guarantees against its transformation into an offensive anti-Ottoman alliance.[44] Moreover, in January 1914 after visiting Belgrade Savinsky reported that from his observations there 'I have become convinced that Hartwig's thought is to set Serbia on to Austria'.[45] The information that Hartwig passed back to Petersburg from Belgrade was on occasion highly selective. Moreover, one looks in vain in his published despatches for an appreciation of the dangers posed by organisations such as the Black Hand to a power which, while guaranteeing Serbia from Austrian invasion, nevertheless had every interest in avoiding a European war. In addition, Hartwig could not always be relied on to fulfil his instructions loyally, nor was the effect of the Russian government's counsels of restraint in Belgrade likely to be great when its representative 'has not endeavoured to conceal the fact that he considered M. [Monsieur] Sazonov's policy despicable and misguided'.[46] This was especially true given general knowledge about the Russian Minister's powerful connections in Petersburg and the imperial approval seemingly signified by the award to Hartwig of the Order of the White Eagle in the spring of 1913. Hartwig's enthusiastic identification of Russia's interests with the Serb national cause and the semi-imaginary 'Slav idea' justified Nicholas Giers' comment, echoed by Neklyudov, 'that it would be better if in the first place he pursued only Russia's interests'.[47] Giers' biting statement that in Belgrade Hartwig, a former correspondent of *Novoye Vremya*, 'shows the activity of an irresponsible journalist' was in part justified.[48]

Hartwig's activity in Belgrade was, however, only the extreme manifestation of that general fear of Austrian ambitions which underlay Russian foreign policy in the years 1909–14. To block any Austrian advance to the south the Russian government had from December 1908 been urging that Belgrade and Sofia should draw together[49] but it was only in the autumn of 1911 that external circumstances, disillusionment with Turkish promises and the advent of the Russophile Geshov-Danev coalition made the Bulgars willing to heed Russian advice in this respect. In the negotiations for a Serb-Bulgar alliance which culminated successfully in February 1912 the Russians played a major role, urging concessions on both sides and finally taking upon themselves the burden of arbitrating the allocation of disputed territory in Macedonia. From the start Petersburg was warned by its able representative in Sofia, Neklyudov, that the alliance had 'one dangerous element – the temptation to use it for attack'.[50] Later despatches explained that the Bulgarians, more powerful and much less fearful of Vienna than the Serbs, would be more difficult for Petersburg to control. Moreover, in the first half of 1912 the mission in Sofia left its government in no doubt that for the Bulgarians the great advantage of the treaty lay not in the protection it offered against Austrian aggression but in the offensive use to which it could be put in Macedonia.[51] As a result, the Russian government strongly pressed moderation on the Bulgars but Petersburg's underestimate of the Balkan states' military capacity, added to the traditional patronising Russian sense that the Slav 'little brothers' would obey elder brother's orders led to the Imperial government failing to grasp the urgency of the crisis before it was too late.[52] Although the Russians must therefore take some responsibility for the outbreak of the First Balkan War in October 1912, condemnation of Petersburg has to be balanced by a sense of Balkan realities in 1912–13. Weakened by internal dissension and the Italian War, the Ottoman Empire was a tempting target for the ever-more powerful Balkan states, whose governments were spurred into action not just by their own territorial ambitions but also by their peoples' well-justified hatred for the age-old Turkish oppressor. As Prince S. Urusov told Petersburg in April 1912,[53] if Ottoman vulnerability had become sufficiently great a Serb-Bulgar offensive alliance would have resulted even without Russian collaboration. Moreover, the Greek-Bulgar alliance was achieved without Russian aid by simply ignoring the two countries' conflicting claims in Macedonia in order to smash the Ottomans before the latter recovered their strength.

Whoever one may hold responsible for the collapse of the Balkan *status quo*, its result was a giant stride towards the outbreak of the European war in 1914. Izvol'sky warned in October 1912 that although the decisive victory of the Balkan states over the Turks was unlikely, of all the possible endings to the war it would be the most fraught with threatening consequences for the general peace; it would bring forward, in its full historical development, the question of the struggle of slavdom not only with Islam but also with Germanism. In this event one can scarcely set one's hopes on any palliative measures and must prepare for a great and decisive general European war.[54]

Izvol'sky's warning was the product of far-sightedness, not of war-mongering. The result of the Balkan Wars was to increase greatly the self-confidence of the Balkan states, the irredentist forces within them and the anti-Habsburg feelings of the subject peoples of the Dual Monarchy. Had Bulgaria emerged triumphant from the Second Balkan War Vienna would have had little reason for concern. Sofia had no territorial ambitions in the Monarchy and its power would have held the Serbs in check and scared the Russians about the safety of Constantinople. The Serb-Rumanian victory was, however, a disaster for Vienna, the growing irredentist movements in these two states representing a threat to the internal stability of the Dual Monarchy. Austria's response to this threat was arrogant and unwise; whatever may justly be said about the difficulties of fundamental internal reform in the Monarchy, the latter should certainly have been attempted since it could scarcely be more dangerous than the blind attempt to solve internal problems by the external adventurism which led to a European war. Russia too was, however, not wholly blameless as regards the growing Balkan crisis of 1913-4. Offering in effect a guarantee to both Belgrade and Bucharest against Austrian intervention, Petersburg would inevitably be in the firing line should its clients' activities arouse fear and anger in Vienna. Even leaving aside Hartwig's activities, Sazonov's own encouragement, however theoretical, of Rumanian aspirations in Hungary, together with his foolish trip into Transylvania with I. Bratianu in June 1914 showed a certain tactlessness and lack of caution given Russia's need for peace.

In 1913-4 Petersburg was, however, too concerned with its own weakness and with what it saw as threats to vital Russian interests to spare much thought for Vienna's feelings. The Russians were, with some justice, indignant that the concessions they had made after the first Balkan War in the interests of European peace had not been reciprocated by the Central Powers. Austrian intransigence over Serbia's Adriatic port had helped channel Serb ambitions southwards and thus aided the break-up of the Balkan League. Vienna's refusal to see the Montenegrins in Scutari had angered the Russians, while Austrian ultimatums to Serbia and Greece to evacuate Albanian territory had convinced Petersburg that by threats of war the Central Powers were attempting to impose their own views in all contentious problems that arose in the Balkans. This would have mattered less had the Russians not been scared by increasing German influence throughout the Middle East. William II's reign had witnessed the huge expansion of Germany's role in the Ottoman Empire and once the Baghdad railway was completed the same process seemed likely to begin in Persia. Moreover, not merely did German economic domination inevitably entail considerable political influence, the activities of German consuls showed that their government was by no means only interested in financial profits in the Middle East. In November 1913, for instance, M. N. Giers reported that Consul Anders in Erzerum was spreading propaganda throughout his region and that plans were afoot for a huge expansion of German-run schools in the area.[55] A year earlier Consul Schunemann in Tavriz had been caught distributing arms to local tribesmen.[56] Given the great instability of Russia's Caucasian territories any government in Petersburg would have been alarmed by the spread of German influence in the Ottoman and Persian border areas.

Above all, the Russians feared for the future of Constantinople. History and sentiment alone would have made it difficult for the successor-state of Byzantium to accept the possession of Constantinople by any other great power but strategic considerations were also significant, for control of the Straits would have allowed any maritime power to dominate the Black Sea. Still more important were economic considerations. Between 1903 and 1912 37 per cent of Russian exports and over three-quarters of her grain shipments went through the Straits, whose brief closure in 1912 and 1913 had enormously alarmed Russian society. Any attempt to shift these bulky exports to overland routes would, as Basily wrote,[57] have been extremely expensive; moreover these routes were mostly controlled by the Central Powers. There was therefore some truth in Sazonov's statement that 'the Straits in the hands of a strong state . . . would signify the complete subordination of the economic development of the whole of southern Russian to this state'.[58] It was thus an axiom of pre-war Russian policy that although the survival of a weak and therefore malleable Turkish control of the Straits was acceptable, even indeed desirable, should the Ottoman Empire collapse Russia would fight rather than allow any other power to hold Constantinople. The announcement in October 1913 that a German officer was to be appointed to command the garrison at Constantinople therefore inspired fury in Petersburg. Liman von Sanders' influence over promotions and appointments was likely to ensure the existence of a pro-German Turkish high command, a point of special significance given the key political role played by the Ottoman army since 1908. Moreover, should the Ottoman Empire collapse the presence of German-commanded troops in Constantinople might seriously impede Russia's determination to seize the Straits. In bidding farewell to the Liman von Sanders mission William II called on its officers 'to create for me a new strong army which obeys my orders'. Expressing the hope that 'the German flag will soon fly over the fortifications of the Bosphorus', the Emperor stressed that the mission's first priority was 'the Germanisation of the Turkish army through (German) leadership and direct control of the organisational activity of the Turkish ministry of war'.[59] Though William's hysterical outbursts always require to be discounted somewhat, taken as they stand these comments amounted to not much less than a declaration of war on Russia.

German policy in the Middle East was not, however, wholly unjustifiable and the principles on which it was based were shared by many Russian diplomats. Benckendorff, scarcely a pro-German, well understood that growing economic power entailed the expansion of German influence and conflicts with the established interests of other states. 'At the root of everything', he wrote in July 1911,

I see the gigantic force of expansion of Germany which carries along with it its influence and inevitably its flag . . . . This expansionist force in no way necessarily means that the Berlin cabinet is deliberately waging an aggressive policy; but it entails countermeasures on the part of the other powers which always create the danger of conflict.[60]

Writing a month later, the Russian *chargé d'affaires* in Brussels was still more outspoken. The tremendous growth of the German population and economy in recent decades, coupled with the small size of the Empire's territory in his view made the Germans' 'struggle for existence' very difficult. Knowing her strength, Germany had a 'natural desire' to use it and to 'make a run at her weaker neighbours, along the line of least resistance'; thus war would indeed 'become for her a vital necessity'.[61] As regards the Middle East, in May 1912 the Russian Military attaché in Berlin, Bazarov, wrote that if the Ottoman Empire collapsed Germany was less well placed than any other European power to pick up Turkish territories, yet her investments in the Empire were vast and likely to suffer badly. Should Germany suffer without compensating gains from a Turkish collapse, there would 'naturally' be 'a very serious protest' in German society which 'may force Germany to seek compensation with sword in hand'.[62] Even the appointment of Liman von Sanders, though a major example of German risky diplomacy, had some excuse. This was recognised by both the French and British military attachés in Constantinople. The latter wrote that German desire for tighter control over Turkish troops was understandable given the ridicule to which the previous military mission had been subjected after the Balkan Wars.[63] L–M Bompard and Sir R. Paget both felt that in practice the mission's effect would be slighter than Petersburg imagined, though to do the Russians justice one must add that the British and French missions in Constantinople were notoriously ill-disposed towards Russian interests. Nevertheless, it is not without interest that the British military attaché believed that Liman von Sanders' power would probably be sufficient to win him great unpopularity in the Ottoman officer corps but inadequate to exercise effective control or push through real reforms. Moreover, if the Germans were foolish not to negotiate in advance with Petersburg about Liman von Sanders' position and powers the British Foreign Office was no better informed than German diplomats about the precise status of its own naval mission in Constantinople. When the Liman von Sanders crisis broke, Grey and Nicolson respectively 'did not realise' and 'had no idea that Admiral Limpus *commanded* the fleet'.[64]

The Liman von Sanders affair persuaded Sazovon that unless Russia took a stronger stand than she had adopted in 1912–13 her vital interests might be ignored by her allies and would be trampled upon by the Central Powers, whose 'ever more irreconcilable and unstable tone in all questions touching their interests' the Foreign Minister described to Nicholas II in December 1913.[65] Had British support been available, Sazonov would have been prepared to answer any German refusal to shift Liman von Sanders by the occupation of selected Ottoman ports, a dangerous policy for which he was rightly chided by Benckendorff and V.N. Kokovtsov.[66] The latter's fall in January 1914, caused largely for internal political reasons, strengthened the tendency in Petersburg which argued that any further Russian concessions to the Central Powers' demands would merely whet German and Austrian appetites and convince Berlin and Vienna that Russian views might be treated with disdain. In its commitment to the resolute deterrence of German aggression Petersburg had the full support of Paris. Angered by Berlin's tactics in the Agadir crisis the French government in 1912–14 was determined not to submit to German pressure and was willing to give far greater support to Russia's Balkan policies than in the past. In September 1912 Raymond Poincaré assured Izvol'sky that if an Austrian invasion of Serbia or any other Balkan crisis brought on a war between Russia and the Central Powers, 'the French government recognises this in advance as a *casus foederis* and will not waver for one moment to fulfil the obligations lying upon it with respect to Russia'. If Petersburg needed any encouragement towards adopting a tough line towards Austria it would have derived it from Poincaré's further comment that the French General Staff was confident of victory in the event of a European war.[67] These assurances were repeated in October and November 1912 and in Izvol'sky's view represented 'a completely new French view . . . that territorial grabs by Austria affect the general European balance and therefore France's own interests'.[68] They become still more impressive when one considers that in December 1912 the French government was actually chiding the Russians for not taking a stronger stance in response to Austrian military preparations.[69] Nor indeed was the advice given to the Russians by French diplomats during the Liman von Sanders crisis likely to induce Petersburg towards restraint. For Sazonov French support was, however, insufficient. As he stated on 31 December 1913,

> Russian action with the support of France is not especially dangerous for Germany. Both powers are scarcely capable of dealing Germany a mortal blow even in the event of success on the battlefield, which is always uncertain. But a struggle in which England took part might be fatal for Germany, which well understands the danger of being reduced to total internal social catastrophe given English action.[70]

Like Nicholas II and Kokovtsov, Sazonov believed that the Germans were so scared of Britain that a firmly-based defensive alliance between the three Entente powers would effectively deter any German dreams of aggression, thereby forcing Berlin to treat with respect the interests of Europe's other powers.[71]

To the Foreign Minister's rage, however, London's 'vacillating and self-effacing policy' knocked the major prop from under his strategy of deterrence and, in his view, allowed Berlin to believe that it could succeed in pushing around its continental rivals.[72] This was doubly dangerous given the growing evidence flowing into Petersburg about Germany's aggressive intentions. Both Bazarov[73] and the agents of the Russian secret political police in Germany reported the concern aroused in public opinion by the press war against Russia which raged in the spring of 1914. The chief of the Russian police forces reported to the army's General Staff in May 1914 that there existed a widespread belief in Germany that, fearing Russia's growing military might, Berlin would utilise 'some sort of insignificant pretext in order to declare war on Russia' while victory was still a possibility.[74] Meanwhile Russian military intelligence in February 1914 presented the government with two German memoranda it had acquired which discussed measures to prepare public opinion for the war on two fronts which was regarded as inevitable in the near future. In addition, the first memorandum emphasised German determination to control the Straits, even at the cost of European war, should the Ottoman Empire collapse; the second stressed William II's hope that tactful persuasiveness on the part of the head of the German military mission would lead to the Turks agreeing to the modernisation of the shore batteries covering the Bosphorus and to command over these batteries being given to Germans.[75] Sazonov himself told Sir George Buchanan, the British ambassador, that this 'secret military information . . . might, or might not be correct'[76] but it is worth noting that the diplomats' scepticism about the accuracy of military intelligence reports from Vienna had in the Bosnian crisis proved unfounded.[77] In any event, whatever Sazonov's doubts, the attitude of the Russian high command during the July crisis must surely have been influenced by these reports of German preparations for a preventive war.

# 3   Who Ruled in Petersburg?

It would in many ways be surprising if Field Marshal Conrad von Hotzendorff's famous question in July 1914 about the location of political power in Berlin did not have a certain relevance to Saint Petersburg as well. After all, at least on the surface the Russian and German political systems had much in common. In both states the control exercised by hereditary monarchs over the executive branch of government, though spasmodic, was real and important. In both these traditionally military empires the armed forces were, even in 1914, still subordinated to the monarch rather than to the civilian government or to a parliament. At the same time, neither state was merely an old-style autocracy; in both, elected legislatures existed which put some constraints on the government's freedom of action and sought to influence governmental policy in the name of public opinion. Few historians of the First World War would deny that the German political system and, in particular, the diffusion of political power in Berlin between a number of conflicting individuals and institutions was in part responsible for the erratic, uncoordinated and at times seemingly suicidal course pursued by the Second Reich in the years immediately prior to 1914. The question therefore almost asks itself, to what extent could a similar charge be levelled with justice against the Russian system of government? The present chapter aims to answer this question by attempting to see how and by whom decisions were made and executed in the years 1905–14 and what influence the Russian governmental system can be said to have had on the state's foreign and defence policies in these years.

The institutions of central government through which Imperial Russia was ruled in the last decade of its existence were set out in the Fundamental Laws promulgated on 23 April 1906 (O.S.). These Laws denied the principle of popular sovereignty by asserting, in Article 4, that 'the supreme autocratic power' remained in the hands of the Emperor, who owed his authority to God alone.[1] The Emperor retained full control over the executive, ministers and officials being

chosen by him and in no sense responsible to the legislature. Nevertheless, as a result of the 1905 Revolution an elected legislature was
created for the first time in Russia; the lower house, the Duma, was
wholly elected, the upper house, the State Council, being filled half by
Imperial appointment and half by elected representatives of the
nobility, the local government councils (zemstvos), commercial and
industrial corporations, the Church and the institutions of scholarship and higher education. All laws required the consent of the
crown and of both the houses, as did the budget and new state loans.

The Fundamental Laws went further than the constitution of any
other European state to underline the Emperor's complete control over
all questions of foreign policy and defence. Article 13, for instance,
reserved to him the exclusive right to make war and peace and to sign
treaties with foreign powers, while Articles 14 and 96 spelled out in
some detail his all-embracing rights as commander-in-chief of the
armed forces. Nevertheless, even as regards foreign and defence policy
the legislature was not toothless. Its budgetary powers, together with
its control over the size of the annual intake of recruits into the armed
forces enabled it to affect the level of the state's military and financial
resources, on which Great Power politics wholly depended. It is true
that the legislature's rights in this respect were circum-
scribed. Rejection, partial or wholesale, either of the budget or of the
recruitment quota resulted, according to the Fundamental Laws, in
the previous year's legislation remaining in force. Thus if on the one
hand the legislature could veto increased levels of defence spending
and military cadres, on the other it could not undermine the state's
position at home or abroad by stopping supply or denying the armed
forces the already established level of new recruits. In addition, in the
last resort the state possessed the power to override any attempt by
the legislature to undermine its foreign policy. The Emperor could at
any time dissolve the existing legislature, though he was bound by law
immediately to hold elections in order to summon a new one. Moreover, if the state chose to use unconstitutional methods to assert its
will, the legislature could offer little effective resistance, as was shown
in 1907 and 1911. On the other hand, the use of such illegal methods
not merely ran the risk of increasing public resentment against the
régime but also undermined faith in the new constitutional order and
the attempted compromise between state and society which had
emerged out of the debacle of 1905.[2]

In the years 1906–14 the most clear-cut conflict between crown and parliament in the sphere of defence and foreign policy concerned the reconstruction of the navy. Nicholas II was committed to the immedi- ate restoration of Russian naval power after the disastrous defeat by Japan and he imposed his views on a somewhat unwilling Council of Ministers. The latter's attempt to steer through the legislature a bill for the construction of four battleships in the Baltic was, however, rejected by the Duma, which reflected Russian public opinion's general lack of enthusiasm for navies and its disbelief in the honesty or efficiency of the naval department. Despite the Duma's refusal for three successive years to vote the necessary credits, construction of the four battleships went ahead and the lower house was ultimately faced by a *fait accompli*. This occurred because the government was able to get the support of the State Council for the credits, the upper house's obedience to clearly expressed imperial wishes outweighing even some of its own members' scepticism about the fleet's usefulness. Since, according to the constitution, deadlock between the two houses of the legislature over individual appropriations resulted in the sum closest to previous years' credits being adopted, the government was able to build its ships on the basis of the money voted for naval construction in 1906. When to the already existing budgetary rights possessed by the state there was added by the decree of 24 August 1909 a still greater freedom to neutralise legislative opposition to specific items of defence expenditure it is not surprising that the British military attaché came to feel that the Duma's financial control over the armed forces was 'practically nominal'. This view was, however, somewhat exaggerated, as subsequent events were to show. Even as regards its plans for a Baltic battlefleet the government did to some extent compromise with the Duma by partly acceding to the latter's demand for a full-scale inspection by non-naval personnel of the administrative and financial practices of the Ministry of the Navy. Moreover, in the period 1911–14 the government, and in particular the Minister of the Navy, Admiral I.K. Grigorovich, made a real and successful effort to achieve a harmonious relationship with the legisla- ture as regards naval questions, a policy aided by the genuine com- mitment to reform both of the Minister and of many of his subordin- ates. Quite apart from the general political reasons why such an understanding with the Duma might prove of value, the legislature's financial powers were by no means irrelevant for naval authorities seeking extra credits for the fleet's expansion at a speed and on a scale for which there were no budgetary precedents. Study of the constitutional relations between Crown and Duma over the issue of naval armaments suggests that although the former held most of the cards in its hand, the latter's financial powers meant that its opinions did possess a certain significance.[3]

When one looks at the relationship between government and society in the light not of constitutional law but of political realities then the attempt to gauge the significance of forces such as the Duma, the political parties and the press becomes more complicated, the factors involved more numerous and imponderable. For a number of reasons, in formulating its foreign policy the government could not afford wholly to ignore public opinion. Alarmed by its isolation and weakness in 1905–6 the régime sought in the following years to achieve a compromise with at least some elements of society in order to strengthen its position. In the period 1907–11 the premier, P. A. Stolypin, worked hard to achieve a *modus vivendi* with the majority parties in the Third Duma, namely the Octobrists and Nationalists. The Russian nationalist policies pursued by Stolypin in internal affairs were in part designed to win the legislature's support but their effectiveness in this respect would certainly be reduced if in its external policy the state disregarded Duma sympathy for the Slavs or failed to maintain Russian prestige. It is true that after 1909 Stolypin shifted his support from the Octobrists to the Nationalists and that the latter were much less interested than the former in foreign policy. It is also the case that after Stolypin's death in 1911 the régime paid less attention to the Duma's wishes and valued its support less highly than before. Nevertheless, the government could never wholly disregard the legislature and was, in addition, aware that in time of war the Duma's backing might help cement national unity and secure the co-operation both of the elected local government councils (zemstvos) and of landowning, professional and commercial elements whose support for the war effort would be of great use. Even the relatively moderate railway workers, whose lack of co-operation during mobilisation could well prove a serious menace, might perhaps be influenced by the Duma's views.[4]

More than short-term political considerations were involved when the government considered the impact of its foreign policy on society. The régime had always derived a major part of its legitimacy from its claim that the autocracy alone had been capable of creating a Great Russia and ensuring that the Empire was respected and accepted as an equal by the leading European powers. Humiliation in foreign policy thus struck directly at the régime's *raison d'être*. This was all the more dangerous given the existence since 1905 of political groups anxious to steal the patriotic card from the government's hands and pose as more resolute and effective defenders than the régime of national interests and traditions. The links being forged between some party leaders, notably A. I. Guchkov, and certain generals and admirals were as yet only an embryonic danger but they already worried some high officials and courtiers[5] and were in the longer term an additional reason to think twice before pursuing a foreign policy too flagrantly at variance with the nationalist sentiments so prevalent in the armed forces. Moreover, as was stated in the previous chapter, any weakness revealed by failures in foreign policy was sure to have unpleasant implications for a régime whose ability to maintain control within Russia depended in part on its reputation for strength and invincibility. Moreover, if all these factors ought to have meant that public opinion exerted a significant influence on the state's foreign policy, in fact in the crises of 1909 and July 1914 the government was indeed to some extent swayed by its awareness of the views of Russian society.

Nevertheless, one must not exaggerate. The Emperor, together with the ministers and officials he appointed, controlled Russian foreign policy. In the formulation of this policy public opinion was only one of the factors to be taken into account by the government, moreover the workings of secret diplomacy to some extent meant that society could be presented with *faits accomplis* or provided with distorted information by the Foreign Ministry. A. P. Izvol'sky and S. D. Sazonov, the heads of this department between 1906 and 1914, were it is true liberal-conservatives, anxious to cultivate public opinion and secure the Duma's support for their policies.[6] No Minister, and least of all a Minister of Foreign Affairs, who was felt to be more responsive to public opinion than to Imperial wishes would, however, have survived for long. His fate would have been similar to that of A. A. Polivanov, the Assistant Minister of War, who was dismissed in 1912 because of his close links with Guchkov. Ministers like Grigorovich who were skilled at securing the Duma's backing for Imperial policies were valued; those with divided or suspected loyalties were not tolerated for long.[7] Nicholas II's power therefore ensured that his views on foreign policy were of crucial significance.

For a number of reasons the Emperor was scarcely very susceptible to the influence of public opinion. In contrast to the persecution by press and society at times suffered by Izvol'sky and Sazonov not merely the monarch's status but also his geographical isolation made him almost invulnerable to criticism. Living outside Petersburg in the very small circle of his family and a handful of friends, Nicholas II's contacts with representatives of the public were few and formal.[8] Nor did the views of those very few relatives, high officials or acquaintances who might have exerted an influence on the Emperor by any means necessarily reflect the attitude even of that relatively narrow élite generally described as Russian public opinion.

The Emperor's independence was, however, based not just on geographical but also on ideological factors. The party leaders and the press founded their claim to exert an influence on foreign policy on the assertion that, to quote Guchkov, it was 'our' money and ultimately 'our' blood on which the state's foreign and defence policy rested. In addition, should war come, 'we can give you one other thing; the guarantee of victory, that enthusiasm without which struggle and victory is impossible'.[9] In fact this claim was largely unfounded since those who actually paid most of the state's taxes and would fill the ranks of its armies in time of war were barely represented in the Duma and did not read the newspapers. Moreover, not merely had the mass of the Russian people always been distinctly suspicious of the Westernised elite, whose representatives dominated the legislature but under the strains of rapid modernisation suspicion was often turning towards hatred, as the revolution of 1905 had shown. Not just conservative high officials but also Nicholas II were well aware that neither the Duma nor the press truly spoke for Russia as a whole and this greatly reduced the latter's influence. Unlike some of his more hard-headed advisers, the Emperor believed despite the evidence of 1905 that the mass of the population, though perhaps ignorant and easily confused, were still at heart loyal patriots and monarchists. After meeting Nicholas in 1909, Matton, the French Military Attaché, wrote that though the Emperor believed Petersburg to be disloyal he still counted on the support of rural Russia.

> He is certain that the rural population, the owners of land, the nobility and the army remain loyal to the Tsar; the revolutionary elements are composed above all of Jews, students, of landless peasants and of some workers.[10]

The welcome given to the monarch in his periodic visits to rural areas suggested both to him and to some observers that peasant loyalty and respect for the crown was still strong and this, in the words of O'Beirne, the British Counsellor in Petersburg, 'enables the Government to disregard to a great extent the agitation of politicians'.[11] Such disregard in any event fitted in with Nicholas II's own conception of kingship. Convinced that he was accountable to God for the country entrusted to his care, he believed it to be his duty to direct governmental policy according to his own conscience and understanding.

It is true that on occasion the Emperor spoke to foreign diplomats of the impossibility for his government to stand up to pro-Slav and nationalist feeling in society if the latter were sufficiently aroused. Up to a point this was true, for reasons already explained in this chapter. Nevertheless, like Sazonov, Nicholas II was no doubt aware that reference to the powerful pressures exerted by public opinion could strengthen the hand of the Russian Foreign Ministry in its negotiations with other powers. When the Emperor wished to convey other messages to foreign governments his interpretation of the balance of forces within Russian politics could be very different. In December 1908, for instance, aware of Berlin's anxiety about anti-German feeling in Russian society, Nicholas told Hintze, William II's representative at the Russian Court, that 'I am the master here'. The Duma, said Nicholas, might be a useful safety valve 'where everyone could air their views and where one might gather advice and even approval' but as regards important policies, 'I myself decide.'[12]

These words were not mere bombast, for as the Chairman of the State Council, M. G. Akimov, recalled,[13] Nicholas II was by no means as malleable as some imagined. Despite his gentle and impressionable nature, where Nicholas II's convictions were in question he could be extremely stubborn, as Stolypin discovered to his cost. It is most unlikely that the Emperor would ever have consented to the adoption of an overall line in foreign policy to which he was opposed. One must remember that the various forces which before 1914 urged the support of a more determined and pro-Slav foreign policy only truly coalesced in the summer of 1915 when the Progressive Bloc was formed in the Duma. This Bloc had the support of the great majority of the legislature, the press, public opinion and, to a considerable extent, most of the Council of Ministers as well. A grand coalition of forces implored Nicholas II not to assume command of the army and to create a government of 'public confidence' which would compromise and indeed merge with the Progressive Bloc. This pressure was exerted at a time when, after the military defeats of 1915, the régime's position was especially weak, its prestige badly shaken. Now if ever was the time to bow to patriotic public opinion. Instead Nicholas II assumed the supreme command, rejected the formation of a government of 'public confidence', in time removed most of its advocates from the Council of Ministers and in 1916, in the midst of the strong anti-German sentiment current during the war, appointed B.V. Stürmer as Chairman of the Council. These were not the actions of a man easily swayed by public opinion. They add weight to the view that one must explain the considerable degree of agreement on foreign policy before 1914 between Emperor, government and society not by society's pressure on the Emperor and government but rather because all three shared common instincts about Russia's honour, prestige and history together with a common interpretation of how her interests were affected by international developments.

Within the executive branch of government the Emperor's power was in theory supreme. Ministers and officials were the Emperor's servants who executed his wishes until he chose to relieve them of the burdens of office. In practice their power was far greater than this, for the monarch's ability to master and direct the many and often highly complicated tasks facing the government was limited, especially given Nicholas II's lack of an effective personal secretariat. In most areas of internal administration Nicholas was merely consulted on the broadest guidelines of policy, intervening occasionally when specific matters aroused his interest[14] Foreign policy was, however, a different matter for here the monarch maintained a close and detailed watch on events. Nicholas read conscientiously the despatches and telegrams which were submitted to him every day and, blessed by an excellent memory, was exceptionally well-informed on questions of international relations. It is true that the disastrous results of his Far Eastern policy in 1904–5, added to his discomfiture at Bjorkoe, seem to have largely convinced the monarch of the need to avoid acting in future in isolation from his Foreign Minister. Moreover, neither Izvol'sky nor Sazonov would have been prepared to follow Lambsdorff's example of allowing policies to be pursued behind their backs but under their names with which they were in disagreement. On the other hand, when faced by serious disagreement with the monarch the Foreign Minister still had little recourse but the threat of resignation. Even if one were sufficiently indispensible to make this threat effective, it was, however, a dangerous weapon to use against Nicholas II, who hated to feel that his hand was being forced.[15]

Two collegiate institutions established in 1905 might, on paper, have been expected to have played a major role in co-ordinating the state's foreign and defence policies. The Council of State Defence was indeed set up with precisely this aim in mind but, proving a failure, was abolished in 1909. The Council failed in part because it undermined the position of the Minister of War without creating an alternative executive authority capable of imposing co-ordinated reforms on the many semi-autonomous branches of the army. In addition, the navy fought hard to preserve its independence from the army-dominated Council, whose views on defence expenditure it inevitably found unpalatable. Nicholas II's enthusiastic support for the admirals ensured that even before its abolition the Council lost all its authority or effectiveness.[16]

With the Council's disappearance in 1909 the Ministers of War and of the Navy again resumed sole control of their departments. At least in theory only they, and not even the two Chiefs of Staff, had the right to report directly to the Emperor. In any case the army Chiefs of Staff between 1909 and 1914 were not on the whole strong characters and changed too often to know their jobs properly. The Minister of War's influence on Russian foreign policy depended both on the extent of his political experience and on the degree to which he enjoyed the Emperor's confidence. Unlike D. A. Milyutin, who exercised a great influence on Alexander II, V. A. Sukhomlinov, the Minister of War in the five years before 1914, seems to have been largely ignorant about foreign affairs. In addition, he was discouraged by Nicholas II from any attempts to exercise an influence in this sphere,[17] though the former minister's determination in his memoirs to shift responsibility for the outbreak of war on to other shoulders certainly results in his exaggerating his powerlessness. Whatever its chief's character, the Ministry of War's role in Russian foreign policy was, however, bound to be crucial. The whole tone of the state's foreign policy depended on the army's ability to wage war. In crises the armed forces' operational plans and their readiness or otherwise to back diplomatic moves by military action became important, as the long-drawn out debate in 1912–14 within the government over the fate of the Straits clearly illustrates. If a crisis became sufficiently serious to make war a possibility then the military and naval chiefs' views on the chances of victory became crucial and these views were inevitably affected not just by technical considerations but also by the generals' and admir-

als' conceptions about Russia's honour and interests. The armed
forces' views on Russian foreign policy were reflected in some newspapers and in particular in *Novoye Vremya* and thus came to the attention of the Emperor and the government. Russia was of course not
Serbia or Bulgaria and, save in the long run, its rulers had no reason to
fear the army's intervention in politics should military views on Russia's honour or interests be ignored. On the other hand, Nicholas II
spent much of his time with his army, whose views on patriotism and
national honour he largely shared. In the autumn of 1912 foreign
diplomats were convinced[18] that Nicholas was strongly influenced by
the pro-Slav and aggressive military atmosphere by which he was
surrounded at Spala and they may well have been correct, especially
since the leading advocate of a stronger Russian stand in favour of the
Balkan League was the Grand Duke Nicholas Nikolayevich, a cousin
of the Emperor.

The second major collegiate institution established in 1905, the
Council of Ministers, was designed to co-ordinate legislative and
administrative policy between the various departments of state,
whose chiefs were *ex officio* members of the Council. Similarities between the Council and the British Cabinet are, however, superficial.
Appointed and dismissed by the Emperor, ministers remained largely
autonomous and in some cases pursued policies sharply at variance
with the views of the Council's chairman. So long as Stolypin was
regarded as the indispensible saviour of the régime his authority over
the monarch and his fellow ministers was strong but after 1909 even
his hold somewhat weakened. His successor, V. N. Kokovtsov, lacked
Stolypin's prestige, never controlled the powerful Ministry of the
Interior and was increasingly unable to impose his views on his fellow
ministers, who split into warring factions. These internal divisions
inevitably weakened the civilian government's ability to influence the
state's foreign policy.[19]

In addition, not merely did many ministers lack either the time or
knowledge to take a detailed interest in international relations, the
constitution made it difficult for the Council to interfere in the military or diplomatic sphere. Article 14 of the law of 19 October 1905 [O.S.]
stated that 'matters relating... to the defence of the state and to
external policy are submitted to the Council of Ministers where there
is an Imperial command to this effect, when the heads of the relevant
departments see this as necesary or when the affairs in question
concern other departments.' Military and diplomatic affairs were

thus regarded as being peculiarly an Imperial prerogative, which explains how Izvol'sky could negotiate with Aehrenthal at Buchlau without the Council's prior knowledge or approval, subsequently indeed at first refusing to divulge to his colleagues what had transpired. In the aftermath of Buchlau Stolypin forced Nicholas II to allow the Council a greater role in foreign policy, Kokovtsov stating that during the rest of the annexation crisis Izvol'sky 'had taken no steps without consultation with the Russian Cabinet', the latter even seeing in draft a telegram from Nicholas II to the Kaiser. In the following years, though the Council never again exercised this close a watch on the Foreign Ministry, it was from time to time informed of diplomatic events; in 1913, for instance, it discussed the collapse of the Balkan League, the possible fall of Constantinople and the threat of European war. The Council's Chairmen, first Stolypin, then Kokovtsov, joined the Emperor and Foreign Minister as junior members of the triumvirate which ultimately decided questions of foreign policy. Moreover, in the crisis of July 1914 the full Council of Ministers debated how to respond to the Austrian ultimatum to Serbia both in the presence and the absence of the Emperor.[20]

If the Council did therefore have some say in foreign policy its advice was nevertheless only taken on sufferance and individual ministers' ability to exercise an influence on Russian diplomacy was strictly limited. Even when consulted, as in July 1914, many Russian ministers' reactions were likely to be somewhat different to those of their British counterparts. In the British cabinet there existed an instinctive knowledge of the equality and collective responsibility of all its members which encouraged and even to some extent forced ministers to stand up and be counted on the issue of peace and war. Russian ministers, generally specialists in a specific field, were more likely to feel a sense of individual responsibility to the Emperor for their own department, coupled in some cases with the comforting thought that ultimate responsibility was at least shared with the monarch. Moreover, unless like A.V. Krivoshein he enjoyed an unusual degree of Imperial confidence, a minister would be shy of attempting to influence the state's foreign policy since it was wellknown both that Nicholas II preferred heads of departments to confine themselves to their own specific spheres and that he regarded foreign affairs as being peculiarly the business of himself and those to whom be chose to turn for advice. Even Kokovtsov, who was both Chairman of the Council and Minister of Finance, at times faced

Imperial suspicion because of the role he came to play in diplomatic and military affairs.[21] The chances of ordinary ministers exercising an influence in these spheres were therefore relatively small.

Much more important were the officials of the Foreign Ministry serving both in Petersburg and abroad, on whom the government relied for advice, information and for the execution of its foreign policy. As elsewhere in Europe, Russian diplomats were in general drawn from a narrow social circle; a considerable number, of whom the many able members of the Giers family provide the best example, came from diplomatic dynasties. Those who handled Russia's relations with Western and Central Europe tended in particular to be well-connected and looked down on other sections of the department, not to mention the largely separate consular service. Appointments and promotions, though in theory based on the almost unworkable Civil Service Regulations, in practice depended greatly on one's ability to know or catch the eye of powerful figures at the Choristers' Bridge.[22] (The Choristers' Bridge in Petersburg was the geographical location of the foreign ministry. Russians spoke of the ministry as the Choristers' Bridge just as Frenchmen or Austrians referred to the Quai D'Orsay or the Ballhausplatz.) As a result a few playboys and a larger number of mediocrities reached important positions but most of the foreign service was competent and part of it was very able. Of those who held key posts before 1914 Count A.K. Benckendorff, N.N. Shebeko and A.V. Neklyudov were among the most effective as was, for all his vanity and egoism, Izvol'sky, to whom on the whole history has been unfairly harsh. On the other hand, even able men were too often allowed to serve almost into their dotage, as the example of Count N.D. Osten-Sacken, the Ambassador in Berlin from 1895 to 1912, makes clear.[23] Indeed the Russian Foreign Ministry in general showed an excessive indulgence towards the whims and comforts of its officials, something owed in part to the easy-going nature of the Russian gentry but which was also linked to the fact that the powerful connections of many of these officials made their brusque treatment inadvisable.[24]

In general in the Russian civil service the more dispersed geographically officials were and the higher their social status the more difficult it tended to become for a minister to control his subordinates. The Foreign Minister's position was therefore particularly trying. In addition, the lack of any clear distinction in Russia between politics and administration had unfortunate effects. Political disputes, intrigues and ambitions sent ripples down the administrative system. In the intrigue-ridden world of Petersburg ministers could never be quite sure that their senior officials did not have an eye on their own port-folios. Assistant Ministers were particularly suspect in this respect and there was therefore a tendency in some departments to appoint trusted rather than brilliant subordinates to these positions.[25] Both Izvol'sky and Sazonov chose former schoolmates for these posts, per-sonal friendship guaranteeing a loyalty which could not always be totally relied on in a professional relationship. The somewhat ineffec-tive role played by A.A. Neratov, Sazonov's deputy, becomes easier to understand in this context and was very much in the tradition of A.K. Vlangali and N.P. Shishkin, both N.K. Giers' Assistant Ministers.[26] Unlike his British counterpart the Russian Foreign Minister was himself of course an official and in that sense much more an equal of his fellow diplomats. Sazonov had served for many years under Benckendorff and Izvol'sky and the letters in particular of the former take on at times an avuncular and critical tone in which no British diplomat would ever have dared to address Grey.[27] When the inex-perienced Neratov substituted for Sazonov advice flowed even more freely from London and Paris.[28] This of course had its advantages. Benckendorff and Izvol'sky were both abler and far more experienced than Sazonov or Neratov; they were also too loyal and discreet to flout their instructions or openly criticise their chiefs. Sometimes, however, the insufficiently strong control exercised by Petersburg over foreign posts had unfortunate results. If N.V. Charykov's 'natural im-petuousness' was partly responsible for the embarassing disclosure of Russian ambitions at the Straits in 1911, Neratov's self-effacing and nervous handling of an ambassador many years senior to him both in the service and at school was also partly to blame for the confusion reigning between Petersburg and Constantinople in that year. More serious were the activities of Hartwig, who followed an independent and dangerous line in Belgrade in part because he was sure of his support in nationalist and, so it is said, Court circles in Petersburg.[29]

To what extent then can one 'blame' the Russian governmental system for the Empire's involvement in the First World War? Much less beyond question than is the case as regards 1904, when the woeful lack of co-ordination between the Emperor, Foreign Ministry, armed forces, civilian government and Far Eastern Viceroy played a major role not just in Russia's involvement in the unnecessary war against Japan but also in ensuring that she entered the conflict unprepared.

The uncontrollable forces pushing Russia towards war in 1914 and the national interests at stake were much greater than had been the case ten years before. Nevertheless, weaknesses in the executive branch of the Russian governmental system did play a certain role in bringing on the conflict. One can, for instance, neither deny the importance of Hartwig's activities nor doubt that it would have been impossible for an early twentieth century British diplomat to act in his independent manner. The extraordinary and dangerous ignorance of Sazonov and Sukhomlinov about each other's profession stemmed in part from the Russian governmental tradition that each ministry was an empire unto itself.[30] The lack of control exercised by the civilian government over the armed forces contained a threat that a combination of the latter's fears and aggressive instincts would push aside the Emperor's resistance and involve Russia in war. If hatred of Sukhomlinov perhaps leads Kokovtsov in his memoirs[31] somewhat to exaggerate the wickedness of the War Minister's plans in November 1912, it was nevertheless, given the existing international tension, dangerous that anyone could even think of ordering any sort of partial mobilisation without consulting the Foreign Minister and Chairman of the Council. Although in July 1914, as we shall see, the Council of Ministers played the key role in formulating Russia's response to Austria's threat to Serbia, by 27–28 July the crisis had largely slipped beyond the grasp of the civilian government and into that of the diplomats and generals. Typically, on 30 July Nicholas II lacked the time to see Krivoshein, the key figure in the government. Nevertheless, one must stress that the Minister of Agriculture wished to see the Emperor in order to support the line being urged by Sazonov and by N.N. Yanushkevich, the chief of the General Staff. In fact for the period 1905–14 as a whole, though the closer involvement of the civilian government in foreign policy was desirable, it is unlikely that it would have radically shifted Russian diplomacy on to a more pacific course. As we have seen, for instance, Izvol'sky's policy of cooperation with Vienna in 1908 was undoubtedly the line most conducive to the preservation of peace but it was overruled by the civil government in part for internal political reasons. In the following five years Stolypin, Kokovtsov and Krivoshein all had a major say in Russia's foreign policy and if the Russian stance in external relations became tougher in 1914 that was not because the civilian government had been pushed aside but rather because its key figure, Krivoshein, had come to share Sazonov's view that determined deterrence of

Germany was the best means to preserve both peace and Russian interests.

In the decade before 1914 Russia stood somewhere between the old absolutist era and a more modern age in which social forces begin to invade the hitherto sacrosanct world of kings and diplomats. Those who governed Russia were still representatives of an old ruling class determined to live up to their ancestors' glories and imbued with an ethos that was by no means pacific, or, for better and worse, based on modern conceptions of enlightened individual self-interest. To the limited extent that public forces had begun to make an impact on state policy their influence was, however, not in general for moderation or restraint. The dominant parties in the third and fourth Dumas shared the ethos of the ruling class, to which most of their members belonged. In addition, they sometimes tried to make a nationalist or pro-Slav policy a major weapon in their party's political arsenal. Finally, they generally lacked the realism or experience in international relations of part at least of the established 'bureaucratic' ruling group. Had Russian politics shifted to the left, as seemed likely in 1905–6, matters might have been different since, as we shall see, the Constitutional Democratic (Kadet) Party before 1914 was less nationalist than its opponents on the right. Further still to the left, the Social Democrats' hostility to Russian nationalism was even more unambiguous. More important however than party programmes is the fact that any government in Russia responsive to mass pressures and interests would have been forced to concentrate a much larger share of national resources on internal rather than external goals. Britain before 1914 might be able to afford Dreadnoughts and an emerging welfare state; Russia could not, and there was a clear connection between the authoritarian nature of the political system and its ability to channel a very high percentage of the national wealth into the armed forces. One could argue that democratisation would have spared Russia from aggressive foreign policies and unnecessary wars or, on the contrary, that given Russian backwardness, her geographical position and the threats to her territorial integrity and interests only an authoritarian government could adequately mobilise national resources for purposes of defence. There is probably some truth in both views but the important point to grasp at this stage is that the authoritarian nature of Russian government was a key factor underlying the whole of Russian foreign policy in these years.

# 4  Actors and Opinions

Nicholas II was a patriot and was devoted to what he interpreted as the interests and dignity of Russia. Given family traditions and his own training it was inevitable that the Emperor's values should have had a strong military hue. In his eyes, to allow Russia's standing in Europe to suffer a permanent and major decline would have seemed a dishonourable betrayal of his duty and his inheritance. Nicholas II felt deeply Russia's humiliation in the Japanese war and was incensed by the further blow to her pride caused by the Bosnian annexation crisis of 1909. The sense that Russian views and interests were being treated in a cavalier way by the Central Powers both in the settlement following the Balkan Wars and, more importantly, in the Liman von Sanders affair made the Emperor, along with most of his advisers determined to show that the Russia of 1914 was neither militarily, economically nor spiritually the Russia of 1906–9. As Nicholas said to Delcassé in January 1914, 'we will not let ourselves be trampled upon'.[1]

If considerations of pride and patriotism, especially strong after the disasters of 1904–9, led Nicholas II to wish for a determined assertion of Russia's views and interests, fear of war pulled equally hard in the opposite direction and all sources are unanimous in stressing the Emperor's intense desire for peace. The conflict with Japan had shown both the weaknesses of the Russian armed forces and the tremendous risks to dynasty and Empire of any unsuccessful struggle. The war had also cured Nicholas II of any hankering for diplomatic or military adventure and in July 1914 he showed a genuine horror at the suffering and death which conflict with the Central Powers would inevitably entail for tens of thousands of his subjects.[2]

The Emperor's ability to balance correctly conflicting pressures and concerns in foreign policy was, however, weakened by his, at times, somewhat naive and over-optimistic view of political affairs. As we have seen, he had exaggerated notions about the patriotic and monarchist feeling of the Russian people. As regards diplomacy, he did not always distinguish between hopes and practical possibilities. His major personal initiative in this sphere, the signing of the Treaty of Bjorkoe, was seen by Nicholas as the transformation of the Russo-French alliance into a league between the Continent's three major powers. He argued that the Triple Alliance, against which the Franco-Russian link had originally been aimed, was by now 'in essence only a historical memory' and that Germany, 'which then seemed very aggressive, is persistently proposing to ally itself to us in order to form, with an exclusively peaceful goal, a common alliance of the continental powers, able to resist English aspirations which have just been sharply confirmed in the new Anglo-Japanese Treaty'.[3] The Emperor's faith that France could be persuaded into a continental league showed a lack of insight into Russia and France's relative power, into the French psychology of 1905 and into the views of French ruling elements about both external and internal political realities. In 1913 – 14, as before the Russo-Japanese War, Nicholas tended to believe that his own deter- mination to preserve peace, added to the awe that Russian power inspired in her neighbours, would be sufficient to avoid war.[4] He failed to understand the fear generated by Russian actions in Vienna and Berlin and had an exaggerated conception both of the power and of the pacific intentions of the German and Austrian Emperors. Neverthe- less, Nicholas' refusal to believe that Germany would willingly unleash a European war was based in large part on reason, logic and history. 'War', he told Peter Bark on 24 July 1914, 'would be disastrous for the world and once it had broken out it would be difficult to stop.' Moreov- er, it was not just that the 'German Emperor had frequently assured him of his sincere desire to safeguard the peace of Europe' and that 'it had always been possible to come to an agreement with him, even in serious cases.' Nicholas II also recalled

> the German Emperor's loyal attitude during the Russo-Japanese War and during the internal troubles that Russia had experienced afterwards. It would have been easy for Germany to level a decisive blow at Russia in those circumstances – which were particularly favourable for such an attempt – since our attention was engaged in the East and we were left with insufficient protection against an attack from the West.[5]

If Germany had not taken the opportunity to overrun Europe at a moment when the continent was hers for the taking, why should she attempt to do so subsequently when the risk of defeat was already considerable?

Like his cousins George V and William II, Nicholas II was extremely interested in naval and imperial questions.[6] He, not Russia's two rather puny 'naval leagues', was responsible for the re-creation of a high-seas fleet after the debacle of 1904–5. He attached immense importance to Russia's Siberian and Far Eastern possessions, seeing in them the main centres for the nation's creative efforts and the main guarantee of future generations' well-being and might. Partly for this reason foreign policy in the first decade of Nicholas' reign, when Asian questions were to the fore, carried a more distinct imprint of the Emperor's personal views than it did in the second decade when Russian diplomacy was above all concerned with the developing European crisis. Here Nicholas seems to have shared the instincts and opinions of the majority of Russia's statesmen, diplomats, soldiers and politicians. Resentment at Russia's humiliation in the Bosnian crisis and fear of the growing strength and aggressiveness of the Central Powers led to the Emperor's firm commitment to the French alliance and to a desire for stronger ties with London.[7] A lingering sympathy and considerable respect for Germany meant that Nicholas, again like most of the ruling élite, channelled more of his feelings of resentment against Vienna than Berlin.

The Emperor's preference for Germany rather than Austria was also in part based on dynastic considerations. For religious reasons the Habsburgs and Romanovs had never intermarried and links between the two imperial families were by no means close. Although relations between Nicholas II and William II were much less warm than had been the friendships existing between their grandfathers and their great-grandfathers, nevertheless the two Emperors did meet at relatively frequent intervals and helped convince each other of their mutual goodwill and desire for peace. In contrast, Nicholas II in 1912 had not met the Austrian heir-apparent, the Archduke Francis Ferdinand, for nine years.[8] In addition, the Russians had never fully forgiven Austria for the foolish ingratitude with which it had repaid Nicholas I for his help in 1849. Austria's abandonment and humiliation of Russia in 1855–6, together with a series of subsequent conflicts of interest in the Balkans meant that even when relations between the governments were good no great warmth or trust existed in Russia towards Vienna. In the aftermath of the Bosnian crisis Nicholas II exhibited an intense bitterness towards the Austrians which, unlike his resentment of German action, was never really dissipated. Austrian efforts in the period prior to 1914 to persuade Nicholas that the two dynastically-based, multi-national empires shared major common interests fell on stony ground, in part no doubt because the Emperor felt that, unlike the polyglot Habsburg dominions, his own state was firmly based on Russian national ideals.[9]

From his conversations with Buchanan in the years immediately prior to 1914 it is clear that Nicholas II was expecting the disintegration of the Habsburg Empire in the relatively near future. So long as Francis Joseph lived he believed stability in Central Europe to be secure but was by no means confident about what would happen after the Austrian monarch's death. In the spring of 1913 Nicholas stated that the disappearance of the Habsburg Empire would be no loss since Austria 'was at present a source of weakness to Germany and a danger to the cause of peace, and it would make for peace were Germany to have no Austria to drag her into war about the Balkans'.[10] The Russian Emperor also had little sympathy for 'trialism', in other words for the attempt to give Austria's Slavs a political weight within the Empire equal to that possessed by the Germans or Magyars.[11] Presumably this lack of sympathy was owed to fears that a liberal-democratic trialist Austria would be a rival Slav great power, a magnet to Poles and Ukrainians within Russia and a reproach to Romanov authoritarianism. Altogether Nicholas' attitude to Austria was short-sighted and naive since he failed to grasp that an unreformed or disintegrating Habsburg Monarchy would probably entail a continental conflict brought on either by Vienna's own efforts to solve internal problems by external adventure or by battles between the various races within the Empire and the rival great powers which supported them.

Nicholas was not a Panslav but he did believe that Russian interests, history and national feeling required him strongly to defend Russia's influence in the Balkans.[12] Above all, however, he was interested in Constantinople. In 1896–7, for instance, the young Emperor had been an enthusiastic supporter of schemes to seize the Ottoman capital.[13] In the period immediately prior to 1914 Nicholas' concern about the fate of Constantinople was increased enormously as the rapid demise of the Ottoman Empire seemed ever more imminent and German influence at the Porte ever greater. In February

1912 he stated that his only reason for distrust of Berlin lay in German policy in Turkey. He had often told William II that he saw no reason why the Germans should maintain military instructors in the Ottoman army, which in time of war would be used either against Russia or the Balkan Christians. Unfortunately, the German Emperor had never given him 'any satisfactory explanation in this matter'.[14] Nicholas' indignation was greatly increased by the Liman von Sanders affair and by Russian discovery of Germany's intention to gain direct military control of the Straits in peacetime and to seize the area should the Ottoman Empire collapse. It was in the light of this knowledge, gleaned from secret German documents, that Nicholas told Buchanan in April 1914 that 'he had reason to believe that Germany was aiming at acquiring such a position at Constantinople as would enable her to shut in Russia altogether in the Black Sea. Should she attempt to carry out this policy he would have to resist it with all his power, even should war be the only alternative'.[15]

Before looking at the opinions of Nicholas II's 'Court' it is necessary to stress that in this chapter the term Court is used to cover not merely the officials of the Emperor's household but also all those relatives, friends and acquaintances of the monarch who had access to him without holding governmental positions. In comparison to this broader group the Household officials were in fact of limited significance. It is true that among these officials, most of whom were former officers of the Horse Guards regiment, sympathy for Wilhelmine Germany was strong . Prussia was seen as a bulwark of European conservatism, a model of ordered patriotism and an old ally of Russia's dynasty and army. Count V.B. Frederycksz, the Minister of the Imperial Court, more than once voiced such sentiments and expressed fears about the dangerous possible consequences of Russia's pro-*entente* policies. As Frederycksz himself stated, however, his complete lack of political experience or training made him wholly unfitted to debate issues of policy with the officials at the Choristers' Bridge. In any event, the Minister made it a principle never to discuss politics with Nicholas II unless the Emperor directly asked for his advice. The considerations which stopped Frederycksz from exercising any influence on foreign policy applied even more strongly to his subordinates. According to A.A. Mosolov, Frederycksz's deputy, 'the only one among the members of the Suite who had any real political ability' was Prince V.N. Orlov, the head of Nicholas II's Campaign Chancellery. Orlov did enjoy, for many years at least, the 'great regard' of the Emperor and his sentiments were very close to those of Frederycksz, as both Mosolov and von Hintze, William II's representative at the Russian Court, make clear. Although Orlov may have exercised an influence even as regards foreign policy on Nicholas II his importance should, however, not be overestimated. The Emperor did not in general discuss political, let alone foreign policy, questions with his Suite, nor would he for long have tolerated any member of his entourage who attempted to force opinions upon him. Moreover, as von Hintze understood, Russian courtiers, like their counterparts elsewhere, tended to be more anxious to discover and echo their master's views than to urge upon him advice which might prove unpopular.[16]

In looking at the broader circle of people who enjoyed private access to the monarch the Romanov family is a logical starting point. Even in the early twentieth century a number of Grand Dukes held key political or military posts and in the first years of his reign Nicholas II had stood somewhat in awe of his uncles. Of the latter all but the ineffective Grand Duke Paul were, however, dead by 1909 and the influence exerted by his relatives on the increasingly experienced and confident Emperor was by this time in decline. Even Nicholas's wife, the Empress Alexandra, seems to have had no impact on foreign and defence policy in the pre-war years and the same was true of all but three of the other Romanovs.

The major influence exerted by the Empress Marie Fyodorovna on her son goes back to well before the twentieth century. Born a princess of Denmark, the Empress carried to her grave a resentment against Prussia dating back to the German-Danish war of 1864. This, together with Alexander III's own suspicion and resentment of German policy, ensured that Nicholas II was brought up in a home far less sympathetic to the Hohenzollerns than was traditional in the Romanov family. There is no evidence that his mother's anti-German feelings had any direct influence on the Emperor in the period 1905–14 but her strong support for Izvol'sky, the son-in-law of a close friend, certainly contributed to the latter's appointment and retention as Foreign Minister. Even here, however, the Empress' influence should not be exaggerated. Izvol'sky was widely regarded in 1905 as one of the ablest men in the Russian diplomatic service and had been recommended to Nicholas II by William II among others.[17]

The other two influential Romanovs were both military men: Serge Mikhailovich was the Inspector-General of Artillery; Nicholas Nikolayevich the Inspector-General of Cavalry and commanding officer of the Petersburg Military District. The former's influence was strictly limited to the technical military sphere but Serge Mikhailovich's admiration for the French artillery and general friendship for the French armed forces was a factor making for closer trust and co-operation between the allied armies.[18] The Grand Duke Nicholas' influence was certainly greater than this, though its precise limits, exaggerated by General V.A. Sukhomlinov and underestimated by General Yu. N. Danilov, are difficult to gauge.[19] In the period immediately following his appointment as Chairman of the State Defence Council in 1905 the Grand Duke's influence was very great. Indeed in the following November the well-informed General Moulin, the French military attaché, described Nicholas Nikolayevich as 'the chief arbiter of military affairs'.[20] Nor was the Grand Duke's sphere of influence confined to the armed forces, for he had a decisive influence on Nicholas II's decisions in 1905 to abandon the Bjorkoe Treaty and grant a constitution.[21] For a number of reasons Nicholas Nikolayevich's influence declined in the following years, a fact symbolised by his resignation as Chairman of the State Defence Committee in 1908.[22] Nevertheless, the German and Austrian ambassadors blamed the Grand Duke for turning Nicholas II's views in a more pro-Slav direction in the early autumn of 1912.[23] Moreover, the Grand Duke Nicholas did not merely attend the crucial meeting of the Council of Ministers, chaired by the Emperor, on 25 July 1914 but also, according to Sukhomlinov, had a long private conversation with Nicholas II before the meeting took place.[24]

According to Nicholas Nikolayevich's biographer, Yu. N. Danilov, the Grand Duke was always suspicious, though never blindly hostile, towards Germany and regarded Austrian ambitions with grave misgivings. He inherited from his father, Nicholas Nikolayevich the elder, a tradition of support for the French alliance, and Laguiche, the French military attaché in Petersburg from 1912, records that the Grand Duke was much moved by his warm reception in France that year and greatly impressed by the efficiency of the French army.[25] Nicholas Nikolayevich was the most pro-Slav male member of the Imperial family. His father had commanded the army that liberated the Balkans in 1877, an army in which the Grand Duke himself had served as a young man. Moreover, both Nicholas Nikolayevich's wife and the wife of his much-beloved brother Peter were daughters of the King of Montenegro and fiery Slav patriots; though there is a general consensus that the Grand Duke was little influenced by his wife, Laguiche wrote in April 1913 that he was 'completely under the thumb of his sister-in-law'.[26] The attaché's description of conversation at a lunch he attended in Nicholas Nikolayevich's palace in November 1912 is striking. According to Laguiche, the Grand Duchess Anastasia, having lived for long in military circles had added 'their belligerent aspirations' to her own Montenegrin patriotism. Apart from wild comments about the forthcoming reconquest of Alsace-Lorraine and ambitious schemes for Montenegrin aggrandisement at Ottoman expense in the ongoing Balkan War, the Grand Duchess was already looking forward to the approaching demise of the Habsburgs. 'As to Bosnia and Hercegovina,' she told the attaché, 'they are dependencies of Montenegro both through their origins and their history and they will return to the bosom of their motherland. This will be the concern of a further war'. Laguiche records that 'the Grand Duke nodded his head in agreement and let her talk'.[27] Even if one discounts much of the significance of excitable table talk, Laguiche's letters do nevertheless convey the correct impression of the mood of Panslav and militant belligerence which existed in the Grand Duke's household in the years immediately prior to 1914. Moreover in judging Nicholas Nikolayevich's attitudes not just ideological but also psychological factors have to be taken into account. Though an honourable and hard-working man, wholly devoted both to the army and to Russia, the Grand Duke was highly excitable and by no means devoid either of arrogance or of the strong sense of his own personal dignity which one might indeed expect many members of the reigning family of an absolutist Empire to possess. This factor made it highly unlikely that Nicholas Nikolayevich would bear with patience the feeling that either he or the country with which he associated himself were being pushed around or humiliated by foreign powers.[28]

Outside his immediate family Nicholas II had few close friends and still fewer unofficial contacts to whom he turned regularly for political advice. As Kireyev records, though the Emperor did at times discuss politics and request the opinions of acquaintances over a limited period, he made almost a point of not consulting these 'favourites' regularly or for any length of time.[29] Nevertheless, there were a few exceptions to this general rule, the most important of whom in the context of this book was Prince V.P. Meshchersky, the editor of *Grazhdanin*. Like his father, Nicholas not merely at various moments in his reign had important private discussions with Meshchersky, he also read and subsidised his newspaper. In the spring of 1913 the Emperor consulted Meshchersky about the central problems of Russian foreign policy and took to heart the Prince's call for better relations with Berlin.[30]

Meshchersky has become part of the demonology of late Imperial Russia, almost taking his place alongside Rasputin as one of those 'dark forces' which doomed the old régime. Though the Prince was certainly not without his failings, his black reputation is by no means wholly justified and owes something to the following three circumstances. Firstly, Meshchersky was a highly conservative editor in a journalistic world dominated by liberals; secondly, he used Imperial protection to criticise officials and policies with a freedom and, at times, harshness which no other newspaper editor prior to 1905 would have dared to employ; thirdly, he was a homosexual. These three facts ensured that Meshchersky received more than his fair share of the mud that flew around Petersburg society in abundance in the last years of the old régime but the latter-day reader of his newspaper may find it difficult not to agree with the contemporary British expert on Russian affairs, H.W. Williams, that the Prince was 'an able and witty writer, and a keen observer, and retains in old age a remarkable freshness'.[31]

Meshchersky's views on foreign policy in the decade prior to 1914 were by Russian standards both extreme and eccentric. Not merely did he advocate friendship with Germany, he also made it clear that he was a supporter of the Dreikaiserbund. In May 1908 he wrote that Alexander III had wanted an *entente* with France, not a rigid alliance binding Russia's hands once and for all. Meshchersky made no secret of his contempt for the French Republic, which was, he wrote in July 1911, rapidly approaching political death.[32] Less contemptuous of Britain, he was nevertheless deeply scared that Russia's links with her would lead to a war with the Central Powers which would bring revolution and disaster to Russia. Meshchersky's harshest criticism was reserved for *Novoye Vremya*, whose campaign to stir up Russian nationalist feeling by fanning Panslav sentiment in external policy and hatred for non-Russian minorites in internal affairs he regarded as suicidal.[33] He believed that foreign policy should be controlled by professional diplomats who should follow the dictates of experience, prudence and reason and should ignore the trumpetings of self-appointed representatives of 'patriotic opinion' drawn from the press and the political parties, who falsely claimed to speak for the Russian people. In response to *Novoye Vremya's* line that Russia's survival depended on the population's patriotism and sense of involvement in the state's foreign policy, Meshchersky retorted that the nationalist sentiments cultivated by the rival newspaper were an empty fraud, wholly alien to the interests and the true patriotism of the Russian people. He argued that the latter neither were nor could be made interested in Balkan quarrels, which they felt to be none of their business. In Meshchersky's view the mass of the Russian people would fully support a government which kept rigidly to the defence of Russia's own essential interests, left the Balkan peoples to work out their own fate and avoided entanglement in external political rivalries which might well endanger not merely Russian lives but also the continued existence of the Russian Empire.[34]

If the term 'Court' requires some definition, that of 'elder statesmen' is if anything still more vague. Nor indeed are the two groups wholly distinct, as Kireyev's example shows. At the centre of the group of 'elder statesmen' stand the appointed members of the State Council, of whom there were 114, active and retired, in 1914 but the term must be understood to cover a wider group of former and present top officials. Although for our purposes the major interest of the elder statesmen lies in the fact that it was from their ranks that there came the most thorough and impressive criticism of the foreign policy pursued by the Russian government in the period 1906–14 it would be wrong to label a majority of this group 'pro-German'. It is true that within the Russian bureaucratic élite there was considerable respect for the Second Reich which many saw as a model their own empire would do well to copy.[35] Even Kireyev, a virulent Panslav, admired Imperial Germany with which he hoped Russia could live on friendly terms.[36] As twentieth century Germany increasingly backed Austria in the Balkans and clashed directly with Russia in the Near East, pro-German feeling in Petersburg inevitably suffered.[37] In Kireyev's case it was killed forever by the Bosnian crisis, after which he was resigned to an inevitable clash with 'Germanism' in the near future, though it is significant that even Kireyev, a great optimist, anticipated war with Germany with considerable fear.[38] Most of Russia's ruling élite did not share Kireyev's extreme Panslav sympathies but as Thurn, the Austrian Ambassador in Petersburg, commented with slightly exaggerated gloom in 1912, there was 'a certain degree of Slavic solidarity in all of them'.[39] Moreover, quite apart from such feelings, for a ruling élite strongly nationalist in sympathy and legitimising its position in part by its claim to defend Russian national traditions, interests and ideals it was difficult to accept increasing German influence in Russia's traditional Near Eastern sphere of interest, especially when Russo-German conflict led to humiliation as in 1909. In the years prior to 1914 Austro-German policies converted many members of the ruling élite from advocacy of reconciliation with Berlin into advocates of a policy of deterrence against the excessive ambitions of the Central Powers. Of these individuals none was more important than Krivoshein, who was to play a key role in July 1914 in Russia's decision to resist Austro-German pressure even at risk of war. Four years earlier Berchtold had described Krivoshein as 'a convinced supporter of the idea of a *rapprochement* between Russia and both the central imperial powers', a key member of that conservative pro-German group to which Berlin and Vienna looked for a fundamental shift in Russian foreign policy.[40]

The events of 1909–14 had thus weakened the pro-German element even among the group in which such sentiments were strongest, namely the bureaucratic élite. In addition, by 1914 the pro-Germans were in a small minority in Petersburg high society, the press, the officer corps and educated society as a whole. Nevertheless, the pro-German cause was by no means dead and, spurred on by the fears of war caused by the Liman von Sanders affair, its advocates mounted in the spring of 1914 a campaign to bring their views to the attention of the Emperor and the government. In describing the pro-German group caution is, however, required. Pro-Germans did not even constitute an organised faction, let alone a political party. Rather, they were a number of individuals, some but by no means all of whom on occasion gathered informally to discuss international events and the means by which their views could best be propagated. Moreover, if the pro-Germans were not united in any organisational sense, the same was true as regards their opinions. All pro-Germans of course believed that Russian foreign policy had been mistaken in risking Berlin's friendship for the sake of closer links with Britain. All feared war and believed that it might well lead to revolution in Russia. On the other hand, they differed as regards the value of the French alliance. Moreover, as regards internal politics, while most pro-Germans stood on the right and believed that only strong authoritarian government was in present circumstances suitable for Russia, some of those who advocated *rapprochement* with Berlin, especially from among the ranks of present and former diplomats, held more liberal views.[41]

The two outstanding figures among the pro-Germans were S. Yu.
Witte and P.N. Durnovo, both men of very sharp intellect and great
political experience. Though Witte and Durnovo's intellectual and
political calibre are unquestionable, in the period 1906–14 neither of
these members of the State Council and former ministers was well
placed to exercise an influence on Nicholas II or on the conduct of
foreign affairs. The State Council played no part in the formulation of
foreign policy and its members' access to the Emperor was very limited. Witte and Durnovo could bring individual memoranda to the
monarch's attention but constant influence of the sort available to
Izvol'sky or Sazonov was denied them. In addition, neither Witte nor
Durnovo was personally at all close to Nicholas, Durnovo for instance
complaining in 1908 that it was two years since he had even spoken to
the monarch. Witte and Nicholas II loathed and distrusted each
other, while Durnovo had no faith in the Emperor's firmness or consistency of purpose.[42]

Like most of the 'pro-Germans' Witte was an advocate of a continental alliance between Russia, Germany and France. Only such an
alliance, as he told William II in 1897, could secure peace and material
progress in Europe. Without it European rivalries would lead to conflicts whose major result would be to replace Europe's domination of
the globe by that of the United States, Japan and other non-European
powers which would develop in the future. In Witte's view the road to a
continental alliance lay through patient, tactful diplomacy
not through attempts such as that made at Bjorkoe to bulldoze France
into friendship with Germany. In 1905 Witte urged moderation and
tact to William II during the Moroccan crisis. After 1906 he strove
hard to be appointed Ambassador in Paris in the hope of wooing
French business and public opinion to the cause of *détente*, reduction in
armaments and economic progress in Europe. In the name of the same
cause Witte attacked those Russians who were hostile to Austria and
eagerly anticipated its rapid demise. In March 1914 he stressed both
that Austria, a Christian and cultured Great Power, provided many
advantages to its peoples and that its demise would result in a second
war of the Habsburg succession. Russo-Franco-German unity could
for Witte be built in part on the hostility towards Britain felt in all three
countries. In 1905, for instance, he stressed to William II that reconciliation and *détente* with France would release the continent's resources
for a successful challenge to British maritime supremacy. In Witte's

view the Anglo-Russian *entente* was a disaster because it had made the achievement of a continental allliance far more difficult and brought down German enmity on Russia's head.[43]

Durnovo had much less official experience of international affairs or European diplomacy than Witte. His period in ministerial office was short, if eventful, and his whole civilian career had been devoted to questions of internal administration. Durnovo was above all a policeman, trained to think first of internal stability and the continued survival of imperial state and society. As chief of the state's police force from 1884 to 1893 and again as the Minister of Internal Affairs responsible for crushing the 1905 Revolution, Durnovo had learned much about the nature of the threat to the existing order posed by Russian revolutionary socialism; his memorandum for Nicholas II of February 1914 was in part the fruit of this insight. Since this memorandum provides the fullest and most brilliant exposition of the pro-Germans' views it deserves to be studied in some detail.

The memorandum certainly embodied an impressive understanding both of the nature of a future European war between the Great Powers and of the effects that involvement in such a war would have on Russian society. Durnovo was under no illusions that a European war would be won quickly on the battlefields and understood that the long and bitter struggle it would entail would be decided as much by the economic power, internal cohesion, and stability of the warring societies as by the prowess of their armies. The aim of his memorandum was to show that Russia's society, economy, and army would very likely disintegrate under the strain of war with Germany and that the result would be the complete and revolutionary destruction of Russian society as it was then composed.

Durnovo placed the European powers, Italy, Turkey and the Balkan states in the camps they were subsequently to join. He suggested the possible involvement of Japan and the United States in the war, though he greatly underestimated the scale of the latter's intervention. He also underestimated British willingness and capacity to put large armies on the continent and exaggerated the degree to which Russia would bear the main burden of the fighting. At the same time, however, Durnovo correctly prophesied many of the weaknesses that were subsequently to be revealed in Russia's war effort. He pointed to the shortage of heavy artillery and machine guns, both of which, he thought, would play a major role in the coming war. In addition, he wrote that the backwardness of Russia's own armaments industry and her wartime isolation from Western producers, resulting from the closing of the Straits and the Kattegat, would make a severe munitions crisis inevitable. In Durnovo's view, Russia did not have anything approaching the means to finance the war save by dubious and dangerous means, nor was her railway network capable of withstanding the increased burdens of a European conflict. Finally, a war between the most advanced industrial states in the world would certainly spawn a number of new weapons but Russia's economic backwardness would make it difficult for her to compete in this field.

Most crucial, however, would be the effects of war on Russian society. Durnovo believed that in a war between Russia and Germany, whichever side lost would suffer a social revolution. In Russia, however, as he stated, the danger of social upheaval was especially great given the instinctive socialism of the masses. Durnovo understood and pointed out the conflict between government and educated classes in Russia, but he believed that this conflict was much less important than the gulf which separated educated Russia from the masses. Because the instincts, values, and needs of these two parts of Russian society were so different, Durnovo believed that a purely political revolution was impossible in Russia. In his view the masses cared nothing for the political rights and civil liberties demanded by the educated, but were intent on a full-scale social revolution aimed above all at the destruction of private property and economic inequality.

War would, he wrote, make the chances of such a revolution far greater. It would bring military disasters, though maybe only partial ones, and a full-scale supply crisis. The educated classes, politically naive, excessively nervous, and long since convinced that all failings in Russian life were due to the government, would blame the latter for this crisis and a campaign of denunciations would start up in the Duma and in society. If such denunciations were allowed they would soon set off a propaganda campaign against the authorities in which revolutionary and socialist slogans would play an ever greater role. The best and most reliable elements of the army, the essential bulwark of the state's authority, would have been killed in the war and much of the rest would be lured from the ranks by a desire to get home for the partitioning of private land. Meanwhile the Duma and the intellectual opposition parties would be helpless to stem the revolutionary current they had themselves to an extent unleashed, for they enjoyed no real authority or support in the eyes of the masses. The result would be total anarchy, the issue of which could not be foreseen.

So pessimistic an analysis of Russia's chances in a European war represented more or less a plea for non-involvement at almost any price, but in fact Durnovo also argued that Russian and German interests were not in serious conflict. Neither power had any interest in annexing each other's land, indeed, in Durnovo's view any extension of Russian territory in Europe would be counter-productive. As regards Russia's Asiatic interests, these were more likely to be opposed by Britain than Germany. The advantages of Russian acquisition of Constantinople and the Straits were, Durnovo believed, exaggerated, for even if both were secured for Russia a hostile fleet in the Eastern Mediterranean could still block egress from the Black Sea and thus sever Russian commercial links with the outside world. Moreover, Durnovo argued that Britain was no less hostile than Germany to Russian control of the Straits and Constantinople and that Berlin would willingly renounce both in return for Russian friendship.

As far as economic interests were concerned, Durnovo did not deny that the 'existing Russo-German commercial treaties are not to our advantage' or that there were other points of conflict between Russia and Germany, but he rightly pointed out that these were as nothing when compared to the common interest the trading partners had in each other's prosperity. A war which destroyed the German economy would, he argued, do Russia no good and it was foolish to believe that a ruined Germany would be able to recompense Russia for the immense costs of the struggle. The vast loans necessary if Russia were to wage this war, together with the destruction of the German economy would merely make Russia economically dependent on the Western powers. In addition, she would remain the only authoritarian monarchy in a continent dominated by liberals and republicans.

Durnovo was not an opponent of the Franco-Russian alliance, so long as it was purely defensive and did not oblige either side 'to support unfailingly, with armed force, all political actions and claims of the ally'. In his view, however, Russian foreign policy since 1906 had been based on false principles. Durnovo saw the fundamental conflict in Europe as being between a Britain determined to maintain its vanishing sovereignty of the seas, on which its empire and commerce depended, and a Germany equally intent on challenging this monopoly. He argued that British and German interests were so much in conflict as to make war between them inevitable. Russia had, he believed, no interest in involving itself in this conflict, least of all on the British side. Durnovo denied that Russia had derived worthwhile benefits from the 1907 agreement with Britain. He did not believe that good relations with Japan depended on the *entente* with London, claiming that Russian and Japanese interests were not in serious conflict. Given the level of economic development of Russian Asia it was absurd, in Durnovo's view, to dream of ice-free ports, the acquisition of Korea or naval power in the Pacific. Russia's interests lay in the defence of her existing territories and these were not threatened by Japan. Durnovo argued that the Japanese were 'by nature a southern people' whose territorial ambitions were much more likely to focus on the Phillipines, Indo-China and the Dutch East Indies than on the far less hospitable Russian Far East. Given her 'imminent rivalry' with the USA, Japan had every interest in concentrating her resources on naval expenditure and this demanded good relations with Russia, the area's major land power. In the rest of Asia agreement with Britain had, wrote Durnovo, been of no service to Russia and in Persia it had merely served to limit the Russian government's freedom to defend its interests. Worst of all, however, the agreement with Britain had drawn Germany's enmity on to Russia, for the British-led *entente* states were attempting to block Germany's natural development as a world power. The worst effects of Russia's pro-British policies were to be seen in the Near East, for here the German response to Russian hostility had been to back Austrian aggression in the Balkans and to take the Ottoman Empire under Berlin's protection. In Durnovo's view the Russian government's present task was to disentangle itself immediately from the Anglo-Russian *entente* and seek friendship with Berlin, which must in turn increase German sensitivity to Russian interests and the nervousness of Russian public opinion as regards Near Eastern questions. Durnovo concluded by writing that the government's future aim must be to reconcile France and Germany and to bring the three continental powers and Japan into a non-aggressive alliance which would guarantee peace for years.[44]

Durnovo's memorandum is beyond question a remarkable document but it is nevertheless not without its weaknesses. Its analysis of the causes of European strife is too simple and Durnovo, too much the 'economic determinist', exaggerates the importance and inevitability of Anglo-German conflict while glossing over Franco-German hatred, Russia's rivalry with Austria in the Balkans and the growing threat to both the Habsburg Empire and European stability of the developing nationalist movements of Central and South-Eastern Europe. The validity of Durnovo's thesis depends in considerable part on the correctness of his premise that German population growth required territorial expansion and that the German government had decided that their Empire's main ambitions lay on the seas and outside Europe. This premise is open to question. Both history and geopolitics suggest that it was in many ways easier for Germany to expand within Europe rather than overseas. Land-based expansion, the course adopted by Hitler, stood to benefit from Germany's dominant, central position in Europe. Overseas expansionism on the other hand was confronted by the major problem of a United Kingdom standing athwart all Germany's maritime communications. Moreover, in claiming that the German government had decided that their Empire's future lay on the seas and in a struggle with Britain, Durnovo paid Germany's rulers too big a compliment, for the German governmental system proved unable to make such a clearcut and logical decision about the aims and priorities of the Empire's foreign policy, a failure mournfully admitted by Bethmann-Hollweg in July 1914.[45] If there was a consistent trend in German foreign policy in the years leading up to 1914 it was the attempt to persuade one of the three *entente* powers to abandon its allies. Had this occurred, Berlin would obviously have had more room to manoeuvre and achieve its aims but study of Wilhelmine Germany suggests that there was no inherent reason why she should seek influence in Africa rather than in the Ottoman Empire, or, in the longer run, domination of the seas rather than hegemony in Europe. Of course, skilful Russian diplomacy might perhaps ensure that the price of Russo-German friendship was the direction of German energies overseas but even if successful such a policy was not without risks. By 1914 the Anglo-French *entente* was firmly based and any Russian attempt to steer Germany against Britain was almost certain to undermine the Franco-Russian alliance. Leaving aside the possible economic difficulties this would cause Russia, there was a real danger that if Britain and Germany went to war France would become involved. Should this happen the Russian government would be presented in the sharpest form with that need to make the choice between Paris and Berlin which most pro-Germans were loathe to face. If Russia abandoned France and stalemate resulted on the Western front, then Russian interests might not suffer. Indeed, as the only great power not

weakened by the conflict her security and significance might be enhanced and there might even come the moment when Russia could
intervene decisively in the conflict as a mediator.

If France did not become involved in the conflict then matters
might work out even better for Russia. M.O. Menshikov, *Novoye
Vremya*'s leading columnist, wrote in the summer of 1912 that Anglo-
German rivalry and even war should be regarded by Russians 'as a
special gift of fate'. For well over a century all of Europe had been
harmed by the arrogant use to which the British had put their
sovereignty of the seas. Russia in particular had suffered, having to
defend itself against British hostility at every corner of its empire.
Meanwhile, a new potential threat had emerged in the form of Germany's massive power. That Russia's two possible enemies were devoting so large a proportion of their resources to checking each other
could only be a matter for rejoicing. Should Germany achieve a balance of power on the seas she would deserve the thanks of Europe.
Even should she break and replace British dominion of the seas Russia had no reason to fear. The nature of seapower being what it was,
Germany would soon find herself drawn into rivalry with the French,
American and ultimately maybe even Japanese fleets. 'Germany will
inherit the role of England, that is for a very long time it will find
occupation for itself far from our borders. Ought not the goal of a
healthy Russian policy really be to help this process?' Menshikov
argued that the European situation was now far more complex than
when the system of alliances first came into being and that either these
alliances must adapt themselves flexibly to reality or they must go.[46]

There was, however, a third possible scenario in addition to the two
already mentioned. If France fought alongside Britain and the Germans, as was very possible, overran the former and drove the latter off
the continent then Russia would be faced with something akin to the
position in which she found herself in 1811 and 1940. She would be the
single remaining independent truly great land power and would have
on her western frontier an empire able to mobilise the resources of
most of the European continent against her in the event of a conflict.
Of course that conflict might not come. Menshikov's vision of a Germany locked in a never-ending battle for naval supremacy might be
realised. The pro-Germans' constant assertion that no serious conflicts of interest divided Berlin and Petersburg might be proved true.
Wilhelmine Germany had, however, been an uncomfortable neighbour for the rest of Europe even when she had the balance of power to

contend with and only memories of 1866–71 to boost her arrogance. Were the balance to disappear and German conceit to be augmented by further victories there was little knowing what interests or rights she might be willing and able to defend against any power she chose to challenge. The rest of Europe, including Russia, would be forced more or, given the nature of Wilhelmine Germany, probably less gracefully to submit to the wishes of the continent's dominant power. For a regime whose *raison d'être*, prestige and pride rested on its claim to defend Russia's standing in the world this might prove an intolerable affront and there was a good chance that Russia would ultimately be forced to start a war she stood little chance of winning.

The policy option supported by Durnovo in his memorandum was therefore fraught with risks for Russia but this by no means necessarily invalidates his approach. After all, events were to show that the alternative policy option, that of deterring Germany by maintaining a common front with Britain and France, also entailed enormous and immediate risks, which Durnovo identified in his memorandum with considerable brilliance. Study of the pro-Germans' arguments therefore reveals above all the difficult position in which Russia was placed in the period prior to 1914.

THE FOREIGN MINISTRY AND THE DIPLOMATS

In a now well-known lecture James Joll suggested that to understand the events of 1914 we needed to study 'the unspoken assumptions' of European statesmen of the pre-war era. He further argued that a 'study of educational systems and their content may help to explain the actions and unspoken motives of statesmen and generals in moments of crisis'[47]. As regards Russia's statesmen and diplomats in 1914 an important, and for our purposes useful, fact to bear in mind is that a great many of them were educated at a single school, namely the Imperial Alexander Lycée.[48] Given its small size (the Lycée had only 186 pupils in the early 1880s) and the fact that only a small percentage of its graduates entered the Foreign Ministry, the major role which former pupils played in this department was astonishing. Of the eight men who headed the Foreign Ministry in the half century before 1914 only two had not received their middle and higher education at the Lycée. On the eve of the war not merely Sazonov and his deputy, Neratov, but also the Vice-Director of the Minister's Chancellery, Basily, and a host of junior officials in the Ministry were former pupils of the Lycée. So too were the heads of mission in Paris, Athens, Bucharest, Peking and Tehran, together with A.N. Bronevsky, the *chargé d'affaires* in Berlin during the crucial days of July 1914. Among other former pupils who played a leading role in the events which culminated in the Great War the names of Kokovtsov, Charykov, Count A.P. Cassini and D.K. Sementovsky-Kurilo stand out. There is therefore some justification for narrowing our search for the educational origins of statesmen's unspoken assumptions to a study of the Lycée and of the intellectual outlook and moral imprint it may have stamped upon its pupils.[49]

Anyone who attempts to study curricula in order to discover a Lycée 'line' as regards diplomacy or international affairs will, however, be disappointed. The Lycée did not exist to provide such a line, most of its students entering the Ministries of the Interior or Finance upon graduation. Moreover, at least until the 1880s curricula were dominated by modern languages and literature; modern history, comparative European politics and international law were neither well covered nor, by the Lycée's standards, well taught. In any event almost all students left the Lycée before they were 22, having received a somewhat rushed middle and higher education. As a result the standard of the senior boys was in general a little below that of undergraduates of Russian universities and this was too fragile a base on which to build sophisticated conceptions about international relations.[50]

Tracing the moral imprint left by the Lycée on its pupils is rather more rewarding, though even here some caution is required. Even at a closed institution like the Lycée, where the authorities' ability to influence their charges was obviously much greater than at a dayschool, the degree to which individuals actually were influenced differed greatly. Thus, for instance, while most authorities stress the Lycée's impact on its pupils, L.S. Birkin, who left the school in 1871, wrote that it did not teach him how to think and barely influenced his moral character.[51] Perhaps the same was true of Izvol'sky, whom a classmate recalls as holding himself somewhat aloof from his fellows and from the flow of school life.[52] Nevertheless, it seems beyond question that as regards most pupils the Lycée's impact was considerable. The school's success here was owed in part to the fact that the values it was attempting to inculcate into its charges, patriotism, a sense of honour and a commitment to service, were strongly held by the noble and high official class from which the Lycée drew all its pupils.[53]

Patriotism is an obvious case in point. The Russian nobility looked upon its alliance with the autocracy in the service of the greatness of the Russian state as its major political achievement. In its teaching of Russian history, its various rituals and traditions and in the monarchist ideology it exuded, the Lycée celebrated that achievement and that greatness. It did so by means typical of Imperial Russia, putting its emphasis less on the study of history and, least of all, of the Empire's future political goals and much more on the cultivation of an intense loyalty to the Lycée itself, of a strong sentiment of devotion to the Imperial family and of an awareness of the close historical links which bound the Lycée and the Romanovs together.[54] As we shall see, exactly the same appeal to institutional and dynastic loyalty was adopted in the regiments of the army but the Lycée's authorities' task was eased by the privileged position of their pupils and by the close and flattering attention paid to the school by the crown ever since its foundation in 1810 by Alexander I. The authorities' efforts were rewarded as they turned out group after group of patriotic and monarchist future officials. This patriotism was never stronger than in the late 1870s and 1880s when most of the former pupils who were to hold key positions in 1914 were at the school. Thus, to take but one example, the class of 1884, imbued with the militant patriotism of Alexander III's reign, were so indignant at the lack of teaching of eighteenth and nineteenth century Russian history in the curriculum that they insisted on arranging an evening course privately for themselves in this subject. Charykov, who left the Lycée in 1875, wrote his memoirs in 1931 having been forced into poverty and exile by the revolution of 1917, whose onset was of course directly linked to the outbreak of the First World War. Charykov had therefore good reason to question or at least regret Russia's involvement in the struggle. Questioning and regret are not, however, the dominant note in the memoirs and Charykov, true to the Lycée's tradition and ethic, rather recalls with pride that after the humiliation of 1909, in 1914 'Russia was able – perhaps to Germany's surprise – to hold her head high under the renewed German menace'.[55]

More of course than patriotism was involved here. Also relevant were Charykov's sense of his own personal dignity and honour, closely connected as both were with those of his country. Again, the Lycée's impact in this sphere reinforced existing values in Russian noble society. Members of the upper classes, especially in old régime Europe, were used to having their persons and opinions treated with some respect. Moreover, in Russian noble society even in 1914 the old ethic of the duel, in which an affront to one's honour or dignity was answered by an appeal to arms, was dying but by no means dead. The Lycée itself put great stress on the need to cultivate this sense of honour. As Baron F.F. Wrangel, the Inspector of Students, wrote in the 1880s, a man's sense of his individual worth and dignity was crucial for his moral character, making dishonest or underhand behaviour impossible. Equally important, as the ex-Lyceist Professor Ya.K. Grot told the class of 1856, was the willingness to follow one's own conscience and 'to act nobly' in all circumstances, regardless of any outward advantages.[56] Such sentiments were by no means always followed in later life by the ex-pupils but they did leave their mark and, beyond question, strongly influenced life within the Lycée. The latter was a far more civilised institution than the English public school of the twentieth, let alone nineteenth, century. In distinction to most Russian military schools, bullying of younger boys by elder ones was by the 1870s largely unknown, a considerable degree of solidarity existing between all pupils. Moreover, nor merely was corporal punishment unthinkable but teachers who treated the students with rudeness, harshness or injustice were likely to be faced by strikes or demonstrations of whole classes, which would maintain their solidarity in the face of the damage opposition might cause to their future career prospects. What stopped this Athenian democracy of students from getting out of hand was, above all, that the latter and the school authorities shared a strong commitment both to the same essential values and to the Lycée itself. It is, however, not fanciful to believe that in July 1914, when faced by the prospect of personal and national humiliation and by the need to accept the risk of war and revolution for the sake of what seemed to them a good cause, Lyceists in high positions to some extent reacted instinctively according to values inculcated into them during their youth. Can one not hear something of the Lycée nôte in Basily's reply in July 1914 to the comment of his friend, the Austrian military attaché, that for Russia war would bring revolution and social catastrophe? Basily states that he replied forcefully, 'you commit a serious error of calculation in supposing the fear of revolution will prevent Russia from fulfilling its national duty'.[57]

Though study of the Alexander Lycée may provide clues as to the basic values and instincts of Russian statemen, these clues do not give one any sense of their conceptions about foreign policy or international affairs. Such conceptions were acquired not so much theoretically as by

experience of the practice of diplomacy and, above all, by absorption
from one's seniors of the collective wisdom of the Russian foreign
service. Perhaps the best way to gain some sense of this collective
wisdom is to study the two texts on international law and relations
which candidates for the foreign service in 1912 were recommended to
read in preparation for their diplomatic examination.[58] Though of
course books about international relations cannot fully reflect the latter's reality, it is nevertheless legitimate to assume that those running
the Foreign Ministry must have felt that the two books in question did
provide a reasonably accurate and useful guide to the field in which
successful examinees would subsequently make their careers.

*Sovremennoye mezhdunarodnoye pravo tsivilizovannykh narodov* ('Contemporary International Law of the Civilised Peoples') was written by F.
Martens, a senior official of the Russian Foreign Ministry and one of
Europe's leading experts in international law. The book's title betrays
one fundamental conviction of Martens, the Russian Foreign Ministry and indeed Europeans as a whole, namely that civilisation meant
Europe or the lands which had succumbed to European conquest or
influence. For Martens, international law was the product of European culture, legal consciousness and economic development and
could have no relevance to societies where the latter had not left their
mark. This did not mean, in Martens' view, that Europeans had the
right to invade uncivilised societies which had done them no injury,
indeed he strongly condemned many aspects of Western colonial
policy, but it did mean that it was pointless to attempt to treat with
these societies in the light of modern legal theory. In addition, and this
was significant as regards Near Eastern policy in particular, Martens
believed that Christian states did have the right to intervene in the
internal affairs of non-Christian ones if the object was to save the
Christian population from persecution.[59]

Martens' overall view of the development of relations between
Western states was not devoid of elements of both optimism and
idealism and the same was true of the outlook of some senior Russian
diplomats, Count V.N. Lambsdorff's views on peace and disarma-
ment being a good case in point. Martens argued that the development of Europe's culture and economy had brought the European
peoples ever closer and made them far more interdependent; he stressed that to guarantee their future material and spiritual prosperity the
peoples of Europe had to strengthen the various international codes
and the sense of security and predictability they engendered. The

increasing interdependence and complexity of the world's society and economy made it imperative that states only indulge in war when vital interests were at stake and all efforts at peaceful negotiation were exhausted. War for its own sake was 'unthinkable' and 'criminal' and the diplomat's role was to make conflict unnecessary through negotiation, compromise and conciliation.[60]

At the same time Martens was a realist. Many quarrels between states were, he wrote, the product of history and could only be solved by force. Once political rather than purely economic or cultural elements predominated in a conflict third-party arbitration was impossible. One did not, in Martens' view, need to invoke the 'famous ... struggle for existence' to explain wars. Independent states collided with each other as did independent humans. In the state's case, its inability to 'fulfil its destiny' without conflicting with another state; the infringement of its basic rights or honour; the disparity between its real power and its external standing or activity; the expansionist strivings or inner tensions of its society; all these might lead it into war. Such wars were 'not accidental nor arbitrary but are closely linked with the historical life of a people, its geographical position, the strivings of its society, political ideals, etc., which explain both the causes of conflict and its results'. However undesirable therefore, war was nevertheless a natural and inevitable part of international affairs and a part for which any community which valued its sovereignty had to prepare if it were to enjoy 'the right to be respected and together with that to be independent, the two always going together'.[61]

The second text recommended by the Foreign Ministry was the *Manuel Historique de Politique Etrangère* by Emile Bourgeois. Bourgeois wrote with regret that neither law nor justice underlay the relations between states in the modern era. The French Revolution might, in his view, have laid the basis for a new morality in international relations but any such chance had been ruined by Napoleonic imperialism. Essentially, the principles of international relations remained the same as they had been in the eighteenth century. They rested on the independence of sovereign states, their 'ruthless' egoism and their competition for power. To complicate matters further, the tribal nationalism which had developed in modern Europe had now to be taken into account by governments in the conduct of foreign policy. On the other hand, despite their immoral origins and instincts the established great powers and the equilibrium and jealousies existing between them were a real, albeit expensive and fragile, force for peace.

While in the eighteenth century many small states existed to whet the great powers' appetite for expansion, by now few such states remained in Europe, thus reducing the chances of conflict in this continent. Moreover, the scale and risks of any war between the Great Powers were far greater than hitherto. 'In a word prudence curbs egoism, limits covetousness and inspires states and nations with the fear of an upheaval like that which marked the beginning of the century ... The game is much greater, the stakes higher, adversaries tougher and richer'. For this reason the great powers feared to start a war and so long as this held true, 'the respect for which together they compelled recognition became, in the absence of law and of justice, a guarantee of peace and of equilibrium for the whole of Europe'. Because of this equilibrium and of the intense suspicion and jealousy separating the powers, independent states had been able, in the Balkans and elsewhere, to emerge and survive. Thus Bourgeois was an, albeit unwilling and shamefaced, advocate of that balance between the great powers in which, as we shall see, many Russian diplomats believed.[62]

If one is in search not of the principles of international relations but rather of the priorities of Russian foreign policy, then, clearly, there were as many interpretations of the latter, even within the Foreign Ministry, as there were independently minded, thinking Russian diplomats. It is, however, a crass but not wholly fraudulent generalisation to divide Russian diplomats between a European and an Asiatic 'tendency'. Of course as a Eurasian state Russia had interests in both continents which no Russian diplomat could ignore. Moreover, if one can to some extent talk of the foreign policy of the first decade of Nicholas II's reign as having an Asian and the second a European orientation this was in part because Russian policy was reacting to crises over whose outbreak it had little control. This is, however, by no means the whole story. There were within the diplomatic corps as elsewhere in the Russian ruling élite strong differences of opinion and emphasis as to where Russia's future and her paramount interests lay and these did affect her foreign policy.

The leading figure in the minority Asiatic 'tendency' was probably Baron R.R. Rosen, a diplomat of great intelligence and moral courage. Most of Rosen's career had been spent in Japan or the USA, his last posting before appointment to the State Council in 1911 being as Ambassador in Washington, and his unorthodox experience may have contributed to his adoption of attitudes towards European relations and the balance of power which were unusual in the Russian Foreign Ministry. Orthodox by birth and with a Russian wife and mother Rosen considered himself fully Russian but he had to endure many jibes about his German name and origins.[63] These were particularly virulent because of Rosen's well-known opposition to Russian policies in the Balkans. In a memorandum[64] submitted to Nicholas II in late 1912 Rosen argued that Russia's mission lay outside Europe in the development of Siberia's vast natural resources and in the spread of Russo-European culture in Asia. He believed that no such scope for Russia's creative energies existed in Europe and that the idea of Russia's mission among the Slavs was both unrealistic and dangerous. Firstly, Slav solidarity, even in the cultural realm, was in Rosen's eyes a myth. Secondly, Panslav ambitions led Russia into unnecessary and dangerous conflict with Austria, whose domination of the Western Balkans was in Rosen's view not contrary to Russian interests.[65] Sharing Durnovo's view that possession of Constantinople would bring great expense and little advantage[66] Rosen believed that Russia had no vital interests in Europe save economic progress and the preservation of her territorial integrity, which 'no one shows the least disposition to attack'.[67] In Rosen's view none of Russia's conflicts with the Central Powers were even remotely worth a war, especially since he shared another 'pro-German' conviction that such a conflict would bring on revolution in Russia. Convinced that if need be Russia could live in amity with a Germany dominant in Central and Western Europe, Rosen argued that above all else she must disentangle herself from the war which the Anglo-French *entente*'s rivalry with Germany made inevitable.[68]

Serge Sazonov's view of Russia's mission and priorities was very different to Rosen's, as he made clear to the Duma in April 1912. He said:

'One must not forget ... that Russia is a European power, that the state was formed not on the banks of the Black Irtych but on the banks of the Dnieper and of the river Moskva. Increasing Russian possessions in Asia cannot be a goal of our foreign policy; this would lead to an undesirable shift in the state's centre of gravity and consequently to a weakening of our position in Europe and in the Middle East.[69]

Sazonov's remarks were more than a statement that Russian interests were centred chiefly in Europe or that he would be unwilling to annex peripheral areas of the disintegrating Chinese Empire. The Foreign Minister was asserting that Russia had a right to influence Europe's future development, especially as regards the Balkans. The Russian state would not, in Kireyev's contemptuous terms, be satisfied with civilising the Hunhuzes and thereby playing the role of a tolerated but inferior outrunner of Western culture.[70] Instead, she would assert her right to an independent cultural and political role within Europe, in other words in the continent where the leading world powers dwelt and around which the world's history seemed to turn. It takes no imagination to understand why this claim was soothing for Russian national pride.

If one wishes to understand the attitudes and the thinking behind the foreign policy Russia pursued between 1906 and 1914 study of the personality and opinions of Prince G.N. Trubetskoy is extremely rewarding. Appointed in the summer of 1912 to head the Near Eastern Department of the Foreign Ministry, which covered Balkan and Ottoman affairs, Trubetskoy's importance rested not only on his key official position but also on the fact that, in the words of the well-informed and reliable B.E. Nolde, Sazonov, a fellow Muscovite, 'felt towards Trubetskoy a very sincere trust and was subject to his undoubted influence', which resulted in Russian foreign policy in 1912–14 bearing 'the clear imprint' of Trubetskoy's 'personal creativity'.[71] Fortunately for the historian, Trubetskoy between 1906 and 1912 retired from the diplomatic service and devoted his time to writing lengthy articles about the theory and practice of international relations, Russian foreign policy, and contemporary events and trends in world politics. These articles, together with a secret memorandum Trubetskoy submitted to Nicholas II in January 1914, provide an exceptionally open, well thought-out and intelligent analysis of Russian policy and the problems it faced as seen, without the benefit of hindsight, through the eyes of one of the key policy-makers.

Trubetskoy was moreover important not only because of his ideas and the way these influenced and reflected the opinions of Sazonov. In addition, he served as the key link between the Foreign Ministry and those public forces which articulated what Nolde describes as 'the programme of Russian liberal imperialism'. Through collaborating with his brother Evgeni in editing the liberal and Slavophil Moscow weekly, *Moskovskiy Yezhenedel'nik*, Trubetskoy drew close to Muscovite 'liberal-imperialist' intellectual and business circles, as well as to the Czech Kramar and other leading foreign Slav activists. He and P.B. Struve became firm friends, both men publishing articles in each other's journals. Other leading liberal-imperialist figures who published in *Moskovskiy Yezhenedel' nik* included V.A. Maklakov, S.A. Kotlyarevsky, Professor A.L. Pogodin, and P.P. Ryabushinsky, a collection of names which symbolises the unity of intellectuals, politicians and businessmen behind the liberal-imperialist cause. In the so-called 'Economic Discussions' which Konovalov and Ryabushinsky sponsored in order to bring together the hitherto wholly distinct worlds of the liberal intelligentsia and Moscow business Trubetskoy played a leading role and his contribution was the longest and most impressive part of the two volume work, *Velikaya Rossiya* (Great Russia), which Ryabushinsky published and which provides the best summary of the views of Russia's liberal imperialists. The appointment of Trubetskoy, whose published criticism of the government's internal policy had generally been severe, to a key position in the Foreign Ministry was a remarkable step and shows how very close in sympathy were Sazonov and his assistants to the 'responsible Slavophil' elements in public opinion of which Trubetskoy was such a leading and well-known representative.[72]

To understand Trubetskoy's views and instincts it is necessary to look briefly at his background and his childhood. The Trubetskoys were one of Russia's oldest aristocratic families. G.N. Trubetskoy's two brothers, Serge and Evgeni, were both famous Idealist philosophers and the five brothers and sisters were probably the most intelligent and impressive aristocratic family in Nicholas II's Russia. The family's childhood was, however, less influenced by the aristocratic Trubetskoy heritage than by the traditions of their mother, who was born a Lopukhin. Her family was one of those well-established gentry clans whose life centred on Moscow and which had always provided the central core of the Slavophil movement; Trubetskoy's eldest sister was to marry F.D. Samarin, thus linking him directly to one of the traditionally leading Slavophil families. Like the founders of the Slavophil movement, Alexis Khomyakov and Ivan Kireyevsky, Trubetskoy had a deeply religious mother and was brought up in an atmosphere of Orthodox belief. He remained intensely religious and Orthodox throughout his life, like his brothers being strongly influenced by the ideas of Vladimir Solov'yov about reconciliation and moral unity between the Christian churches. All three Trubetskoy brothers attended Moscow University, at which two of them subsequently became professors, and Moscow remained for them always the centre of their emotional and intellectual world. This is a factor of real importance, for it was easier to breathe the ideals of Orthodox and pre-Petrine Russia amidst the churches of the ancient capital than in the Italianate palaces of the Petersburg ministries. Evgeni Trubetskoy recalls how when in Moscow, and especially in the city's churches, he felt overwhelmingly the sense of the unity of living Russia with the dead generations and their ideals, as well as the moral union of the whole Orthodox population. He recalls also how in 1877 he and his young friends felt an 'elemental hostility' towards the anti-national elements in Petersburg who were holding Russia back from intervention to rescue the Orthodox Slavs from Ottoman tyranny. The roots of G.N. Trubetskoy's patriotism and of his faith that this sentiment was shared by all true Russians, whatever their social background, lay in similar feelings.[73]

Trubetskoy believed that a healthy society had to be allowed to breathe freely, express its opinions and educate itself through the exercise of political power. He held that 'no great people can live without inspiration, without creative animation' and that in Russia the basis of such inspiration had to be Orthodox and Slav ideals.[74] The Slav idea, an essential foundation of which was justice for Poland, could contribute to the development of an unselfish and unifying patriotism. Memories of the glorious role played by Russia's armies in liberating the Balkans could restore Russians' pride in their past. [75] For Trubetskoy ethnic ties were no myth. They defined 'similarity in culture, in ways of thinking and in national ideals' which 'no great people can fail to value, seeing in them the extension of its creative forces, its own spiritual character'. Russia to be true to its role in the world's history had to protect the smaller Slav states' cultural and political independence from Germanic pressure.[76]

For Trubetskoy, external and internal affairs were inextricably linked but it would be a crass error to imagine that his views on Russian foreign policy were dictated by internal political considerations. If anything it would be more correct to stress that in his patriotic concern for Russian security, dignity and interests he was determined that the Empire should be internally united, progressive and therefore sufficiently strong to show a firm front to its foreign rivals and play the key role in the European great power system which he believed the interests of both Russia and European peace demanded. Criticising govenmental conservatism and repression he stated in

January 1909 that 'it is impossible to govern against the people when it is necessary to turn to it for the defence of Russia'. Convinced that Western liberal-constitutional principles contributed to a state's efficiency, unity and power Trubetskoy argued that

> in the struggle for existence organisms less adjusted to the struggle from the technical point of view were inevitably defeated by stronger ones. And given equal strength a state continuing to be governed by personal discretion will similarly not be in a position to stand up to states with a more modern system of administration, just as our clumsy ships with their weak artillery could not fight against the well-equipped Japanese battleships.[77]

Aware that international relations in his day embodied the laws of the jungle, Trubetskoy stressed the vital significance of military power for a state's survival. Unless Russia were manifestly strong she would neither secure the alliances vital to preserve her from isolation nor deter the rivals certain to exploit any signs of weakness she displayed. Although 'Russia's strength and means far from correspond to her tasks as a great power', she was forced to play an active role in both European and Asiatic military and diplomatic combinations, since 'the main threat of war for Russia is really contained in too clear a revelation of our weakness'. As more and more once-great states crumbled under the advance of a handful of super-powers seemingly on the verge of absorbing the whole globe the lesson of recent history did indeed seem to be that 'countries incapable of defending either themselves or their national dignity... become a subject for compensations and possible divisions'. When Russia suffered humiliation in her foreign policy, as for instance in the Bosnian crisis, there surfaced Trubetskoy's insecurity about Russia's position and his fear that she might join the list of recently defunct or dying empires.[78]

If power was the key to international relations, the balance of power between states and alliances was for Trubetskoy the major guarantor of peace. The principle 'of the system of political balance in which rests the guarantee of the whole world's peace' had for Trubetskoy something of the force of natural law or Holy Writ. Appealed to constantly in his writings, this principle underlay his entire conception of international relations. He saw the Franco-Russian alliance as the necessary and almost inevitable response to German unification and increasing power.[79] Confident that the balance between the alliances was a source of stability and peace he saw Russia's temporary removal from the ranks of active Great Powers after defeat and revolution in 1905 as highly dangerous. France's small population and weak economy, together with Britain's lack of an army, meant that 'without Russia England and France are insufficiently strong to form a counterweight to Germany and German diplomacy is trying to exploit this fact'. European security would remain fragile until Russia was seen to take up again her partly forfeited position among the powers.[80]

For Trubetskoy the threat to European peace came from Germany. In 1910 he quoted with approval his brother Serge's likening of Germany to 'a great boiler, developing surplus steam at extreme speed, for which an outlet is required; to close off such an outlet, to deprive Germany of her safety valve, would be to call forth an explosion, dangerous for Germany itself, for its allies and for its neighbours'. Unlike some Russians who wished to encourage Germany to direct her energies, military as well as economic and cultural, westwards, Trubetskoy was insistent that Germany's safety valves should be purely economic. He praised the development of Germany's maritime commerce and justified her desire to protect this immense investment by 'the strengthening of her fleet'. The increasing support in Britain for protectionism scared Trubetskoy because 'if these ideas come out on top in England then that itself will close many of the safety valves for German excess steam'.[81]

As one might expect, when German 'excess steam' sought outlets in the Near East Trubetskoy was less happy. He wrote fearfully in February 1906 about the growth of German influence in the Ottoman Empire. Still more alarming was the threat of German ambitions should the Habsburg Empire disintegrate. Trubetskoy warned that 'the plans of pan-Germanism extend to the taking possession of the whole of Austria with all the latter's claims up to and including Salonica'. Nor in 1906 did he see any fundamental difference between Pan-German claims and the German government's actions. As German activity in Turkey showed, the latter were merely quieter and carried out more astutely. Trubetskoy asked

What is Pan-Germanism if not a vivid expression of the German imperialism which inspires the speeches of the Emperor William and the policy of his Chancellor? This policy can count on the sympathy not just of junkers or even liberals. In the breast of a

German, whether he be a landowner or a socialist, there beats above all a German heart and the watchword 'Great Germany' will be heard more readily by the latter than the call to the unity of the proletarians of all countries.

Such considerations made Trubetskoy feel in February 1906 that 'the Macedonian and Austrian questions are perhaps newly developing phases of world history. In the field of practical policy they influence the character of our relations with Germany, outlining a stage of perhaps peaceful and perhaps violent conflict between Germanism and slavdom'.[82]

These views, written for Struve's journal *Polyarnaya zvezda* in February 1906, were the most outspokenly anti-German comments published by Trubetskoy in the years before 1914. Subsequently he admitted that Pan-German views might not always represent the aims of the Berlin government and in January 1907 stressed that the Social Democrats and the trade unions were 'a serious opponent' of German aggressive imperialism. In October 1908 he emphasised that Slav interests in no way conflicted with the opinions expressed by those who represented truly popular forces in Germany. He underlined that the peoples of the two empires had a huge vested economic interest in each other's prosperity.[83] Yet even when seeking to be conciliatory towards Berlin Trubetskoy's underlying fear and distrust was sometimes evident. For him Germany remained 'the country beating all records of militarism and giving the general tone to the growth of European armaments'. In addition, he understood that in the eyes of the conservative forces which dominated the German government 'only nationalist notes' could serve to delay the advance of democracy. In February 1909 as the annexation crisis reached its height Trubetskoy's bruised patriotic feelings and awareness of Russian weakness led to an unusually open expression of his suspicion about Germany's ultimate aims. 'The Germans,' he wrote, 'are not ... wholly without the thought of removing from Russia at least part of the Baltic coastline in order to place us in the position of a second Serbia and thus finally to solve, for them, hateful slav question which is the main hindrance to German hegemony on the continent'.[84]

Germany's power meant that the policies pursued by her government were of decisive importance for the future of all Europe. This ensured that for the contemporary observer of international affairs the interpretation of German aims was bound to be of central significance. For Trubetskoy, however, Austrian affairs were only marginally less important. His statement in 1910 that 'the existence of an independent Austria is as much a necessity for Russia as for Europe for in it is tied the knot of the European balance' was both sincere and realistic. Aware that the disintegration of Austria would entail serious Russo-German conflict, he hoped that the Habsburgs would preserve their Empire by carrying out major internal reforms. The introduction of universal suffrage in Austria in January 1907 struck him as 'an event of huge importance'. It showed, he hoped, that the Habsburg Empire was neither as moribund nor as doomed as he had previously imagined. Universal suffrage could end the situation whereby Slavs were second-class citizens in Austria, and by creating a genuine Austrian patriotism in place of its inadequate previous substitutes, 'either . . . Pan-German chauvinism or . . . devotion to the dynastic idea', could both greatly strengthen the Dual Monarchy and exercise powerful pressure on the Hungarians to alter their policy of Magyarisation and repression of Hungary's minority races. Trubetskoy believed that in a democratic and racially equitable Austria the various peoples, although desiring the maximum internal autonomy, would become loyal imperial subjects out of an awareness of the advantages they derived, both economically and in terms of security, from belonging to a great empire.[85]

Both in the summer of 1909 and again in 1910 Trubetskoy stressed that Russia had everything to gain from the development of Austria into a federation in which Slav voices would have a major influence. The Slavs should not seek to remove Austria from the Triple Alliance since a sense of total isolation might drive Berlin towards 'a politics of disaster', but they should ensure that the Dual Monarchy was a servant neither of Magyar arrogance nor of a Germanic *Drang nach Osten*. Trubetskoy realised that whatever might be Russian interest in Austria's Slavs she had no right directly to intervene in the Monarchy's internal affairs. His strategy for influencing Austrian developments was two-fold. A determined Russian stand in the Balkans would show Vienna the dangers of expansionism, while Russo-Polish reconciliation would undermine the common hostility to Petersburg which alone held together the ruling Germano-Polish coalition in Vienna. This would bring about a unification of Slav forces in Austria whose influence would be a major force for moderation and peace. As

Trubetskoy wrote in June 1909, whether Austria would develop along these desirable lines depended on complicated historical circumstances which no one could predict but Russia must do everything possible to ensure such development.[86]

Trubetskoy's sense that Austria stood before a crossroads and that the path she chose would be of crucial significance for Europe was even stronger in January 1914 than it had been four years earlier. In an important memorandum submitted through Sazonov to Nicholas II he drew the Emperor's attention to the dangers posed to the Habsburg state by the increasing 'ferment of the nationalities' within the Monarchy, coupled with 'the extreme strengthening of irredentism' in Rumania and Serbia. He added that in the face of these popular movements which were undermining the Monarchy the latter 'will in the perhaps not too distant future face a choice between two paths; either fundamental reconstruction of the state structure on the basis of a federation of the different nationalities or a desperate struggle aimed at the final confirmation of the predominance of the German-Hungarian minority over all the other peoples in the Empire'. This struggle would take the shape of a war aimed at showing both the minorities and the irredentist states the dangers and the hopelessness of opposing the Monarchy and its German and Hungarian rulers. 'At a given moment,' warned Trubetskoy, 'especially if Germany were disposed towards this, the warlike tendency might come out on top in Austria-Hungary and its supporters are pointing out that war is perhaps the only way out of insoluble internal difficulties'.[87]

Russia's three main allies in defence of peace and the European balance of power were in Trubetskoy's opinion France, Britain and the Slavs. His commitment to the French alliance was total, leading him even to criticise Izvol'sky's effort in 1907 to please Berlin by the agreement to preserve the *status quo* in the Baltic. Trubetskoy complained that 'one cannot close one's eyes to the evident necessity as regards the question of mutual security in Europe to choose between France and Germany. To seek a middle way is equivalent to wanting to sit between two stools. This is scarcely either a profitable or an honourable position'.[88]

Trubetskoy was already in 1906 a strong advocate of better relations with Britain. He gladly accepted the 1907 agreement even though unenthusiastic about some of its terms. He felt that the denial to Russia of direct relations with Afghanistan was a harmful leftover of past suspicions which might profitably be removed once trust existed between the two powers. He also became increasingly critical of the Russo-British agreement over Persia. Not just for commercial reasons but also because of the unstable state of the Russian border population the Imperial government could not, in Trubetskoy's view, afford to allow anarchy in Northern Persia. It was nonsense for the British to blame Persia's anarchy on Russian military intervention or support for the Shah. In fact the Russians had sacrificed their own interests in backing the Persian constitution but the latter had, despite British pretence to the contrary, deepened rather than alleviated Persia's anarchy, the sole bulwark against which in Northern Persia was often the Russian army. The Russo-British agreement was making it impossible for the Russians to restore order in Northern Persia as the French were allowed to do in Morocco.[89]

In Trubetskoy's eyes, however, specific colonial grievances against Britain were wholly outweighed by the contribution that friendship with London made to Russian security. Russo-British amity offered at least a 'moral guarantee' that Russia's Far Eastern possessions would be safe from any attack by Britain's ally, Japan.[90] Even more important was the role that Russo-British unity played in preserving European peace. Trubetskoy's trust in Britain was based in part on the fact that she was a satiated, conservative and maritime power and therefore posed no threat to the European *status quo* or vital Russian interests. In addition, the democratisation of British politics and 'the whole character of the development of contemporary English culture' convinced him that 'England does not nourish warlike schemes against Germany'. Nevertheless, Britain's usefulness though important was limited. She lacked the means to guarantee Russian security in Eastern Europe or the desire to uphold Russian interests at the Straits. In addition, too close links between Petersburg and London awoke Germany's traditional nightmare about coalitions and might even lead Berlin to strike decisively against what it saw as encirclement. In the wake of the Bosnian crisis Trubetskoy became much more sensitive to German fears than had hitherto been the case and correspondingly more anxious to stress that a wholly defensive *entente* rather than an alliance linked Petersburg and London.[91]

For Trubetskoy the value of Slav support rested in part on the fact that 'Russia's position in Europe is to a considerable extent defined by her interests in the Black Sea basin and in the Balkans'. These interests were 'vital' and centred on Constantinople, whose fate was 'a question of vast historical and strategic importance'. Slav solidarity suited Russian ideals and interests since it would check German domination of the Balkans and Near East, which Russia individually was too weak to do.[92] Intelligent considerations of *realpolitik* lay behind Trubetskoy's determination that Russia should show the Slav states that she could defend their interests and would stand by them in time of need. So also, however, did an emotional Slavophilism which at times clouded a little Trubetskoy's judgement. In the Bosnian crisis, for instance, his demands for compensation for Serbia were unrealistic; his belief that from an Austrian invasion of Serbia to a future partition of Russia was a relatively short step was also clearly exaggerated, though it does serve to illustrate the insecurity of Russian policy-makers, whose awareness of Russia's weakness had been greatly heightened by the events of 1904–5.[93]

Trubetskoy's views on foreign policy revolved, as we have seen, around two ideas, Slavdom and the balance of power. The former was a weak reed, as he himself at times admitted. As he stated in December 1909, the rulers of the Balkan states used Slav slogans when it suited them but in practice combined the pursuit of self-interest with a love for underhand intrigue which Trubetskoy blamed on their Turkish inheritance. Nor, as he wrote a month earlier, were pro-Slav feelings deeply rooted even in the Russian educated classes, a point ironically confirmed by *Moskovskiy Yezhenedel'nik's* own very limited circulation and ultimate collapse.[94] Given this, it was optimistic indeed for Trubetskoy to expect peasants in the backwoods of Kostroma and Kherson to feel any patriotic upsurge as they marched to defend their Serb 'brothers'.

As regards the centre-piece of Trubetskoy's policy, reliance on the balance of power to deter Germany, the most obvious point to make is that the policy failed. Germany was not deterred and the result was a disastrous war. Nevertheless, one can advance powerful arguments in defence of the advocates of deterrence. One such defence would be that deterrence would not have failed had it been rigorously applied and, in particular, had Britain placed itself unequivocally on the side of Russia and France. This was Sazonov's view. Another point, one made in the previous section, is that the only possible alternative to support for deterrence and the *entente*, namely the attempt to steer Germany westwards, was also by no means without risk. Reliance on the balance of power seemed in addition to be justified by Europe's experience since 1871 and was by no means only 'holy writ' for Russian diplomacy. Moreover, deterrence appeared logical, for it was rational to believe that although Germany might be happy to push around opponents too weak to fight, she would hardly risk her prosperity and indeed existence in a war with a coalition of European powers. The point does have to be made that Germany's behaviour in 1914 was indeed irrational and led precisely to the destruction that the balance of power theory had always suggested would face the state which sought to overturn the equilibrium. This does not mean that the strategy of deterrence was necessarily correct or the conduct of Russian foreign policy between 1906 and 1914 faultless. It may well be that Russian interests would have been best served by adopting a position of dignified second fiddle to Berlin, could the latter have been achieved. The Slav idea, indirect Austrian control over Serbia or even German domination of the Straits do not, in the light of cold reason, seem to have justified running the appalling risks Russia faced in entering a European war. Nevertheless, given both objective circumstances and the psychology of pre-war Europe Russian options were, as was stated in the previous section, both narrow and difficult. If P.N. Durnovo was no fool neither was G.N. Trubetskoy.

THE ARMY AND THE NAVY

The first plans for a future war with Germany and Austria were drawn up by General D.A. Milyutin in 1873 and amplified in General N.N. Obruchev's 'Consideration about Plans for the Conduct of War' in 1880. In view of the greater speed of concentration of the enemy forces both generals accepted that Russia would initially have to act defensively. They hoped, however, that once fully ready the Russian forces would counter-attack and saw the Austrian front as providing the best opportunities for this Russian offensive. Subsequent milestones in Russian military planning were the Franco-Russian military convention of 1894, which pledged the Russians to put 800,000 soldiers in the field against Germany, and the Russian decision, made in 1900–2, that an offensive should be mounted against the Germans as well as the Austrians in the first month of the war. In the wake of Russia's defeat in Manchuria Russian planning once again became far more defensive but on 1 May 1912 (O.S.) the orders for deployment and operations issued to the military districts returned to a more offensive approach. These directives in fact comprised two plans, 'G' and 'A', the former being intended for use in the unlikely event that the Germans concentrated the bulk of their forces on the eastern front.

The latter plan, 'A', was the basis for Russian military operations in August 1914. It called for an offensive by two Russian armies into East Prussia aimed at tying down German troops and occupying Prussia east of the Vistula as a necessary prelude to later operations against Germany. Meanwhile the main thrust was to be against Austria, three and, depending on circumstances, possibly four armies being directed to attack and destroy Austrian forces east of the Carpathians.[95]

A number of factors influenced Russian planning for war with the Central Powers. Geography inevitably was one. The huge Polish salient extended far to the west and was enveloped from north and south by East Prussia and Galicia. Russia troops in this salient, most of which comprised the Warsaw Military District, had to form three fronts, to the north, west and south, and their deployment and operations were of central importance in Russian military planning, a crucial point to which we will return in Chapter 5 when discussing the Russian mobilisation. Russian possession of the Polish salient offered both the chance to mount a decisive offensive from bases west of the Vistula towards Berlin and the danger that Russian forces would be cut off and encircled by an Austro-German pincer movement from East Prussia and Galicia. Both the French and General M.I. Dragomirov were impressed by the advantages of a Russian offensive from Western Poland but the majority of Russian military chiefs regarded such a move as far too risky, especially in view of the superior speed of mobilisation and concentration of the Central Powers' armies. In their view any attempt to concentrate the bulk of Russian forces in Western Poland before the Galician and East Prussian flanks had been secured would result in the Russian armies being taken in the rear and destroyed even before they were fully ready or deployed.[96]

Most Russian planners were much more enthusiastic about an offensive into Galicia than into East Prussia. As General M.V. Alekseyev stated in 1908, the latter was a difficult region to invade for geographical reasons. Some Russian planners also attached great importance to the moral effect which would be produced on the Slav populations of Central and Eastern Europe by either decisive Russian victories or defeats against the Austrians. Moreover, there was deep hatred as well as some contempt in the Russian officer corps for the Habsburg Empire and the French were alarmed lest these feelings together with the Russian generals' respect and fear of the German army might seriously distort what Paris felt to be correct strategy. As

we have seen, the Russians were always to attach primary importance
to their operations against Austria but under consistent French pressure they agreed on an early offensive against Germany as well.[97]

This French pressure was a sign more of weakness than of strength.
France had one main enemy, Germany, and in the twentieth century
it became ever clearer that the Germans aimed to direct the bulk of
their forces westwards in the event of war. Given both the quality and
size of the German army this put France's survival at risk. Unlike
their French counterparts, Russian military planners had various
options open to them. They could attack either Austria or Germany;
on the other hand they could concentrate their forces safely in the rear
and satisfy themselves initially with beating off the Austrian offensive
and the limited 'spoiling' attack which even some French experts
agreed the Germans might make in order to cause havoc to Russian
plans before the slow-moving Russian troops were fully concentrated.
Over and over again the French army stressed that France's security
rested in part on Russian willingness to strike quickly at Germany,
preferably into Silesia but failing that into East Prussia, in order to
ensure that Berlin left at least five or six corps on the Eastern front.[98]

One means of pressure used by the French was financial. This was
true in particular as regards the construction of strategic railways,
which were of key significance for the rapid concentration of Russian
forces. Both in 1901 and in 1913–14 the French attached riders to their
loans to Russia which ensured that the Russians built lines which they
would otherwise not have constructed either at that time or at such
speed. On 27 January 1906 Moulin, the French military attaché,
wrote that France should not let the Russians borrow beyond a certain point without ensuring Russian compliance with French views on
the need to develop railways and supply depots. In April 1906 Russian willingness to accept French-inspired changes in the military
convention probably owed something to the huge and much-needed
loan which the Russian government was on the point of finalising at
that moment in Paris. In the winter of 1913–14 a French General Staff
officer wrote that 'France ought to profit from the financial advantages she has given her ally by obtaining from the latter greater
military advantages but it does not at present seem that in this sense
France is failing in her duty'. Nevertheless, the importance of financial pressure should not be exaggerated, especially in the years 1907–
14. Six months before the outbreak of war Laguiche wrote that those
Frenchmen who believed their financial power allowed them 'to talk

toughly' to the Russians and 'make them pay very dearly' for loans were badly mistaken. Although Russia would for some time continue to need foreign capital the growth of her economy and of domestic investment in recent years had been spectacular and 'the Russia of today is no longer what it was fifteen years ago. She has a power, both financial and otherwise, much greater than in the old days'. Laguiche added that in a decade or two Russia might well be able to free herself from the need for French investment and that even now it was a mistake to imagine that, regardless of other circumstances, France must always remain for the Russians their only possible banker. The Russians, he wrote, were well aware of their new-found power and were much less willing than in the past to accept surveillance, let alone pressure. For this reason the French must measure their demands and only attempt to use their financial weapon when to do so would genuinely further the interests of both partners to the alliance.[99]

In Franco-Russian military relations financial pressures were in fact seldom of primary importance and it is significant that perhaps the most important concession made by the Russians to the French in the eight years before the war, namely the promise that the Russian army would be concentrated and ready to attack the Germans after the fifteenth day of mobilisation, came in 1911 at a time when Russian finances were flourishing and there was no immediate desire for more foreign loans. The key element in Franco-Russian military relations was quite simply that, as a report of the Third Bureau of the French General Staff put matters in August 1912, for France the main advantage of the Russian alliance lay precisely in the possibility it provided for simultaneous offensives against the Germans from west and east in the early weeks of any future conflict. The Russians were aware of the decisive significance of this factor in French eyes which explains, for instance, why the important strategic conference of March 1902 over which Nicholas II presided insisted that unless a rapid offensive against Germany was both promised and if necessary delivered the Franco-Russian alliance might collapse. Russian willingness to commit themselves to attacking Germany was therefore intimately linked to the enthusiasm and trust with which the Russian government and army regarded the French alliance as a whole.[100]

Franco-Russian military relations in 1906–9 were a little cool. Neither side rated the other's army highly and the Russians felt the French had cold-shouldered them, even perhaps twisted their arms, in the wake of the Japanese War. Cooler feelings, added to French failure to support Russia strongly in the annexation crisis, no doubt influenced General Danilov's 1910 estimate that Russia might have to face the Central Powers alone in a future conflict, which of course made his proposed deployment even more defensive than would otherwise have been the case. In 1910–14, however, the relations between the allied armies became better and better as the reports of both the French and British military attachés make clear.[101] The French were impressed by the speed and success with which the Russian army had recovered from the effects of 1904–5, as well as by what Laguiche described as the 'vast . . . enormous' military programme unveiled in 1913–14.[102] Commenting in 1911 and 1913 on growing Russian warmth, French military sources ascribed this in part to the excellent impression which the French army had made on recent high-ranking Russian visitors, including the Grand Duke Nicholas and Gerngross, the Chief of the General Staff. Captain Langlois and Colonel Janin, leading French experts on the Russian army, also noted with satisfaction that as a result of lengthy observation by visiting Russians of French higher military education radical reforms were being introduced into the Nicholas Staff Academy along French lines.[103] Symptomatic of Russian military moods was the appointment in later 1910 of the extreme francophile Colonel Byelyayev as editor of the two journals of the War Ministry, *Russkiy Invalid* and *Voyennyy Sbornik*, both of which played an important role in forming and articulating military attitudes. Byelyayev told Janin, who was on a six-month attachment to the Russian General Staff Academy at the time, that he would suppress any articles or letters hostile to France which might be offered to the journals.[104] If Russian officers had previously suspected France of socialist anti-militarism and her army of lack of proper discipline, the growth of patriotic feeling after the Moroccan crisis, the introduction of three-year service and the personality and foreign policy of Poincaré all tended to disabuse them of such fears. In particular, as Laguiche wrote in December 1912, 'the mass of officers greatly liked our attitude because they felt us to be ready to march for a slav cause in support of Russia whereas in 1908 we were felt to be too cold.'[105]

The growing respect in Russian military circles for the French army and alliance certainly influenced the Russians towards meeting French calls for rapid offensive action against Germany should war occur. In addition, Russian military intelligence was itself stressing that the Germans would indeed, as the French had always claimed, probably be sending the great bulk of their army westwards in an attempt to annihilate France.[106] As Count Ignat'yev, the Russian military attaché in Paris, assured the French, German success in eliminating France from the struggle would be a disaster for Russia and it was therefore logical to expect Petersburg to do everything possible to insure against such an eventuality.[107] The best insurance, as the French always urged, was for the Russians to draw German troops to the east by threatening Germany's own territory. Whatever the Russians did to the Austrian army would not recompense them for the fall of France, moreover the facts of geography and communications made it clear that Germany could destroy French military capacity well before the Russians could inflict decisive damage on Austria. On all these counts the French were therefore right to insist on rapid Russian aid against Germany and the Russians right to grant it.

This does not mean that Russian or allied planning was faultless. In particular, Zhilinsky's promise in 1911 that the Russians would attack after the fifteenth day of mobilisation could only be fulfilled if the army took the offensive before all its units were deployed. According to the military historian, General A.M. Zayonchkovsky, Zhilinsky's promise meant that A.V. Samsonov's Second Army advanced in 1914 without one-fifth of its infantry, for which it paid dearly at Tannenberg.[108] Genuine joint Franco-Russian planning aided by a sensible grasp of the alliance's strategic position would have made this sacrifice unnecessary. The correct allied strategy for a future war was for the French to remain on the defensive until the Russians were ready to commit their forces and had Russian generals been able to infect their French counterparts with some of their much-despised defensive-mindedness this might have been realised. If so, this would have saved France from enormous casualties and spared Russia the need to intervene before her troops were ready. Unfortunately, Russia's own military planning shows evidence of a muddle-headedness and lack of self-confidence which makes it unlikely that her generals would ever have been able to impose their views on the determined, if mistaken, French. Thus Plan 'A', the product of a compromise between the views of the General Staff and those of the Kiev Military District, divided Russian troops between the German and Austrian fronts in such a way as to deprive the latter of the chances of decisive success without guaranteeing the former against disaster.[109]

The destruction of all but the Black Sea squadron by the Japanese meant that in the period 1906–14 Russian admirals were on the whole planning the operations of ships which were still under construction. Nevertheless, the first squadron of battleships of the new Baltic Fleet, laid down in 1909, was nearing completion by 1914, powerful units were being constructed at great speed in the Black Sea and very ambitious programmes for future shipbuilding in both seas had become law. Grenfell, the British naval attaché, correctly commented in June 1912 that the Russians were aiming to have 'a first-class modern navy by the year 1930', adding that 'if a large navy may be justly considered as a luxury for Germany, it is indisputable that the same applies to Russia, but in a vastly greater degree'. Grenfell's sourness was understandable, for the Russian fleet was designed as a weapon of diplomatic pressure which could be used to equal advantage against Britain or Germany. The confidential explanatory note which accompanied the 1912 'Programme of Increased Ship-Construction', apart from stating the obvious need to defend Russia's shores and trade, stressed the advantages of possessing a fleet strong enough to affect the balance between the world's largest navies. Whether in peacetime or as a neutral in time of war a state possessing such a fleet would be either 'a desirable ally' or 'an opponent whose interests need to be seriously taken into account'.[110]

In more specific terms Russian naval planning from 1908 to 1914 was largely occupied by the question of the Straits. Three main fears agitated the Russians. Firstly, the Ottoman Empire might collapse and the Straits be seized by another power. Secondly, in an effort to survive the Turks might build a fleet large enough to challenge Russian domination of the Black Sea. Thirdly, whoever held the Straits might close them to merchant shipping, thus imposing crippling losses on Russian trade. There was, at least in the short run, not a great deal that the Russian navy could do about any of these problems, which explains why the Russian admiralty was so anxious that the final collapse of the Ottoman Empire be postponed until 1918 when five squadrons of their Black Sea and Baltic fleets should be ready for action. Rapid amphibious operations against Constantinople in the period 1912–14 were impossible for lack of the necessary transport and equipment, while the impending arrival of Turkish Dreadnoughts from British naval yards would not only make such operations inconceivable but would also threaten Russia's Black Sea coast and cut the maritime communications which would be vital for any

Russian army seeking to fight the Turks in Armenia or Asia Minor. Since it was impossible to bring Russian ships through the Straits or, at least initially, to build them as quickly in Russian Black Sea yards as in Britain or Germany the Russian navy was at a severe disadvantage in its efforts to compete with the build-up of the Turkish fleet. Matters became worse when the Turks began to purchase completed Dreadnoughts in South America. In response the Russians attempted to block such purchases and to persuade the British to delay the delivery of ships to the Turks. At the same time, they poured money and effort into creating an efficient shipbuilding industry in Southern Russia with results which even the British, usually jaundiced about Russian naval efforts, found impressive. Finally, the Russians planned to send their first Baltic squadron to operate in the Mediterranean in 1914–15 in the hope that its threat to the Turkish coastline and trade would force the Ottomans to deploy their fleet to the west rather than in the Black Sea. It was to secure French support for this scheme, which would entail basing the fleet at Bizerta, that Lieven, the chief of the Naval General Staff, was sent to Paris in 1912 to sign the Franco-Russian naval convention. Russian enthusiasm for a similar convention with the British in 1914 was also owed largely to hopes about future co-operation in the Mediterranean and was therefore a good deal more soundly based than London imagined. At the very least the Russians might have succeeded in opening British eyes to the importance of the Eastern Mediterranean, to which the Royal Navy was extraordinarily blind. Had this occurred the disastrous escape of the *Goeben* to Constantinople, which, according to Marder, the Admiralty and Admiral Milne 'at first almost looked upon . . . as a success' could never have happened.[111]

Not just army and navy planning but also the level of military preparedness was of crucial importance in the period 1906–14. Since a state's weight in international affairs was largely measured by its ability and willingness to use force in support of diplomatic activity this could scarcely have been otherwise. The flat statement of the Minister of War, General Roediger, that the army was not capable even of a defensive war against the Central Powers forced the government to capitulate in the face of German threats in March 1909. Five years later the assertion by the two defence ministers, Sukhomlinov and Grigorovich, that the armed forces were ready for war with Germany and Austria had the opposite effect. Without this assurance it is inconceivable that the Russian government would have adopted the relatively firm stance that it took up in July 1914. Since Sukhomlinov and Grigorovich's statement can with justice be described as one of the key causes of Russia's entry into the First World War it is worth studying in some detail why this statement was made and to what extent it was true.

Grigorovich's assertion of Russian readiness was more remarkable than Sukhomlinov's for the navy was unprepared for conflict with the Central Powers to an obvious degree which was not true of the army. Ironically, however, the clearest sign of the navy's unpreparedness, namely its great numerical inferiority to the fleets of the Central Powers, was to matter very little. However much of the Russian programme of naval construction had been completed, Russia could never have hoped to challenge German naval domination of the Baltic. On the other hand, coastal defence in these waters was well provided for in 1914–17 by Russian proficiency with mines. The strength of the Russian fleet in the Mediterranean and Black Sea would never, as the British found in 1915, have guaranteed that it could force the Straits without military support. The war did, however, come just in time to stop the British despatching to Constantinople the completed Turkish Dreadnoughts which would temporarily have given the Ottoman Empire control of the Black Sea; in these ships' absence Russian supremacy in this area was maintained until the Revolution.

Naval unpreparedness in 1914 turned out to be more a question of personnel than of material, as some observers had always believed would be the case. Unlike the army, the overwhelming majority of whose soldiers were peasants, naval ratings were often drawn from the urban working class. Such conscripts were of course much better equipped than peasants to handle the complicated machinery of a modern warship but they were also deeply influenced by the revolutionary sentiment general in the Russian working class by 1914. Naval ratings had played a major role in the 1905 Revolution and conspiracies and mutinies continued to flourish in the fleet, unlike the army, up to the outbreak of the war. Noting in 1913 the 'rapidly advancing . . .class consciousness' of the workers and believing that in Russian conditions better education would probably only lead to still deeper disaffection, Grenfell wrote that for all the improvements recently made in the navy 'a heavy discount must continue to be made upon its paper value, as opponent or as ally, owing to the uncertainty of the disposition existing among the ships' companies'. The more enlightened Russian admirals needed no warning on this score. The Chief of the Naval General Staff wrote that although it was easier and more comfortable for naval officers' self-esteem to concentrate on rebuilding the fleet and planning naval strategy the question of personnel was the most serious one facing the navy. Lieven stressed the way in which the navy had failed to use available chances to create homogeneous ships' crews, united in a spirit of pride and loyalty to their units and led by officers with whom they were personally acquainted over a number of cruises. He emphasised the crucial significance of the 'vast gap' caused by the lack of long-service NCOs who, belonging socially to the lower deck and professionally to the service and its officers, would hold the two ends of the navy together. In the absence of such NCOs 'our ratings are completely out of our hands and their mood depends entirely on political currents among the masses'. In Lieven's opinion it was almost impossible for officers and men to work together in full harmony since 'between the two there exists an abyss from birth which it is difficult to cross from either side. . . the moral and intellectual level of the two is so different that it is difficult for them to understand one another'. Though long service and in particular war-time comradeship could sometimes bind the two sides together 'in normal times they are completely indecipherable for us. Officers imagining that they know the physiognomy of their sailors, except as regards service matters, are bitterly mistaken'. Though discipline in general ensured obedience, most sailors looked on the officer as a lord and as an 'oppressor', whom he 'always fears, and distrusts'. One could scarcely find a more explicit statement of the extent to which the deep gulf between the educated élite and the masses undermined the military potential of the Russian state. Clearly, the ambitious plans of the naval authorities were based on very insecure foundations.[112]

To some extent similar considerations applied to the army as to the navy. Had the former not been far better prepared than the latter in terms of material, however, the Russian government would never have dared to go to war in 1914. Whereas 1904–5 had witnessed the destruction of the Russian navy, very few of Russia's best military units had seen action in the Far East. On the other hand, European depots and magazines had been emptied to meet the needs of the Far Eastern army and large cadres, in particular of engineers, sappers and other specialised troops had been detached from army units in Europe. On top of this much of the army even as late as 1907 was being used to check internal unrest, with dire effects on its training and cohesion. Moreover, since the bad state of Russia's finances meant that until 1909 little money was available to make up for the weaknesses caused by the events of 1904–7 the efforts of the military authorities were further hampered. In the face of these difficulties the great strides which the army had made by 1914 were remarkable and, as both the British and French attachés agreed, reflected creditably on the Ministry of War. Junior and middle-ranking officers, bitterly ashamed by the defeats of 1904–5, threw themselves wholeheartedly and with considerable success into teaching their soldiers the tactical lessons of the recent conflict and Wyndham, the British attaché, wrote that Russian units were absorbing rapidly the tactics learned by the British in the Boer War. Depots and magazines by 1914 had almost reached, and indeed sometimes surpassed, the levels considered necessary for a European war and the field artillery had been completely rearmed with more modern weapons. Strenuous efforts were being made to increase the numbers of reserve officers and regular NCOs though inevitably, as with all questions of personnel, these changes took time to bear fruit. The system by which reserve units were formed was radically improved, as were the mobilisation and deployment of the army.[113] The Great Programme adopted in 1913–14 and intended to be completed in four years planned for a 40 per cent increase in the size of the peacetime army and a 29 per cent jump in the number of officers. Money was at last made available to abolish the cumbersome 8 gun batteries and to increase the artillery strength of Russian corps to German levels. A whole series of reforms in almost all branches of the army were planned to carry forward the changes already made in 1909–14 and there can be little question that, had the Great Programme been fulfilled, the Russian army would in some respects by 1917–18 have been considerably more formidable than it was on the outbreak of the war. In one sense therefore Sukhomlinov's willingness to assert that the army was ready in 1914 is a puzzle.[114]

It would, however, be a mistake to imagine that had the Russians succeeded in postponing the outbreak of war for three or four years all the weaknesses which helped to undermine their military effectiveness would have disappeared. Many of these weaknesses were the products either of history or of the existing level of Russian social development and could not be eradicated overnight by administrative means. This was even true of a key Russian failing, namely the relatively limited ability of most of the senior commanders. Sukhomlinov told Colonel Matton, the French attaché, in January 1910 that improving the calibre of the high command was 'the most important and the most difficult task' he faced;[115] even Roediger's morally courageous purges of senior commanders had failed radically to improve the standard of Russian generalship.[116] One problem which bedevilled the high command was that personal hatreds and egoistic considerations too often proved stronger than canons of professional or patriotic behaviour. As one senior general told the British military attaché, Alfred Knox in 1912, 'there will never be unselfish co-operation amongst the higher leaders as in the German army'.[117] Sukhomlinov's support for the selection of a rapidly-changing series of nonentities as Chiefs of the General Staff in 1909–14 is an example of the placing of a personal interest in survival as minister above the needs of the state, but unfortunately the Minister was often right not to trust the professional loyalty of such powerful subordinates, who were on occasion quite capable of intriguing with their chief's political enemies.[118] The training and career experience of Russian generals also left much to be desired. The General Staff Academy, through which most high commanders had passed, not merely provided far too theoretical a military education but also plucked officers out of their regiments in their early twenties and then set them on a career which gave them very little experience in the command of fighting units. In addition, the limited self-confidence of top commanders, which the French put down to their wavering between a number of contradictory military doctrines of foreign origin, was increased both by a sense of Russian backwardness in comparison to its German neighbour and by the defeats inflicted by Japan in 1904–5. A. Kersnovsky's comment that little could have been expected of Russian generalship until 1920–5 when the older generation would have been replaced by younger and abler men is too pessimistic. More effective use of wargames and manoeuvres could have taught even the pre-war generation the rudiments of how to command large units. Kersnovsky is, however, right to underline that in itself the creation of ever-larger armies envisaged by the 1913–14 Great Programme was of limited benefit so long as the efficient use of even existing formations was beyond the capacity of many Russian generals.[119]

Perhaps the most important point to grasp in discussing Russian preparedness for war in 1914 is, however, that everything depended on the nature of the war for which one was supposed to be preparing.

The warnings, for instance, of P.N. Durnovo about the fatal strains a future war would put on Russia's weak economy and divided society were only fully relevant in the context of a lengthy conflict. The Russian Ministry of War in 1914 had, however, been preparing itself for a struggle which would last for two to six months. Sukhomlinov wrote in 1909 that 'contemporary political and economic conditions will not allow our neighbours to wage a lengthy war. In correspondence with this all their military system is directed towards guaranteeing the possibility of dealing rapid and decisive blows . . . We also must follow this example'. Two comments are necessary on this statement. In the first place German calculations, based in part on Schlieffen's views about the fragility of a modern economy, were mistaken. Secondly, Sukhomlinov should have been less willing tamely to base his plans on German calculations since, however necessary or advantageous it might be for Berlin to wage a short war, allied interests and calculations might well need to be geared to how to prepare for and survive a longer one.[120]

A lengthy conflict faced not just Russian society and the Russian economy but also the army itself with very difficult problems. This was in part because of the army's structure but even more because of what one might describe as its ideology. Although in theory the Imperial army since 1874 had been a conscript body deriving its strength from the physical and moral forces of the entire population, in practice it still retained some of the characteristics of a dynastic bodyguard. Large-scale exemptions for family and educational reasons, caused in part by financial stringency and in part by the need to leave key cadres in the civil economy, resulted in the number of trained reservists being very low when the overall size of the population is taken into account. This was especially true as regards officers. In 1914 Russia had approximately 41,000 regular and 21,000 reserve officers, Prussia 29,000 and 22,000 respectively.[121] In addition, neither in their backgrounds nor in their beliefs were regular officers typical of educated society as a whole. Drawn in general from gentry or military families, their ideals were on the contrary, as we have seen, largely despised by leading elements in the civilian population. The ideology of the army was, as knowledgeable French officers constantly stressed, by no means based on the Western concept of a patriotic and informed citizenry. Captain Jacquinot, who spent six months in a Russian regiment in 1913–14, wrote that the Russian soldier

lacks enthusiasm and patriotism. He is taught the history of the
regiment but he is ignorant of the history of his country. He is not
kept informed of contemporary goings-on and he would fight just as
willingly against the French as against the Germans and Austrians
. . . . The Russian soldier goes into battle much less through devotion to the country than through discipline and through loyalty to
God and the Tsar.[122]

Though other French sources also stressed the army's regimental
patriotism, its 'cult of former glories' and the loyalties which were
built up in the course of three years between officers and men, some of
them were aware that the religious and even monarchist sentiment
which had in the past bound the army together was weakening.[123]
The real point, however, was not that the peacetime army was fragile
but that it was almost impossible to adapt its praetorian and regimental ideology to the demands of a lengthy war, especially of course once
the bearers of this ideology, the professional officers, were dead. Some
senior officers, of whom A.A. Brusilov and A.I. Denikin are good
examples, were aware of this weakness, in part because of the poor
showing of Russian reservists in 1904–5. They hoped that the spread
of Slavophil and nationalist sentiment through both the civil and
military press, through education and through officers' talks with
their soldiers, would create the basis of a patriotic army. General
Kuropatkin also believed, as he told General Sir Ian Hamilton in
March 1908, that Russian reservists would fight much better in a Slav
cause than they had in the obscure colonial conflict with Japan.
Although such hopes help explain the officers' enthusiasm for the
Slavophil and nationalist campaign waged by, amongst others, *Novoye
Vremya* in 1906–14 they proved to be optimistic. Moreover, the officer
corps was not merely badly trained in the political indoctrination of
conscripts, its efforts in this direction were in general both half-
hearted and looked on with some suspicion by the government
itself.[124]

Study of the Russian army suggests therefore that in some ways
Russia was reasonably prepared for a war on land in 1914, or at least
in many respects not radically less prepared than she was likely to be
in the next few years. Unfortunately, however, the war for which she
was partly ready was the conflict which the generals expected to fight
in 1914, not the one with which they were to be faced in the ensuing
three years. This of course helps explain why Sukhomlinov and

Grigorovich did not insist that Russia should avoid involvement in war in 1914. In addition, narrower personal considerations played a role. Both defence ministers admitted in private that their forces were not wholly prepared and Sukhomlinov expressed the hope through Basily to Sazonov that the latter would bear this fact in mind when deciding on what policy to adopt in the July crisis. Neither Sukhomlinov nor Grigorovich was, however, willing to take upon himself the responsibility for undermining the state's foreign policy by stating openly in the Council of Ministers that their forces could not defend Russia against the Central Powers.[125]

Before condemning either man for moral cowardice one must, however, bear in mind the ethos of the Russian military world before 1914. Indeed such an understanding is essential if one is to make any sense of the aggressive policies supported by the various European high commands in the prewar era. Everything that we have already said about the patriotism, code of honour or sense of personal dignity of members of the Russian ruling élite in general applies with double strength to Russia's military commanders. If, for instance, one takes the continued existence of the duel and its peculiar ethic as providing some clue as to the attitudes of Russian statesmen in 1914 then it is clearly significant that the sphere in which duelling retained most hold was the officer corps. In addition, the experience of Russian generals was one of command, unlike the diplomats who were inured to the process of compromise and conciliation. Nor did most generals have the diplomat's political sophistication or experience. Russian military education did not of course stress the evils of war; on the contrary, it asserted that conflict between states was at worst an inevitable trial and at best a force for national purification, unity and development. Given the nature of war it is not surprising that Russian cadet corps saw cowardice as the supreme vice. The greatest military virtue on the other hand, was a courageous and aggressive spirit, one that would, in Professor Rozin's words, risk its existence in attacking even seemingly impregnable positions or in defence of symbols of regimental history and honour such as a flag.[126]

A senior Russian admiral wrote shortly before the war that the navy must seek above all to breed officers with the aggressive fighting spirit which burned within all great commanders. Using Nelson as his example, he wrote that the whole life of a great warrior was taken up with the thought of combat and with the desire to impose his will on the enemy or die in the attempt.[127] Of course most Russian commanders were by no means Nelsons but they were nevertheless likely to attempt to meet, even if only superficially, the ideal of the military type which their education, their fellow-officers and their leaders placed before them. Whatever the advantages of this military paragon in time of war, it is clear that he was by no means an ideal diplomatic adviser, especially in sensitive negotiations perhaps requiring the acceptance of painful blows to national pride.

The beliefs and political views of the Russian officer corps present few surprises. Overwhelmingly conservative in sympathy, they supported governmental efforts to cultivate Russian nationalism among the masses. The officers' favourite newspaper was *Novoye Vremya*, whose links with the army were, as we shall see, quite close.[128] As one would expect, there was strong sympathy in the army for the Slav cause, so much of which was bound up with Russian nationalist traditions and past military glories. In the 40,000 strong pro-Slav demonstration which occurred in Petersburg on 6 April 1913, for instance, officers 'played a great part', many Guardsmen turning up to the memorial service for the allied dead in full dress uniform. Both in this demonstration and in the packed meeting of the Russo-Galician Society which took place the next day to denounce Austrian persecution of the Ruthenes the numerous officers present were greeted with mingled roars of 'long live the Russian army' and 'down with Austria', to which they responded with enthusiasm. The willingness and ability of serving officers to take part in these, and other, meetings shows the favour with which some military leaders viewed the Slav cause. Indeed not merely were many of the key figures in the various pro-Slav organisations retired generals, Skugarevsky, Parensov and Volodimirov all coming within this category, but the memorial service of 6 April 1913 in the Peter and Paul fortress' cathedral was actually attended by the garrison commander and his entire staff. In 1912–13 pro-Slav feeling strengthened the tendency already existing within the high commmand to support a firm assertion of Russian power, a tendency which was of course all the stronger because of the humiliations of 1904–5 and 1909. Senior General Staff officers in the winter of 1912–13 were determined to face down any Austrian attempts to block Slav demands, regarding these attempts as a bluff which would rapidly disintegrate in the face of firm Russian support for the Slavs' rights.[129] Austria was indeed loathed by most officers, to an extent, in the words of a French observer, 'as to totally take away judgement'. In particular, the Archduke Francis Ferdinand was the officer corps' *bête noire*, all sorts of aggressive schemes being attributed to him.[130] Although they were less hostile to the Germans, Janin wrote in 1910 that officers in the General Staff Academy tended to regard a Russo-German conflict as probable, speaking of 'the coming war with the Germans in terms analogous to those which were used in my time at the School of War'.[131] Other French officers stressed their Russian counterparts' resentment at German contempt for Russia and her army and their 'jealousy' at the successful careers made by Balt officers in the Russian service. Dislike of the Germans was on the whole stronger in the middle and lower ranks of the officer corps than among the generals, most of whom at least respected German efficiency.[132] Actual pro-German sentiment was most widespread among the military courtiers and, at least in Langlois' view, among senior officers of Teutonic origin for whom German was still a mother tongue. The latter, though according to Langlois always loyal and sometimes very able, tended to be well versed in German military literature and 'become unconsciously admirers of the German army and of its methods'. The consensus of French opinion immediately prior to 1914 was that friendship for France and hostility towards Germany within the Russian army were both growing and that, taken as a whole, the army represented 'a faithful friend' of France.[133]

Russian Ministers of War and Chiefs of the General Staff between 1906 and 1914 certainly seem to have been wholly committed to the French alliance, though they were not necessarily hostile to Germany. Palitsyn, Roediger and Sukhomlinov on occasions showed signs of strong suspicion of British motives and hankered after the continental alliance. Thus Palitsyn scared Moulin in December 1906 by the depth of his hostility to Britain and by his desire to cement a German-French-Russian alliance in opposition to the Anglo-Japanese grouping. Like Sukhomlinov six years later Palitsyn stressed to the French attaché William II's personal commitment to this scheme. On returning from a visit to Germany in which he had discussed European problems with the Kaiser and his leading advisers, Sukhomlinov spoke both to Laguiche and, it seems, to his assistant, Wehrlin, in February and March 1913. He explained German armaments by Berlin's growing sense of isolation in Europe, the unreliability of Italy and the increasing weakness of Austria. In Sukhomlinov's view the latter 'hardly exists any more; the cracks in the edifice are clear to the naked eye and are growing from minute to minute'. With the Habsburg Empire likely to disintegrate on Francis Joseph's death it was, said Sukhomlinov, not surprising that Germany desired to be strong. Inevitably, she sought to incorporate 'the German elements of Austria' into the Second Reich but in order 'to compensate for the destruction of the balance' the 'Emperor William would be ready to restore the Rhine frontier to France in exchange for a continental alliance of France-Germany-Russia'.[134]

Despite this rather naive excursion into diplomacy, it is difficult to tie down Sukhomlinov's sympathies, though he does seem always to have respected William II.[135] France's military attachés in Russia never, however, had any doubts about Sukhomlinov's loyalty to the alliance and it is not without significance that he was for many years the chief aide of Dragomirov, the most 'faithful, devoted and sincere friend' France possessed in the Russian army.[136] Sukhomlinov's views on foreign relations are, however, almost certainly less important than his 'military instincts'. The attacks on the Russian army by the German press in the spring of 1914 infuriated the Minister and inspired him to a famous and aggressive response in a well-known article in the *Birzheviye Vedomosti*.[137] In addition, having long since expressed concern at German efforts to build up a powerful Turkish military 'diversion' on Russia's southern front.[138] the Liman von Sanders affair no doubt greatly angered Sukhomlinov. In the early summer of 1914 he was certainly in no mood to submit to German pressure. Partly in order to be disagreeable to Berlin, Sukhomlinov was determined that Yanushkevich should accept, together with Joffre, the chief of the French General Staff, his invitation to British manoeuvres, telling Laguiche on 9 July with some glee that 'he awaits an explosion when the simultaneous presence of the chiefs of the general staffs at British manoeuvres becomes known' in Germany.[139] Sukhomlinov was to get his 'explosion' rather sooner than he imagined and it is difficult not to feel that, given the immense risks entailed in international tension in 1914, his indulgence of his somewhat childish instincts betrayed a rather superficial attitude towards the responsibilities his job entailed.

THE PARTIES, THE PRESS AND PUBLIC OPINION

The main institutions through which public opinion expressed its views in the period 1905–14 were the political parties and the press. 1905 had witnessed both the creation of legislative chambers and the abolition of preliminary censorship and this gave to public opinion a freedom and an importance it had never hitherto possessed. The press boomed. There were 125 daily newspapers in Russia in 1900 and 856 in 1913. Meanwhile not just opposition but even revolutionary parties were able, at least until N.A. Maklakov's crackdown in 1914, both to express their views without restraint in the Duma and to see these opinions published in the press with full freedom because of parliamentary privilege. Of course, in the period 1905–14 Russia was by no means a liberal democracy. The electoral laws of June 1907 ensured the domination of the Duma by representatives of the 30,000 families of the landowning gentry, whose political role was thus enhanced at a time when, in economic terms, much of the gentry was in full decline. Since large areas of the Empire remained in 1906–14 under the sway of, supposedly temporary, emergency regulations the significance of the civil rights granted in 1905 was greatly reduced. The government used these regulations with some success to undermine the efforts of opposition parties to create organisations or cultivate support in the provinces. Heavy fines and the imprisonment of editors severely constrained the freedom of the provincial press, though the major national papers were sufficiently wealthy and strong to shrug off these efforts at control. In the light of Russian history both of the Imperial and Soviet period the fact that the state attempted in some ways to impede the free expression of public opinion is, however, unsurprising. On the contrary, what is remarkable is that in the nine years prior to the war the government was openly and legally deluged by criticism, often of a radical and sometimes of a revolutionary nature, aimed not just at its internal and external policies but also at the basic principles on which the state was founded. This gives to the study of Russian public opinion in the period 1905–14 an interest and importance it would not otherwise possess.[140]

As regards foreign policy, it is possible to divide Russian public opinion in the years 1906–14 into a left, right and centre. Of these groups the generally pro-German right is the least interesting and important. The Duma right, together with its newspapers, *Zemshchina* and *Russkoye Znamya*, merely echoed the opinions which we have already seen expressed by Durnovo, Witte, Meshchersky and Rosen but in a generally cruder, less intelligent and less well-informed way. Moreover, neither the Duma right nor the pro-German tendency had much support in the Russian public whereas, as we have seen, the latter had powerful sympathisers in senior official and court circles. Both the natural inclinations of the leading pro-Germans and good political tactics therefore decreed that they should concentrate their efforts on winning over the Emperor and the government to their views rather than attempt to convert public opinion. It is indeed symptomatic that even the pro-Germans' leading newspaper editor, Meshchersky, should be important because of the impact that his journal made not on its very limited public readership but rather on the monarch.

Nevertheless, the Duma right's history has some relevance to a study of the origins of the First World War, if only because it helps bring out some of the essential differences between Russian and German politics in the prewar era. The Right Group, which accounted for approximately one-ninth of the Duma's members in February 1908, was an unstable coalition of priests, representatives of the most conservative and frightened elements of the landowning gentry and of the various eternally squabbling proto-fascist organisations which had sprung up during the 1905 Revolution. The Right's major weakness, namely its inability to win mass peasant support, sprang above all from the peasantry's determination to seize the estates of the landowners, which made a German-style conservative alliance of rural classes against the liberal and socialist towns impossible. In addition, the very limited franchise of the period 1907–14 made the cultivation of a mass following unnecessary for a right-wing political party. Indeed the demagogic and crude slogans of proto-fascist groups such as the Union of the Russian People were likely to repel a largely gentry electorate, however conservative. The Right Group was united by a belief that only a harsh authoritarian government could hold off the revolution, by extreme and vicious anti-Semitism and by feverish Russian nationalism. The Right's determination that Russian pride and prestige should be upheld to the fullest possible degree made it difficult, however, for many of its members to stomach what they saw as governmental timidity in foreign policy. This, together with the Panslav sympathies of some members of the Right, meant that there were increasing numbers of defections from the pro-German camp especially in the period 1912–14, including that of the Right's most flamboyant leader, V.M. Purishkevich. Even N.E. Markov, whom fear of revolution and admiration of conservative Prussia kept in the pro-German camp until the war, did not in June 1914 hide from the Duma his dislike of Austria or his opposition to reconciliation with her.[141]

The views of the left-wing parties are of more interest and importance than those of the far right. Social Democrats in the Duma opposed all aspects of the state's foreign policy which they saw as being guided solely by the selfish interests of the upper and middle classes. The latter, so the socialists argued, sought to conquer territories and markets overseas in order to fatten their own pockets and divert the masses' attention from internal affairs. No true conflicts divided the peoples of the world, indeed in the opinion of the Social Democrats' spokesman in the Duma even the Kurds and Armenians had only the most brotherly feelings towards each other unless incited to mutual hatred by the wicked forces of imperialism.[142] Given the increasing hold which the Social Democrats, and in particular the Bolsheviks, had over the working classes their irreconcilable opposition to all aspects of the existing state and its interpretation of the national interest was a matter of importance. As *Grazhdanin* emphasised early in 1910, whereas German socialists and their leaders were patriots who had a certain respect for the German state, the same was unequivocally not the case with their Russian counterparts.[143] Awareness of this fact and of the dangers it would represent in time of war, added to memories of 1904–5, powerfully restrained the Russian government from pursuing a risky or aggressive foreign policy, as both British and French sources stressed in 1913.[144] The Austrian embassy in 1913–14 was even more emphatic than Laguiche about the dangers of revolution and the Russians' need for peace. In October 1913, for instance, Count Czernin wrote that although beating the nationalist drum in support of 'great patriotic goals could in other circumstances be a blessing', in present Russian conditions 'the opposite is true'. 'If the iron fist' of military and police repression 'were to turn abroad', then 'the glowing fire' of revolution, already smouldering under the surface, 'would immediately burst into flames'.[145] Such views, repeated on a number of occasions in Austrian despatches, can scarcely have failed to influence those who formulated foreign policy on the Ballhausplatz towards the view that Petersburg would hardly run the risk of war, however much it might protest at Austrian actions. If this is indeed the case then Russian internal politics, or rather the way they looked to Austrian eyes, were a factor of considerable importance in bringing on the crisis of July 1914.

Judged at least by the support it enjoyed in the Duma or the press, what might be described as the centrist view on Russian foreign policy enjoyed far more public sympathy than did the opinion either of the right or of the left. The three major parties in the Third and Fourth

Dumas, namely the Nationalists, Octobrists and Constitutional Democrats (Kadets) can all be described in this sense as 'centrist'. All three parties rejected the Social Democrats' view of international relations as a conspiracy of Europe's ruling classes. They accepted the existence of sovereign states seeking to pursue national interests, though many Kadets were much more hopeful about the peaceful and legal solution of international conflict than were Octobrists or Nationalists. All three parties grudgingly accepted the Imperial government as the defender of Russian interests in foreign affairs, though they believed that it would only be fully legitimate and effective in this role if it followed the wishes of public opinion.[146] There was a consensus that Russia's main interests lay in Europe rather than Asia and a common sympathy for the Balkan peoples and their struggle for liberation. Finally, all three parties supported the Triple Entente, which they saw as a guarantee of peace, Russian security and of the Empire's ability to pursue a foreign policy free from German tutelage.[147]

The parties' attitude towards foreign relations also shared some common weaknesses. Since foreign policy was conducted largely in secret the parties had some difficulty in grasping the course of diplomatic events. In addition, very few of their leaders had diplomatic experience and many showed little understanding of the realities of power politics. Public opinion had a highly optimistic view of the options open to the government and generally allowed its ideological and emotional sympathies to triumph over a hard-headed appreciation of Russian interests.[148] P.N. Milyukov, the Kadet leader, was for instance much more knowledgeable about foreign affairs than most parliamentarians and lacked the chauvinist blinkers of the Octobrists and Nationalists; yet in 1913 even he greatly overestimated the Russian government's ability to impose its own views in its relations with other states and allowed his pro-Bulgar sympathies to warp his interpretation of Russia's role in the Balkans.[149] The events of 1904–5 had strongly affected the public's instincts about foreign policy. They bred a pessimistic sense that Russian diplomacy would always be outsmarted by foreigners and a great fear that backstairs influences at court and in high society would result in further adventurism or in the pursuit of a 'dynastic' rather than 'truly national' policy. Defeat by Japan also caused Russians to feel a considerable sense of insecurity, which led them into exaggerating the threat to the Empire's integrity not just from the Central Powers or the Japanese but also from 'the growing might of China' and the 'Panislamic threat'.[150] In addition 1904–5 made Russian nationalists even of the mildest variety very sensitive to any further blows to their country's pride and prestige. This helps explain the explosion of feeling over the annexation crisis and the largely mistaken view held by most Octobrists and Nationalists that Russia rather than Austria had suffered the more serious defeats in the Balkan crisis of 1912–13. In reviewing Russian attitudes during the annexation crisis of 1908–9 Nicolson wrote that the violent enthusiasms and criticism of the press and the parties, coupled with their adamant refusal to face realistically the logical consequences of the policies they were advocating, was highly irresponsible and made 'a firm and consistent foreign policy almost impossible'. There was truth in this comment, as there was also in Izvol'sky's characterisation of public opinion as 'hysterical'.[151] Ironically, although the Duma leaders denounced backstairs influences and claimed that peace, security and Russian interests would only be safe if the government listened to the voice of public opinion, in fact in the period 1906–14 the opposite was often true. In general, the 'backstairs influences' were considerably more balanced, realistic and peaceable than most of the leading spokesmen on foreign policy of the 'centre' parties in the Duma.

It is important, however, to make distinctions between the three major pro-entente parties in the lower house. Until the war and the political crisis of 1915 provided the basis for a fragile unity, all attempts to bring elements of these three parties together into a 'patriotic' centrist bloc had failed. Although Bernard Pares, for instance, was always hopeful about the chances for such a coalition,[152] the obstacles in its way were considerable. In their views on ideology and internal policy most Octobrists, not to mention Nationalists, differed sharply from the Kadets; moreover the parties also disagreed, albeit not quite so fundamentally, on foreign policy.

Of the three parties the Kadets were probably the most interesting and had the most talented leadership. Although the electoral system ensured that the Kadet Duma faction was less than two-thirds the size of either the Octobrist or Nationalist groups, the K.D.s enjoyed the support of most of the Empire's middle classes. The Kadets were, however, above all the party of the professional middle class and were formed around a core of ideas rather than in defence of any particular economic or social interest. They enjoyed little support from the business class, on which the Russian intelligentsia had always looked with great suspicion, while most landowners had been pushed to the right of the Kadets by the peasant uprising of 1905–6.[153] Kadet views were not unlike those of the British Liberals in the early years of this century. Like their British counterparts they had a liberal-imperialist right wing, whose leading figures were P.B. Struve and V.A. Maklakov. Most of the party remained loyal, however, at least until 1914 to what one might describe as Gladstonian principles. They tended to regard foreign affairs as an annoying and expensive diversion from the essential stuff of politics, namely internal reform. Thus the party programme made no reference to questions of foreign policy or defence nor, according to Liszkowski, a contemporary German historian, were these issues ever discussed at any length in Kadet Congresses.[154] The party was nevertheless the haven for most Russians who advocated the creation of international bodies to arbitrate conflicts between states and to codify and enforce supranational law. In 1906 the Kadets came out for an international court of arbitration and security force which were to be based in Switzerland and the party's leader, Milyukov, played an important role in the European peace movement, in 1911, for instance, bringing Angell's 'The Great Illusion' to the attention of the Russian public by a series of lectures and through publications of his own.[155]

Kadet views on foreign policy were strongly influenced by the party's ideology and its stance in Russian internal politics. Many Kadets were suspicious of all nationalist ideologies, which were seen to threaten the party's ideal of a rational, peaceful world based on the acceptance of law and compromise. In addition, Russian nationalism, though latent in Kadet breasts, was the traditional ideological weapon of the régime and of the right and thus a direct threat to Kadet political interests. Horrified by the slaughter that a European war would entail, some of the Kadet leaders were also aware that neither the military victory of the Russian régime nor its war-time defeat and disintegration would be likely to lead to the orderly, free and tolerant society they desired.[156]

Most Kadets took their line in foreign policy from Milyukov. The party's leader, though not without his share of self-importance and intellectual arrogance was a man of great intelligence and considerable first-hand knowledge of Balkan affairs. Milyukov's commitment to the *entente* owed much to his fear of Austro-German power and adventurism but it was also connected to his deep admiration for the British political tradition and his desire that Russia should ally itself with liberal forces in Europe. For many Kadets alliance with the Western democracies indeed provided a satisfying feeling that Russia had joined the club of 'civilised Europe' and encouraged the hope that the support of London and Paris would somehow ensure the triumph of liberalism within Russia. Milyukov's own stance changed somewhat in 1912–13. Rather like his hero, Edward Grey, Milyukov, while remaining loyal to the Triple Entente, came to fear that deterrence in itself might not be sufficient to avoid war if the arms race continued. In addition, he felt that the German Emperor had shown in the Balkan crisis a determined commitment to peace which made the continued rapid expansion of Entente armaments both unnecessary and provocative.[157] Ironically, while the generally pro-government Octobrist and Nationalist parties denounced Sazonov in 1912–14 for his timidity and his abandonment of Slav interests, Milyukov became to all intents and purposes the Foreign Minister's chief defender in the Duma.[158] A humane and civilised horror at the prospect of war, added to a clear realisation that Serb ambitions were not necessarily Russian interests led Milyukov to advocate the maximum possible degree of compromise in the crisis of July 1914. Though appalled by Vienna's actions he was willing to see the Habsburgs' armies occupy Belgrade so long as a lull in military activities then allowed European mediation to occur and a continental conflict to be avoided. Only when the German declaration of war destroyed Milyukov's last hopes about William II's pacific intentions did the Kadet leader promise total support for the government's policy and the defence of Russia.[159]

Milyukov's support for Sazonov's cautious policy in 1912–13, his criticisms of the more assertive stance adopted by the French government under Poincaré's influence and his attacks on Serb chauvinism exposed him to growing criticism from within his own party.[160] The liberal imperialists both through their journal, *Russkaya Molva*, and in the Kadet Central Committee asserted that Russia should take a much stronger stand in defence of her own and Slav interests. Unlike Milyukov they believed in the efficacy of deterrence and argued that a diplomatically firm and militarily powerful Triple Entente was the best guarantee of peace.[161] V.A. Maklakov spoke for his fellow liberal imperialists in denouncing Austria as anti-Slav and encouraging the Serbs to look to Russia for support in their ultimate ambition, namely the unification of all Serbs, which 'in the future must naturally' come about, though to overcome the obstacles in its path 'will cost much blood and tears'. Maklakov's Slavophil and nationalist views owed something to political calculation. Nationalism, he wrote in November 1908, had always been the régime's great prop. In seizing this ideal for themselves the liberals would take from the government's hands 'this flag, its only psychological resource'.[162]

The chief liberal imperialist thinker in prewar Russia was, however, Struve. This fascinating and exceptionally intelligent man had in the 1890s been the leading young theoretician of Russian Social Democracy. Subsequently moving to the right he had become the editor of the newspaper *Osvobozhdeniye*, which had spearheaded the liberals' assault on the autocracy in 1903–5. Experience of the anarchy of 1905–6 convinced Struve that a Russian revolution would prove a purely destructive force and pushed him still further rightwards. The origin of his and Maklakov's conflict with Milyukov lay indeed not in external policy but in their differing views about the possibility of reconciliation with the régime in 1906–7. In 1908–9, however, a number of important articles by Struve made public his split with Kadet orthodoxy and carried it into the field of foreign policy as well. Struve never abandoned the key foundations of his liberalism. He continued to assert that individual freedom, individual responsibility for one's actions and the rule of law were the essential bases for a prosperous, just and healthy society. At the same time he expressed views about the state, nationalism and foreign policy which flew in the face of all the traditional principles of the Russian intelligentsia, from which the Kadet party drew its roots.[163] For Struve the state was a beneficial institution based not on class oppression but on the necessary organisation and disciplining of society. Together with its still more powerful partner, the cultural and linguistic community which Struve defined as the nation, the state answered 'the ineradicable religious need of man' to belong to a body wider and longer-lasting than himself. Loyalty to state and nation filled the human soul with warmth, light and purpose, which explained why men were willing to die for these abstractions. The state was an organism, not just a collection of citizens, and it had interests and laws of development of its own which by no means necessarily corresponded to the interests or desires of the population. Making no secret of his intellectual debt to Nietzsche and Darwin, Struve argued that the state had an inner striving and need to be powerful, for it was a law of history that weak states became the victims of their neighbours' appetite for expansion. A great nation was one in which government and people shared a common concern for the state's external power. Turning the

Russian radical tradition on its head, Struve argued that the desirability or otherwise of internal revolution must be gauged by the extent to which it increased or decreased the state's external power and the unity of its people. Praising both the revolutionary Cromwell and the conservative Bismarck for their creation of united peoples dedicated to the construction of great empires, Struve stressed the nationally cohesive effects of imperialism and argued that British and German experience showed 'the strength of a state which puts the national idea into its service'. A Great Russia required reconciliation between state and people around the banner of liberal imperialism. It needed the concentration of Russia's economic and cultural expansion in the areas bordering on the Black Sea, which both the Empire's history and the growing economic power of Southern Russia required to be the key region for Russian foreign policy. The Triple Entente guaranteed Russia peace with honour and must stand up firmly to the Central Powers. Concessions born of weakness would merely lead to further pressure, while alliance with Berlin would turn Russia into Germany's vassal and would sacrifice 'the historical mission, the might and the dignity of the state'. Both Struve's intelligence and his liberalism made him see that the policy of russification supported by the right-wing parties merely weakened and divided the Empire and he favoured full autonomy for Poland and Finland. On the other hand, he believed that for the other minorities membership of the Russian Empire was an asset and that as far as possible these races should be encouraged to gain access to the world's science and learning through the medium of the Russian language and culture. In particular, he was a violent opponent of Ukrainian nationalism and, above all, of efforts to create a separate Ukrainian high culture.[164] The Russian nationalist sentiments which increasingly dominated Struve's thinking came to full flower in the course of the Great War, which, he envisaged, would end with Russia, ensconced in Constantinople, both as the Slavs' defender from external foes and as the arbiter of all squabbles within the Slav brotherhood.[165]

Given their author's past career, it is not surprising that Struve's ideas caused alarm and resentment in liberal and radical circles, especially since they were coupled with a strong attack on what he described as the intelligentsia's fanatical devotion to inherited political dogma in the teeth of both logic and empirical evidence.[166] On the other hand, Struve's works provided a basis for agreement with elements to his right, firstly of course with small groups such as the

Progressists which were the Kadet's immediate neighbours in the political spectrum but also with the Octobrists and Nationalists.

Both these parties above all relied for support on the landowning gentry and both pursued Russian nationalist policies but their ideologies, structures and aims were nevertheless distinct. The Nationalists, by 1914 the larger of the two parliamentary factions, were above all an interest group formed by Russian landowners of the Western Borderlands of the Empire for their own self-defence. In perpetual conflict and competition with Polish nobles and Jewish businessmen the Western Russian landowners successfully used the Nationalist Party to gain supremacy in their own region and to express their resentment of their non-Russian enemies. The Party's horizons did not extend far beyond its own region and most of its members showed little interest in articulating a nationalist ideal which would be of general appeal within Russia. R. Edelman, the Party's historian, states that few Nationalists were very interested in foreign policy or the Slav cause, the party in this sense being much less truly nationalist than the Octobrists, Progressists or right wing Kadets.[167] The party's main spokesman on foreign affairs, Count V.A. Bobrinsky, was in his background, education and interests much more akin to most Octobrists than to his fellow Nationalists. Like the core of the Octobrist Party, Bobrinsky was a landowner from Great Russia where the racial tensions of the Western Borderlands barely existed and the gentry tended to elect men to the Duma more for their local standing than because of their precise political allegiance. He was also better educated than most Nationalists and had passed his political apprenticeship, like many Octobrist leaders, in the pre-1905 Liberation Movement. The Octobrists were less wholly committed to the defence of narrow sectarian interests than the Nationalists and, like Bobrinsky, more interested in principles and ideals.[168] Of the latter, patriotism was the most important. Perhaps more than by anything else the Octobrist Party was united in its commitment to Imperial unity and to the restoration of the Empire's power and pride after the disasters of 1904–5. For both Octobrists and Bobrinsky an element of political calculation entered into their patriotic campaigns. Patriotism would, it was hoped, provide their parties with a useful ideological banner and might, as Guchkov put it in 1908, help to create the unity and purpose needed if Russia were to emerge unscathed from her internal difficulties.[169] The element of calculation should not, however, be exaggerated; for these scions of the gentry or, in Guchkov's case, of traditional Moscow commercial society, Russian nationalism was in general instinctive, sincere and deeply felt, as was, for many of them, their commitment to the Slav cause.[170] Much Octobrist effort in the Duma went into aiding the reconstruction and reform of the armed forces and Knox, the British Military Attaché, wrote in May 1912 that 'on questions of national defence the Octobrists have shown a knowledge and a patriotism beyond those of any political party in the world'.[171] Unfortunately, the Octobrists' interventions in the field of foreign affairs were less successful. In March 1913, for instance, M.V. Rodzyanko, the Octobrist President of the Duma, told Nicholas II that 'the Straits must become ours. A war will be joyfully welcomed, and will raise the government's prestige'.[172] Even Guchkov, a far more intelligent man than Rodzyanko, was in August 1912 'inciting the Serbs to war' in a manner that Artamonov, the Russian Military Attaché in Belgrade, correctly described as incomprehensibly reckless given the clear dangers to Russia of a Balkan conflict and Guchkov's own attacks on the unpreparedness of the Imperial army for war.[173] Bobrinsky's major intervention in foreign affairs, namely the Galicia-Russia Society which he founded to oppose Austrian persecution of Ruthenes, was if anything still less defensible. As the Austrian foreign minister, Berchtold, rightly complained, for all its failings Vienna was a good deal more tolerant towards its minority nationalities, even including Slavs, than was Petersburg.[174] Bobrinsky's campaigns for the Ruthenes therefore not merely provided an extra and by no means minor irritant to Austro-Russian relations, they were also, at least objectively, hypocritical. Had Bobrinsky and the Octobrist leaders, or for that matter the Progressists and right-wing Kadets, had their way Russia would indeed have found herself at war with the Central Powers in 1912–13 rather than a year or so later.

Like the Duma politicians the Russian press was for the most part strongly in favour of the Triple Entente. Some papers, of which *Rech'*, *Golos Moskvy* and *Utro Rossii* were the most important, indeed belonged to leading party politicians and therefore acted as mouthpieces for their pro-Entente line. The major independent papers, *Novoye Vremya*, *Russkoye Slovo* and *Birzheviye Vedomosti* all, however, adopted the same stance, in part forming, in part reflecting the pro-Entente and anti-German feeling which Dmowski, Pares and Nicholas II all agreed to be dominant in upper and middle-class Russia even in 1908.[175] In June of that year the Emperor deplored the press' hostility to Berlin, whereby 'every incident that occurred in a distant province of the Empire, such as an earthquake or thunderstorm, was at once put down to Germany's account'[176] and O'Beirne agreed that 'a constant suspicion of German designs' had 'become a sort of *idée fixe* even with serious writers'. In his view the much greater freedom of expression existing since 1905 had allowed the latent anti-German sentiment in Russian society to come into the open. In addition, there were specific reasons in recent years for the growth of anti-German feeling.

> 'Liberal politicians dislike the Germans, because they attribute many of the illiberal acts of the Administration to German influence, and because the Germans have furnished many of the Generals, who, as provincial Governors, enforced repressive measures ... Patriotic Russians ... of the reactionary type, hold Germany indirectly responsible for Russia's unfortunate adventure in the Far East. They see Germany thwarting Russian aims in the Balkans, Asia Minor and Persia, and their resentment is embittered by a sense of the military weakness of Russia as compared with her powerful neighbour.'[177]

Nicolson added that in the press, as indeed in Russian society, there existed 'a feeling of mistrust of German diplomacy and policy, and it is thought that friendship with Germany soon lapses into vassalage, and that a considerable price has to be paid to enjoy even that invidious position.'[178] From 1907 to the outbreak of the war the British Embassy, which kept a very close eye on the Russian press, stressed that, although inevitably the latter on occasion expressed resentment at specific British or French policies or attitudes, its overall commitment to the 'liberal entente' never wavered. Hostility to Germany swelled or diminished, according to the British, as diplomatic conflicts waxed or waned but it remained always at least a constant undercurrent in Russian public opinion. Among the factors which explained this feeling, O'Beirne in 1910 felt the most significant to be

> the racial struggle that is proceeding in south-eastern Europe between Slavdom and Germanism; jealousy of the German superiority in culture, energy and the moral qualities; the industrial intrusion of Germany into Russia; the fact Germany thwarts Russian policy at various points in the Near and the Middle East; and the dominant fact that Germany is a too powerful neighbour who seems occa-

sionally to abuse her superior strength.[179]

For foreign diplomats the most important Russian newspaper was the
Petersburg daily, *Novoye Vremya*, which O'Beirne described as 'the
most prominent champion of the policy of co-operation with the western powers'.[180] With a circulation of approximately 150,000 in the
period 1911–14, *Novoye Vremya* was one of Russia's most popular papers. Moreover, unlike the still more popular *Russkoye Slovo* and *Birzheviye Vedomosti*, *Novoye Vremya* devoted most of its attention to politics,
both Russian and European. Whereas most of the Russian press was
liberal in sympathy, *Novoye Vremya* was conservative and, above all,
nationalist and it had a wide following in high official and landowning
circles. Nicholas II read *Novoye Vremya* daily, considering it 'our most
serious and our principal' newspaper,[181] and so too did a great many
officers. Indeed the paper's editor told the French Ambassador in
1912, á propos of the nationalist, anti-Austrian and pro-Slav articles
which were jamming the paper's columns at that time, that 'we would
not carry on such a lively campaign if we did not have the army with
us'.[182] A British observer wrote in 1914 that *Novoye Vremya* was 'not an
official paper, the views it expresses do not by any means always
represent the views held by the government. They rather represented
a shrewd compromise between official views and public opinion'.[183]
Foreign diplomats were not always sure whether the paper was expressing its own or official views and confusion was increased by the
editorial policy of its owner, A.S. Suvorin, who, while maintaining a
generally nationalist and conservative line, allowed wide latitude to
contributors and encouraged the expression of opposed points of view
in his newspaper.[184]

In the period 1906–14 *Novoye Vremya*'s editorials were torn between
knowledge of Russia's need for peace, and an aggressive assertion of
national interests and patriotic sentiments designed in part to boost
internal cohesion in Russian society. The paper's ideology is best
summed up in the editorial with which it greeted the new year in 1914.
For a great people, it stated, bread was not enough, indeed it was only
of secondary importance. A country's prestige in the eyes of the world
together with successes in war and foreign policy 'arousing and feed-
ing the people's sense of pride and at the same time a feeling of
patriotism, give such moral satisfaction that even if they are obtained
at the price of great material sacrifices, these sacrifices are accepted
calmly and without a murmur'. The editorial contrasted the nation's

patriotism and unity amidst the constant suffering and wars of the eighteenth and early nineteenth centuries with the present decline of patriotic sentiment, which had led to the loss of Russian self-confidence and the growth of centrifugal and anti-Russian forces within the Empire. As was often the case in the period 1906–14, *Novoye Vremya* compared Russia's present position to that of Prussia after Jena. Patriotism had, wrote the editorial, enabled Prussia to rise from disaster after 1806 so that within two generations she had grown to enviable 'power' and 'glory' and within four was competing successfully for first place among the states of Europe. Russia must follow her example. She must

> conduct a great power policy which was the best school of patriotism for our ancestors and which beyond question will be the same school in our time. One must trust in Russia! One must raise the spirit of the great Russian people. One must satisfy its still terrible thirst for greatness . . . . The fatherland's glory is the people's right to happiness.[185]

In *Novoye Vremya's* view, as it stated in an important editorial on 14 June 1908, the path to Russia's glory and to the fulfilment of its national destiny lay along the cultivation of Russian nationalism within the Empire and support for the Slav cause outside it. It was impossible 'without ceasing to be Russians' to allow German cultural domination of Southern and Eastern Europe. Russians must oppose to the powerful German *Drang nach Osten* 'a similar cultural force, the slav one'.[186] Although *Novoye Vremya* insisted that the competition should be peaceful, its Slav sentiments were already even in 1906 leading it to attack the Murzsteg agreement whereby Russia and Austria agreed to co-operate in the Balkans in defence of the *status quo*.[187] The events of 1908–9 seemed to *Novoye Vremya* to justify its previous opposition to co-operation with Vienna and at the same time greatly strengthened its hostility to Berlin. In January 1909, for instance, welcoming the links which bound Russia to the Western powers, *Novoye Vremya* wrote that 'the enemies of enemies are friends to each other'.[188] The newspaper's reaction to Russia's capitulation before German pressure to recognise the annexation of Bosnia-Hercegovina was fierce. Calling this capitulation a disgrace and a 'diplomatic Tsushima', *Novoye Vremya* blamed it in part on Russian diplomats' 'blindness to Russia's wideawake national feeling . . . lack of faith in Russia, in her vital power, in her ability to fulfil her historical tasks'.[179] With one German out of every three now a socialist Germany was not as strong as Russians imagined and its pretensions should be opposed. Its present policy was 'to frighten' Russia's rulers 'by the imaginary dangers of war, to humiliate Russia in the eyes of all slavdom and to tear her away from the Triple Entente'. This policy would not succeed, for

> Germany's actions have only deepened and finally made clear those contradictions between German and Russian vital interests which were until this time unclear for a certain part of Russian society . . . Germany is striving to move forward across the Balkan Peninsula to the Aegean Sea and further into Asia Minor and Persia. Russia can either give in to this movement or oppose it. In the first place it will be surrounded by Germany from the west and the south. In the second it must strengthen and widen its agreements with England and with France.

In *Novoye Vremya*'s view the second course was obviously correct,[190] for if the Triple Entente were weakened 'German preponderance would at once be established over all the continent of Europe.'[191]

Though in the course of the next five years *Novoye Vremya* often wrote in far politer terms about Germany and always stressed the great common interest both empires shared in peace, it never wavered in its support for the Entente, the balance of power and a confident and determined policy of deterrence which would check German pressure and ambitions, in the process securing peace with honour. The quality of *Novoye Vremya*'s interpretation of international affairs over this period varied greatly. In the six months prior to the war the paper was at its worst in its baiting of Vienna and in the hypocritical and pseudo-sentimental articles with which it backed Bobrinsky's campaign on behalf of the Ruthenes.[192] Typically, even on 29 June the paper's editors managed nothing better than a grudging expression of regret at Francis Ferdinand's assassination, which they placed beneath a leader denouncing Austrian persecution of the Slavs, whose growing unity *Novoye Vremya* extolled.[193] On the other hand, the paper's better side was revealed by an excellent response by Menshikov to the anti-Russian press campaign being conducted in Germany.[194] By moderate and rational arguments Menshikov destroyed the case for a German preventive war against Russia. He stressed the benefits

that Germany's colossal achievements in the last century had brought
to the whole world and pointed out that, far from being constrained,
German energies were still finding every sort of successful outlet. He
could not, he wrote, believe that Germans could fail to see the threat
to all their past achievements and future prospects which a new era of
conflict would entail. He begged the Germans to ponder the devastation of the Thirty Years War and of the Napoleonic era and to abandon support for the Austrian war party, which if it continued to
pursue its present programme would soon be forced into policies
which would entail colossal risks.[195]

The Russian public's attitude to Germany was influenced not just
by questions of politics, ideology and national security but also by
economic factors. Russo-German trade in 1905–14 was colossal and
growing. In 1913 Russia sent 44 per cent of her exports to Germany
and took 47 per cent of her imports from her. The two empires had
therefore both a vast stake in each other's prosperity and many issues
over which conflicts of economic interest could occur. Most Russo-
German squabbles in the economic field centred on the periodic negotiations for the renewal of the treaty which regulated trade between
the two empires. Russian feeling that the 1904 trade treaty was balanced in Germany's favour certainly helped sour public attitudes
towards the Second Reich and the run-up to the renewal of the treaty
in 1917 would no doubt have been accompanied by polemics between
the two empires' presses. The Russian economic interests affected by
the Treaty had, however, little chance of seriously influencing the
Foreign Ministry's overall policy towards Germany, which was
guided above all by considerations of national security. In any case,
the Russian economic interests hostile to the treaty had conflicting
aspirations. Agrarians sought lower tariffs and in particular the abolition of the German import licences system, which had the effect of an
export premium and was enabling German grain to drive Russia out
of the Scandinavian and Polish markets. Industry on the other hand
wanted higher tariffs to protect itself against German imports, which
grew 2.7 times between 1905 and 1913. Industry itself was, however,
very divided. Small and middle-sized firms were hostile to big business, the interests of the various branches of industry clashed, while
parochial loyalties and wholly differing traditions ensured that Moscow's textile barons would never co-operate effectively with Petersburg high finance and heavy industry for any length of time whatever
common interests they might share.[196]

The only major effort by Russian business to enter politics and affect the state's foreign policy came from the younger generation of Muscovite tycoons and was led by Ryabushinsky and Konovalov. Inheriting the Muscovite commercial traditions of independence from the state and contempt for Petersburg, these two men were also fired by anger that for all their wealth, members of their class remained second-class citizens in Russia's monarchical and noble state. They also resented the intelligentsia's traditional contempt for businessmen. Beginning in 1908–9, the so-called 'Economic Discussions' and the publications funded by the two industrialists established close links between them and figures such as Struve, the Trubetskoy brothers, Kovalevsky and N.N. Lvov who stood spiritually between the gentry Octobrists and the intelligentsia-dominated Kadets and were the heart of Russian liberal imperialism.[197] The ideology which Ryabushinsky and Konovalov began to articulate combined their conviction that Russia's future belonged to the bourgeoisie and that the Empire must protect its industrial base from German imports, with Struve's imperialistic ideas and the instinctive nationalism of Moscow's old business families. Entering the Duma as a Progressist in 1912, Ryabushinsky preached his views in his newspaper, *Utro Rossii*. He argued that the government's timid and repressive domestic policy was holding back the free development of the vigorous bourgeois forces which would create a Great Russia and was therefore making almost inevitable the régime's corresponding failure in external policy to defend Russian interests and prestige adequately.[198] Thus one finds yet another group entering the political arena anxious to seize the patriotic flag out of the government's hands and to associate itself with the national and Slav cause. Unfortunately, where foreign policy was concerned, Ryabushinsky and Konovalov also shared the lack of realism and logic already seen in a number of other Duma leaders. Thus in April 1912, for instance, Ryabushinsky in one breath attacked the premier, Kokovtsov, both for his weak-minded willingness 'to give way to foreigners to the detriment of national interests' and for harbouring 'warlike designs, not in accordance with the people's true precepts'.[199]

In studying Russian internal affairs as a means to understand the origins of the First World War it is important to grasp how Russian developments seemed to German eyes. One must remember that in July 1914 Germany's rulers took most of the vital decisions which led to war and that in so doing they were in part guided by fears not only of the rapid growth of Russian military power but also of the effects that present and future political developments might have on its use.[200] The evidence presented in the four sections of this chapter shows that these fears had some justification. Any neighbour might justifiably fear a Russian Empire of the future based on Struve's ideology of state power, *Novoye Vremya*'s vision of patriotism or much of the Duma leadership's desire to cement national unity and secure party advantage by a vigorous foreign policy. In the Progressists one can also see business interests clothing their ambitions in the nationalist flag. Meanwhile a large Russian navy was being built on the basis of ideas akin to Tirpitz's risk theory. A potentially vast army, its officers animated like their German counterparts by aggressive, Social Darwinist and nationalist conceptions, was being created and some of its leaders, present and future, were forging close links with liberal conservative and national liberal politicians. This coalition was hostile to Germany and still more so to Germany's sole reliable ally, Austria; indeed most of the coalition's leaders were expecting and some positively encouraging the disintegration of the Habsburg Empire, which would face Germany with great external difficulties. It was logical to expect that the crown would be forced to share ever more of its power with this coalition, indeed most Western historians blame Nicholas II's refusal to do this for the fall of the monarchy. Moreover, if German panic at the Russian menace was exaggerated it was scarcely more so than the perpetual British alarm about the Russian threat to India.

Still, it is important to stress that German fears *were* exaggerated. Russia was not about to become a larger and more powerful variation on the theme of expansionist, nationalist militarism whose leading European embodiment was the German Empire itself. The nationalist ideology which united and motivated Wilhelmine society could never be so effective, might indeed even prove counter-productive, in multi-national Russia. The two empires' geopolitical positions were also entirely different. With the possible exception of the Straits, Russia was a territorially satiated power; Germany was not. Given the beliefs current in pre-war Europe German politicians could advance plausible, if misguided, arguments for expansionism in a way that was not true in Russia. There existed a common European view that a nation's prosperity and standing depended on the possession of colonies which would provide both markets and areas for colonisation. Nor was it wholly illogical for Germans to fear lest protectionist tariffs should one day shut them out of the huge empires controlled by the other powers. If one took seriously the idea that the state's goal was the maximisation of its power it was self-evident that, unless the territorial *status quo* were changed, in the longer term Germany could never compete with Russia, the United States or, so it was thought, the British Empire. If, however, Germany was the growing adolescent bursting his tight-fitting clothes by the speed of his development, the Russian child, though also growing rapidly, was struggling not to be engulfed in the ample robe left to him by his ancestors. Not for nothing did German capitalists dream of conquering foreign markets while Russian ones, though increasingly anxious to export, above all prayed for the preservation of their domestic one from European domination.[201] As Kokovtsov was fond of saying, all Russia's expansionist energies must for generations be confined within her own borders.[202]

Economic and financial leaders, such as Kokovtsov and Witte, could expect to find allies in their opposition to external adventurism among Russia's security chiefs. Russia was still decades from the creation of the conservative peasantry and the essentially reformist and 'patriotic' working class which were among the key strengths of Wilhelmine Germany. Social and ethnic tensions were sufficiently fierce to arouse doubts whether anything but a harshly authoritarian régime could hold the Empire together, Refusal to liberalise, however, ensured the ever greater alienation of educated society from the state. Russia's rulers were thus faced with a deep and contradictory political crisis which was likely to make external adventure exceptionally dangerous for a considerable time. It did not need security chiefs of Durnovo's intelligence to recognise this. Moreover, even as regards the middle classes nationalist sentiment was much less widespread in Russia than in Germany. The Kadets placed far more emphasis on internal than on external policy, the Octobrists had very limited mass support and Ryabushinsky's 'nationalist bourgeois' campaign could not even secure the sympathy of most of the Moscow business community, let alone of broader social forces. Prince G.N. Trubetskoy[203] and M.M. Kovalevsky, both of whom were at the centre of the pro-Slav current, believed that it did not as yet run very deep. Kovalevsky records that for all the talk about neo-Slavism and the fears it generated abroad he was struck by how insubstantial was real interest in it or the Balkans in Petersburg educated society. Indeed he states that whereas in early 1912 he could get 2000 people to a lecture on Rousseau, barely 150 attended talks designed to give educated Russians a real grasp of South Slav contemporary politics.[204] Though nationalist and pro-Slav enthusiasm grew and was evident in the demonstrations in the spring of 1913, it is difficult to be sure how deep it went. Certainly the feelings then paraded had not inspired a reading public large enough to keep *Moskovskiy Yezhenedel'nik* alive three years earlier. Nor, as General Danilov states, did patriotic sentiment run deep enough either to stop many educated Russians from evading front-line service in 1914-17 or much of society from winking indulgently at those who did so.[205]

On balance, therefore, study of Russian internal affairs helps explain but does not justify Germany's decision to wage war in July 1914. A contemporary German pessimist might no doubt have feared that Russian power would be used by a nationalist élite to achieve the same advantages that the German right had secured from the triumphs of 1866–71. His more realistic brethren should have realised both that Russia was still ill-placed to follow Prussia's example and that should she attempt to do so the self-regulating mechanism of the Balance of Power would turn against her. The stronger and more aggressive Russia became, the less chance there was of Britain standing by her side against Germany. Nor indeed would even Poincaré's France be willing to fight Germany so that Russia could break up the Habsburg and Ottoman Empires.

# 5 The July Crisis

THERE is no reason to suspect that Petersburg had any foreknowledge of the conspiracy which led to the murder of the Austrian heir-apparent though it is conceivable that Hartwig or Artamonov knew of the plot. Albertini indeed states that the military attaché's foreknowledge 'seems certain', though he makes this claim on the basis of the uncorroborated statements of suspect witnesses.[1] Russian documents published by the Soviet government do not prove that Hartwig and Artamonov knew nothing of the conspiracy. On the other hand they do illustrate that both men were unsympathetic to the Black Hand's struggle against Pasic[2] and were well aware that Serbia needed a long respite before running the risks of involvement in any further external crises.[3] Unless reliable evidence shows the contrary, one must therefore assume that neither Hartwig nor Artamonov would have lent any support to a conspiracy which could not fail to exacerbate Austro-Serb relations.

The Russsian government's ignorance about the conspiracy played an important role in the July crisis. It is now known that although the conspirators were Young Bosnians fired by their own hatred of Vienna's policy, they were armed and smuggled across the Austrian frontier by Serbian officials who knew and sanctioned their intentions. Moreover, that sanction came from the head of Serbian military intelligence, Dimitrijevic, and may well have been connected in a roundabout fashion with his own desire to topple Pasic, the prime minister. The fact that the Serb government could not control its own army or nationalists only in part diminishes its responsibility for the murder; indeed, as Szapary (the Austrian ambassador in Petersburg) told Sazonov, such a situation strengthened the case for Austrian intervention to crush the otherwise uncontrollable radical and nationalist hydra[4]. As Apis' nephew later wrote, had his uncle's role in the conspiracy been revealed in July 1914 this 'would have done untold harm to his country'.[5] Even as it was, Szapary reported on 29 July, with a possibly false degree of optimism, that Sazonov was looking hard for some evidence in Vienna's dossier on the crime which would justify his distancing himself from Belgrade.[6] Had the truth been known about the conspiracy it is possible that Sazonov would have from the outset of the crisis been more willing to compromise with Vienna, while the revulsion against Serbia in London would have been very great. As it was, however, the Austrians neither discovered the link with Apis nor actually communicated their dossier of evidence to Petersburg. Sazonov was therefore faced with unproven Austrian statements about Serbian involvement in the conspiracy which, given Vienna's past history of basing anti-Serb claims on false documents, he rightly regarded with great suspicion. The best evidence he had about the assassination came from a report of Prince M.A. Gagarin, whom Shebeko had sent to Sarajevo to study the crime. Gagarin stated, correctly, that Princip and Cabrinovic were Bosnians and that the Austrian authorities had shown vast incompetence in their efforts to protect the Archduke. For the local officials, he wrote, it was very convenient to blame the conspiracy on Belgrade and to claim that the plot's ramifications were so great that the heir could not have escaped his fate. Gagarin, however, doubted that Belgrade was behind the plot, arguing that the conspirators would have been better armed had the Serbs provided their weapons. This information can only have strengthened Sazonov's belief that Austria's accusation against Belgrade was unjust and that 'pan-Serb agitation in Austria was an internal growth'.[7]

Although during the first three weeks of July 1914 the Russians were alarmed at times by reports of impending harsh Austrian action in Belgrade they were reassured by firm Austrian statements that such rumours were untrue. When the crisis broke on 24 July the Russians therefore both felt gulled and were taken by surprise. This increased their distrust of Vienna and meant that for much of the last week in July Russia was represented by chargés d'affaires in Paris, Berlin, Vienna and Belgrade, the three ambassadors being on holiday and Hartwig having suddenly succumbed to a heart-attack. Danilov, the Quartermaster-General, was also on leave and the absence from Petersburg of the General Staff's strongest personality and leading expert on mobilisation was to have important results.[8]

On receiving the text of the ultimatum at 10 a.m. on 24 July Sazonov, according to the Director of his Chancellery, Schilling, 'considered war unavoidable'. Immediately reporting, for the first time ever, on the telephone to Nicholas , Sazonov stated that given the

ultimatum's demands and its brutal wording Austria must know that
it 'could not be complied with by Serbia' and must therefore be
intending to attack her neighbour. It was obvious, said Sazonov, that
such an ultimatum could not have been sent without German consent, which strongly suggested that the Central Powers were intending to use their present military superiority to start a European war.
Calmer and less pessimistic than his Foreign Minister, Nicholas
ordered the Council of Ministers to discuss Russia's response to the
ultimatum.[9]

Before the Council's meeting, which took place in the afternoon of
24 July, Sazonov discussed the crisis with the British and French
ambassadors. Paléologue urged a tough line and promised Sazonov
unequivocal French support. With his President and Prime Minister
very difficult to contact on the battleship *France* a great burden rested
on Paléologue's shoulders but although nothing precise or detailed is
known about Russo-French discussions during Poincaré and
Viviani's visit to Russia in July 1914 one can only assume that the
ambassador's self-confidently vigorous line echoed the approach
taken by his country's leaders in the previous week. It was, in any
event, in accord with France's diplomatic stance over the previous
eighteen months. Buchanan, as one would expect, was far more non-
committal and urged Sazonov to gain the maximum time possible in
which diplomacy might find a peaceful solution to the crisis.[10]

Russia's response to the Austrian move was decided at a meeting of
the Council of Ministers which began at 3 p.m. and lasted for over two
hours. Given the crucial importance of this meeting it is worth studying in some detail the statements of Russia's ministers on the afternoon of 24 July.[11] Sazonov spoke first. He stressed Germany's

> systematic preparations, which were calculated to increase her
> power in Central Europe in order to enable her to carry out her
> wishes, not only as regards matters in the Near East, but in all
> international questions, without taking into consideration the
> opinion and influence of the powers not included in the Triple
> Alliance.

In the course of the last decade Russia had shown great moderation
and made many concessions wherever her interests and Berlin's came
into conflict but 'Germany had looked upon our concessions as so many
proofs of our weakness and far from having prevented our neighbours

from using aggressive methods, we had encouraged them'. Now had to come the moment to make a stand. The Austrian ultimatum to Belgrade was beyond question drawn up with German connivance and would if accepted turn Serbia into a *de facto* protectorate of the Central Powers. In the past Russia had 'made immense sacrifices' to secure the independence of the Slav peoples and if she now abandoned under threat 'her historic mission, she would be considered a decadent state and would henceforth have to take second place among the powers', losing 'all her authority' and allowing 'Russian prestige in the Balkans' to 'collapse utterly'. Nor would concessions now ensure peace even in the near future since there was nothing to stop Germany from mounting still further challenges to Russian interests. A firm stand would, however, mean a real risk of war with the Central Powers, whose consequences were all the more dangerous 'since it was not known what attitude Great Britain would take in the matter'.[12]

Next to speak was Krivoshein, the Minister of Agriculture. Krivoshein's illness in January 1914 coupled with his awareness that the chairmanship of the Council of Ministers entailed more responsibility than power had resulted in I.L. Goremykin's appointment to replace Kokovtsov as the nominal head of the civil administration. Nevertheless, in the first half of 1914 Krivoshein was the most powerful figure in the Russian government. His success in administering the vital and complicated programme of agrarian reforms, together with his clear mind, simple manner and political skill had won him the full confidence of Nicholas II, which gave him a considerable influence in the state's overall internal and external policy. Peter Bark, the Minister of Finance, records that on the afternoon of 24 July Krivoshein's 'declaration was the most instrumental in influencing our decisions'.[13]

The Minister of Agriculture stated that only the army's loyalty had saved the régime from collapse in 1905. Since then a constitutional system had been established, Russia's financial position vastly improved and major reforms in the armed forces undertaken. 'However, our rearmament programme had not been completed and it seemed doubtful whether our Army and our Fleet would ever be able to compete with those of Germany or Austro-Hungary [sic] as regards modern technical efficiency', since in cultural and industrial terms Russia was far behind the Central Powers.

On the other hand, general conditions had improved a great deal in Russia in the past few years and public and parliamentary opinion would fail to understand why, at the critical moment involving Russia's vital interests, the Imperial Government was reluctant to act boldly . . . . Our exaggeratedly prudent attitudes had unfortunately not succeeded in placating the Central European Powers . . . . No one in Russia desired war. The disastrous consequences of the Russo-Japanese War had shown the grave danger which Russia would run in case of hostilities. Consequently, our policy should aim at reducing the possibility of a European war (but) if we remained passive we would not attain our object. War could break out in spite of our efforts at conciliation . . . . In his view stronger language than that we had used hitherto was desirable. All factors tended to prove that the most judicious policy Russia could follow in present circumstances was a return to a firmer and more energetic attitude towards the unreasonable claims of the Central-European powers.

In private conversation after the session Krivoshein added that although the policy he advocated entailed 'serious risks', the latter would not be reduced by a conciliatory stance. 'He thought that the only hope of influencing Germany was to show them, by making a firm stand, that we had come to the end of the concessions we were prepared to make. In any case, we should take all the steps which would enable us to face an attack'.[14]

Bark, the Minister of Finance, records that 'Krivoshein's speech made a profound impression on the Cabinet'. Goremykin then turned to the service ministers for their views. Sukhomlinov and Grigorovich stated that although great improvements in the armed forces had occurred since 1905, the programme of rearmament was not completed and Russian military superiority over the Central Powers could not be assumed. 'They stated nevertheless that hesitation was no longer appropriate as far as the Imperial Government was concerned. They saw no objection to a display of greater firmness in our diplomatic negotiations.' Next Peter Bark, and a friend of Krivoshein, confirmed that although Kokovtsov's careful management had built up a considerable surplus in the Treasury, as a result of inevitably excessive wartime expenditure 'the financial and economic stability of the country would be endangered'. Bark did not of course foresee the economic collapse that three years of war would ultimately entail and stated that since further concessions in no way guaranteed peace and 'since the honour, dignity and authority of Russia were at stake, the

Finance Minister should adhere to the opinion of the majority of the cabinet'. The other ministers also 'shared the opinion of Sazonov and Krivoshein', and Goremykin summed up by saying 'that it was the Imperial Government's duty to decide definitely in favour of Serbia'; that firmness rather than conciliation was likely to secure peace; but that if it failed to do so 'Russia should be ready to make the sacrifices required of her'. The Council resolved that Vienna should be asked to extend her time limit; that Belgrade be urged 'to show a desire for conciliation and to fulfil the Austrian Government's requirements in so far as they did not jeopardize the independence of the Serbian state', and that the defence ministers should request Imperial permission for the mobilisation, if events should require it, of the Odessa, Kiev, Kazan, and Moscow Military Districts. Nicholas II accepted the Council's policy and himself chaired an extraordinary session on the morning of 25 July which confirmed the previous day's decisions.[15]

At about 7 p.m. on 24 July Sazonov conveyed to the Serbian Minister in Petersburg both Russia's desire for peace and her commitment to Serbia's independence, a message which Spalaykovic then passed on to Belgrade. Russia's support came as music to the ears of Pasic and Prince-Regent Alexander who, while horrified at the prospect of war, felt some of Austria's demands to be unendurable.[16] Albertini states that Russian promises of support convinced the Serb cabinet to reject point 6 of Vienna's ultimatum and to return a more equivocal response to some of the other demands than they would otherwise have made.[17]

As a result of the decisions of the Council of Ministers on 24 and 25 July the Russian armed forces began preparations for war. On 26 July the law of 17 February / 2 March 1913 on the Period Preparatory to War came into force.[18] Magazines and supply depots were to be made ready, railway repairs to be completed and all units and departments were to check on their instant readiness to carry out their tasks during mobilisation. Railway personnel were to be brought up to full complement for mobilisation, while covering troops were to take up positions on threatened fronts and, in border areas, some reservists to be recalled not to their units but to training camps. On the evening of 25 July at a conference of officers of the General Staff Yanushkevich called for energetic fulfilment of their tasks, stating that if necessary it was permissable slightly to overstep the strict limitations of the law in preparing the army for war.[19] Meanwhile, as we have seen, it had been decided in principle to mobilise four military districts, Sazonov initially intending to do this should Austria invade Serbia. As later became clear, the military leaders had, however, led the Council of Ministers into error, since they failed to bring to the government's attention the difficulties that any partial mobilisation would put in the way of a subsequent general mobilisation. Most to blame here was Yanushkevich, since the Chief of the General Staff was responsible for all questions of mobilisation; unfortunately, new in the job, he was neither a sufficiently strong character to resist Sazonov's desire for partial mobilisation nor well enough informed to make out an unanswerable case against it. Only when the Quartermaster-General, Danilov, returned to Petersburg on 26 July did the General Staff resolutely bring its objections to the attention of the civil government. Sukhomlinov himself must, however, share responsibility for the mistakes committed between 24 and 26 July. Though his job was more concerned with administration than operational planning, it was the Minister of War's duty to know enough about the problems of mobilisation to advise the Council of Ministers on the subject correctly.

The results of the generals' error were not, however, immediately apparent. On 26 and 27 July Sazonov became more optimistic about the chances of avoiding war, to a degree which both Pourtales and Szapary rightly found exaggerated.[20] Although part of the explanation for this lies in Sazonov's unstable temperament, other factors also played a role. Like Grey, Sazonov believed that Austrian assurances that a Serb rejection of the ultimatum would not at once lead to military operations 'makes the immediate situation rather less acute'.[21] In addition, from his calm conversation with Szapary on the afternoon of 26 July Sazonov drew the impression that much of the Austrian ultimatum might after all prove acceptable to Russia and that Vienna might well be willing to discuss the remaining contentious points with Petersburg. His optimism was buttressed by Pourtales' statement, which was admittedly purely personal, that he welcomed Austro-Russian negotiations and felt that Vienna might be willing to tone down some of its demands.[22] The events of 28 and 29 July were to disillusion the Russian Foreign Minister completely. Like Europe's other leaders he found the Serbian reply to Vienna's ultimatum astonishingly conciliatory and Austria's brusque declaration of war therefore all the more appalling. The bombardment of Belgrade convinced him that Vienna was fully committed to the immediate invasion and destruction of Serbia, while Berlin's failure to

stop Austria's headlong rush into war made the Russian Foreign
Ministry believe that Germany had either lost all control over its ally
or, much more likely, was in spite of its assurances actually conniving
at Austria's actions and doing nothing to check them.[23] The final
blow came on the afternoon of 29 July when Pourtales delivered
Berlin's warning that unless Russia ceased her military preparations
these would lead to German mobilisation and to war.[24] Already on 28
July Sazonov had secured Nicholas II's agreement to partial Russian
mobilisation in response to Vienna's declaration of war on Serbia.
The events of 29 July convinced him that war with the Central Powers
was inevitable and that the vital point was to prepare to wage it with
the greatest possible chance of success. He joined with the military
leaders in successfully pressing general mobilisation on Nicholas II,
only to see the Emperor rescind his decree and revert to partial mobilisation late in the evening of 29 July in response to a telegram from
William II. On 29 and 30 July Sazonov and Yanushkevich, backed by
Krivoshein, urged general mobilisation on Nicholas II on the grounds
that the Central Powers were bent on war and that if Russia delayed
or, still worse, threw her plans into disarray through partial mobilisation, she would lose the war before it had even begun. On the other
side Goremykin, with the backing of at least one other minister and
some of the military courtiers, urged the monarch to stick to partial
mobilisation in order not to precipitate a Russo-German conflict and
thus to gain time for diplomacy to find a peaceful solution.[25] The
Council of Ministers was not recalled, everything depended on Nicholas II's judgement and the impression made on him by individual
advisers. Finally, on the afternoon of 30 July Sazonov persuaded the
Emperor of the need for general mobilisation. German countermeasures were immediate and in Germany, unlike Russia, military
planning ensured that mobilisation led automatically to war. Russia's
armies could remain mobilised but behind their frontiers almost inde-
finitely; Germany planned for military operations almost from the
first day of mobilisation in order to avert the risk of a two-front war by
destroying France at the outset of the conflict. Almost precisely two
days after Nicholas II's final decision for general mobilisation Pourtales informed Sazonov that the two empires were at war.

To what extent can the Russian government be faulted for its handling
of the July Crisis? Russia's key decision was the one taken on 24/25 July
to support Serbian independence even at the risk of war. Given Austrian
determination to crush Serbia and German willingness to back

Vienna even if war with Russia and France should ensue, Petersburg's stand made a European conflict probable. Yet it is not easy to see how Russia could have acted differently in July 1914. Even leaving aside the moral, psychological, ideological and political factors which played a role here, capitulation to open Austro-German coercion would have dealt a tremendous blow to Russia's prestige and thus to her ability to defend her interests and retain her clients and allies in the Near East. Russia's heads of mission in Sofia and Constantinople, A.A. Savinsky and M.N. Giers, were both moderate men without Panslav leanings. The former, however, stated on 29 July that in the event of capitulation 'our prestige in the slav world and in the Balkans would perish never to return',[26] while the latter wrote that if Russia thus recognised the irresistible nature of German power the Turks and the Balkan states would unfailingly swing into the camp of the Central Powers, which would 'result in the total destruction of our prestige and of our position in the Near East'.[27]

Even if the Russians had pushed Belgrade into accepting every clause of the Austrian ultimatum in July 1914, it is, moreover, by no means clear that war could have been avoided save in the very short run. In the weeks and months that followed capitulation to Vienna the Serbian government would probably have tried to wriggle out of the consequences of its action. By 1914, however, Austria was unwilling to tolerate such behaviour, believing that after the events of 1906–13 only Serbia's humiliation and reduction to the status of a semi-protectorate could give Vienna a chance of checking Serb nationalism and breaking the increasing hold of Belgrade on the sympathies of the Serb and even to some extent Croat population of the Monarchy. No Serbian government which surrendered the nation's independence would, however, have survived for long. The proud and courageous Serbian people, whose nationalist sentiments were reflected by the Serbian army, would in all likelihood have overthrown such a government with as complete a disregard for the international consequences as they showed in 1941. In the inevitable Austro-Serb war which would have followed it is not easy to see Russia standing aside.

Once Russia had decided to back Serbia the only means for the Triple Entente to avoid war lay in speedy action in London and patience in Petersburg. The British had immediately to make it clear in Berlin that should the Austro-Serb crisis develop into a European war the United Kingdom would fight on the side of Russia and France. Meanwhile, the Russians had to avoid military preparations which would precipitate armed conflict before London's message had time to be absorbed in Berlin and could result in German pressure for moderation in Vienna. It has often been argued, most recently by L.C.F Turner, that in this respect Russia was badly at fault.[28] He states, firstly, that there was no need for Russia to mobilise against Austria since the mere threat to do so would have deterred Vienna from invading Serbia; secondly, that there was no cause for precipitate Russian intervention in an Austro-Serb war since the more deeply involved became Habsburg troops in Serbia the better for subsequent Russian military operations; thirdly, that the Russian generals were incorrect to argue that a previous partial mobilisation gravely hindered a later general one.

The first argument is clearly wrong since even Russia's actual mobilisation did not stop Conrad's large-scale invasion of Serbia. Unfortunately, mere Russian warnings, however strong, could not have restrained Vienna or Berlin in July 1914. As Buchanan wrote four months earlier, the powers had learned somewhat to discount Russian statements since in the past strong words had been followed by weak actions. As a result, the conviction had grown in certain capitals that Russia would under no circumstances fight in defence of its interests, which, added the able British Ambassador, was both a mistake and a major danger 'to the cause of peace'.[29]

Turner's second point has more weight, especially in view of our subsequent knowledge of the superb performance of Serbia's army in the First World War. Pre-war Russian generals lacked this knowledge and were determined that Vienna should be forced to divide its strength between the Serbian and Russian fronts.[30] Thus a conference of the chiefs of staff of Russia's military districts had agreed in November 1912 that only if Russia stood aside in the initial phase of an Austro-Serb conflict

would Austria be able to transfer overwhelming forces to the south in order to settle accounts with the Serbs by rapid and decisive blows . . . .In view of this the conference put forward two conditions: firstly, not to delay the moment of the announcement of mobilisation by Russia, so that this action could be carried out more or less simultaneously with the enemy, and secondly to tie the declaration of war to the calculation that the actions of the Russian armed forces should be fully developed at a time when Austria had still not finished its struggle with Serbia.[31]

According to Zayonchkovsky, the Russian General Staff discovered to its horror that in the winter of 1912 Austria had succeeded in gradually mobilising all its forces in Galicia without Russia being aware of the fact. The generals were determined not to be caught napping again. In Zayonchkovsky's view, 'the experience of 1912 . . . was not without influence as regards Russia's unwillingness to put off her mobilisation in the July days of 1914'.[32] In addition, although all Europe's general staffs were obsessed by the need for rapid mobilisation, fearing delay and last minute tinkering with their plans and believing that the war would be decided in its opening weeks, Russia's generals had particular reason to be alarmed on these scores. The vast size of the Empire and the relatively sparse density of the population, administrative infrastructure and railway network made the efficient mobilisation and rapid concentration of the Russian armies very difficult. French observers particularly stressed that Russian railways, often built on the cheap, could not be used intensively. Rails were too light and bedding for the track often too weak; there were too few watertanks and crossings; the use of coal, oil and wood burning locomotives complicated problems of fuelling. These and many other hazards ensured that even on the good lines the average troop train could not travel more than 320 kilometres a day. Railway movements were further complicated by the fact that while most of the population lived in the Kazan and Moscow military districts the majority of army units had to be deployed even in peacetime on the western frontier.[33]

These difficulties help explain the Russian generals' impatience but they do not answer Turner's third point about the compatibility of partial and subsequent general mobilisation. Without a detailed knowledge of the problems of mobilisation and railway movements it is impossible to come to a final conclusion on this question but it does seem clear that the General Staff's opposition to partial mobilisation was genuine and not a front for warmongering. In December 1912 Monkevitz, the Assistant Quartermaster-General, had for instance told Laguiche and Wehrlin that the patchwork manner in which the Austrians had so far gone about the mobilisation and concentration of part of their forces made any subsequent general mobilisation impossible. He added that 'when a huge machine is to be brought into play and is ready one cannot set off certain wheels of the machine in isolation, without the risk of compromising the proper running of the whole machine'.[34]

A major problem about partial mobilisation was that Russian regiments did not draw their reserves from a single military district. This was largely the result of the multi-racial nature of the Empire. The government wished Poles to serve in Asia and Caucasians in Europe. A rule existed that units should be three-quarters Slav and, if possible, one-half Great Russian, which, together with the need to distribute evenly scarce skilled cadres often living in a very few urban centres, ensured that units drew their recruits from a wide area.[35] This became a particularly pressing issue when partial mobilisation was under consideration. The diplomats wished to mobilise four districts to show Vienna that Russia meant business without threatening Berlin. In military terms, however, this was difficult to achieve. Many reservists from the Moscow and Kazan districts went to units deployed against Germany. Either these reservists must be sent to the Austrian front or remain milling about at the mobilisation centres. Meanwhile of course the Kiev and Odessa districts drew some of their reservists and relied on the concentration on their front of units from outside the four mobilised regions. If for instance the Guards Corps, situated in the Petersburg military district and recruited from the entire Empire, was neither to be mobilised nor to be deployed in the Kiev district then a large gap would immediately exist on the Russian south-western frontier.[36] Finally, the Warsaw military district, which faced both Germany and Austria, was both the key to military operations and the area whose railways had to carry much the greatest number of troop trains.[37] Delay or confusion here would not merely cripple Russia's planned offensives but also might render impossible an effective response to the Austrian main attack northwards from Galicia, of whose details the Russian General Staff was well aware. For all these reasons it is easy to understand why the thought of partial mobilisation threw Russian military planners into panic. One could of course argue that this merely shows how foolish were the Russians in not having planned for partial mobilisation but one has to remember both that the generals' mobilisation plans were concerned with military not diplomatic operations and that it seemed pointless to contemplate an isolated move against Austria since in any Austro-Russian conflict immediate German intervention was inevitable.

How important was the general mobilisation of the Russian army on 31 July? At first glance it would seem to have been crucial since Russia's move was answered immediately by Germany's mobilisation and within two days by the outbreak of war. Even without the Russian mobilisation there is, however, every reason to doubt whether by 30

July a European conflict could have been avoided since, as Russian
diplomats stressed,[38] by then Austria and Germany had gone too far
to retreat without serious damage to their prestige and to the stability
of their alliance. By the time awareness of the likelihood of British
intervention had caused Berlin to urge its first counsels of restraint in
Vienna the Austrians were only prepared even to listen to London's
calls for compromise if Russian mobilisation ceased and their offensive into Serbia was allowed to continue.[39] Bethmann-Hollweg's half-
hearted calls for moderation were in any event being undermined by
Moltke's bellicose advice to Conrad. Moreover, even before he heard
the news of general Russian mobilisation the German Chancellor was
intending to send Petersburg a further virtual ultimatum demanding
the cessation of Russia's military preparations and, as Albertini rightly states,[40] the inevitable rejection of this demand was almost bound
to lead to war. Study of the July Crisis from the Russian standpoint
indeed confirms the now generally accepted view that the major immediate responsibility for the outbreak of the war rested unequivocally on the German government.

# Conclusion

RUSSIA entered the First World War because mankind had not devised a method whereby conflicts between sovereign states could be resolved by peaceful means. Deterrence and the balance of power, on which most Russian statesmen had pinned their hopes for peace, did not stop Europe from sliding into war, though they might have done so had the power of the European rival blocs actually been balanced and had the British commitment to deterrence been unequivocal. Unfortunately, the nineteenth and early twentieth centuries had witnessed a horrifying increase in states' capacity to wage war without a corresponding development on a pan-European level of political institutions and popular attitudes which would have made the use of these weapons impossible. This particular imbalance is still very much with us.

Russian foreign policy in the pre-war years was, as we have seen, influenced by the nature of the Imperial governmental system. A great amount of power remained in the hands of Nicholas II, who, although neither as weak nor as foolish as most Western commentators have imagined, was certainly not the ideal man to carry such an immense burden of responsibility. There was also on occasion a disquieting lack of co-ordination or even mutual comprehension between the state's diplomatic, military and political leaders, which made the handling of international crises less efficient than it should have been. This lack of co-ordination also affected Russia's planning for war. Thus, whereas the army had prepared exclusively for a short conflict, Professor P.P. Migulin, probably Russia's leading expert on the economic aspects of war, was gleefully informing his fellow citizens on 3 August 1914 that 'Germany's opponents have only to draw out the war for a year, or still more for two years, and Germany will no longer have the strength to continue it through exhaustion; she will be forced to give up.'[1] Looking at Russia's failings in isolation is, however, somewhat unfair. No European state planned in advance for a long war, nor was mutual incomprehension between statesmen and soldiers confined to the Russian Empire. Though naive, Nicholas II lacked the hysterical inconsistency which made William II so dangerous. Sazonov had neither an outstanding brain nor an equable temperament and some of his subordinates, notably Hartwig, were dangerously insubordinate. But Russian policy in 1912–14 was no more bellicose than that of France; nor was it as self-contradictory as Berlin's wavering between its continental and colonial options, or as prone to self-delusion as was the Germans' faith in British non-intervention. Trubetskoy's writings display a clear and intelligent comprehension of European relations which provides a rationale for Russian foreign policy not much less reasonable than Eyre Crowe's submissions to his superiors in the British Foreign Office.

Russian foreign policy was influenced by internal political factors. To preserve its legitimacy or its hold over its subjects the Russian state could afford neither to seem consistently weak nor entirely to ignore the claims of Russian national feeling. This constrained the government's freedom of action, especially as regards events in South-Eastern Europe. The rise of political parties and ideologies seeking to make capital out of nationalist and Panslav attitudes and policies had obvious parallels with events in Germany. Yet, as I have sought to explain, Russian society and politics were very different from Germany's. As regards the link between external and internal politics three connected factors most strongly differentiated Russia from its western neighbour. Firstly, the groups pushing the Russian government towards external aggression had far less popular backing than in the Second Reich. Secondly, the more intelligent leaders of the Russian right were well aware of the great fragility of their society and were terrified lest war bring social and political revolution. Finally, Russia's huge size and potential resources guaranteed the Empire its place in the sun so long as existing territories were retained and developed. These three factors, together with the Empire's military weakness after 1905, go far towards explaining why Russian policy was much less aggressive than Germany's in the decade prior to 1914. At the same time, the nature and psychology of the Russian ruling élite meant that there were strict limits beyond which it was not willing to be pushed by its desire and need for peace. It would not accept a clear and insulting demotion to the ranks of Europe's second-class powers. Since German unity and strength did in fact temporarily place the Second Reich in a different league from the other continental powers a determinist might feel that the very nature of Russia's rulers in itself made conflict likely, especially once Russia had linked its fate to France, which had never fully accepted demotion from its position as *La Grande Nation* in 1870.

Looked at from a certain angle there seems a ghastly inevitability about Russia's drift into the anti-German camp and ultimately into a European war. There was a clear logic behind the alliance between Europe's two second-ranking Great Powers to ensure that their interests and traditions were not trampled on by the continent's super-power. Germany's commitment to Austria's survival, however justified, was always likely to be a source of tension between Petersburg and Berlin given Russia's long rivalry with the Habsburgs in South-Eastern Europe. When Austro-German perceptions of the best means to preserve the Dual Monarchy led to policies which infringed on Russia's position in Europe tension turned into armed conflict. The result was to bear out in full Durnovo's prophecies and to justify Rosen's statement that, short of preservation of its territorial integrity, Russia's supreme interest was the avoidance of conflict on its western frontier. Rather than simply blaming the Russian government for its miscalculation, one would perhaps be wiser to state that both in Berlin and Petersburg too many people ignored the fact that war between the two empires would be the supreme evil not just for the Russian and German peoples but also for continental Europe as a whole. Though conflict might occur on the seas and in limited areas of the continent, so long as Germany and Russia did not go to war a large measure of stability could be preserved in Europe. Any clash between the continent's two titans was, however, likely to lead not just to horrifying devastation but also to lasting instability. Ironically, the First World War, which had begun as much as anything as a struggle between Russia and Germany for the domination of Central and Eastern Europe, ended with both countries among the defeated.

This fact alone virtually doomed the Versailles settlement, especially since the Anglo-Saxon powers whose intervention had overthrown Germany were unwilling and unable to guarantee the *status quo* of 1919. France alone could never maintain a European order to which neither Germany nor Russia was committed. Together, the two defeated empires of the First World War first tore up the Versailles settlement and then in 1941 resumed their struggle to dominate the continent.

# Chronological Table

| 1856 | 30 March | Treaty of Paris ends Crimean War |
| 1861 | 3 March | Emancipation of the serfs |
| 1871 | 10 May | Treaty of Frankfurt ends Franco-Prussian War |
| 1874 | 13 January | Introduction of universal military service in Russia |
| 1877 | 24 April | Russia declares war on Ottoman Empire |
| 1878 | 3 March | Treaty of San Stefano |
| | 13 July | Treaty of Berlin |
| 1879 | 7 October | Austro-German Dual Alliance signed |
| 1881 | 13 March | Accession of Alexander III |
| | 18 June | Dreikaiserbund agreement signed |
| 1882 | 9 April | N.K. Giers appointed head of Foreign Ministry |
| | 20 May | Italy joins Austria and Germany in Triple Alliance |
| 1886 | 21 August | Russians abduct Prince Alexander of Bulgaria |
| | 19 October | Alexander III orders breaking off of diplomatic relations with Bulgaria |
| 1887 | 18 June | Russo-German Reinsurance Treaty signed |
| | 10 November | Berlin Reichsbank rejects Russian securities as collateral for loans |
| | 12 December | Anti-Russian Mediterranean *entente* signed by Austria, UK, Italy |
| 1888 | 15 June | Accession of William II |
| 1890 | 15 March | Dismissal of Bismarck |
| | 18 June | Reinsurance Treaty lapses |
| 1891 | July | French fleet visits Kronstadt |
| | 27 August | Russo-French political agreement signed |

| 1892 | 17 August | Obruchev-Boisdeffre military agreement (accepted in principle by Alexander III) |
| | 30 August | S. Yu. Witte appointed to head Ministry of Finance |
| 1893 | October | Russian fleet visits Toulon |
| 1894 | 4 January | Russo-French military alliance ratified |
| | 10 February | Russo-German commercial treaty signed |
| | 2 December | Accession of Nicholas II |
| 1895 | 26 January | Retirement of N.K. Giers |
| | 23 April | Russia, France, Germany force Japan to abandon Liaotung Peninsula |
| 1896 | 5 October | Nicholas II begins first visit to France |
| 1897 | 27 April | Francis Joseph visits Russia; start of Austro-Russian *entente* over Balkans |
| 1898 | 27 March | Russia leases Port Arthur from China |
| 1899 | 18 May–29 June | First Hague Peace Conference |
| 1900 | 7 August | Count V.N. Lambsdorff appointed Minister of Foreign Affairs |
| 1902 | 30 January | Anglo-Japanese treaty |
| | 16 March | Russo-French agreement on Far East |
| | 28 March | Russian Main Staff conference chaired by Nicholas II decides on rapid military aid to France in event of European war |
| | 9 November | Mobilisation Plan 18 confirmed |
| 1903 | 11 June | Murder of King Alexander Obrenovic of Serbia. Karageorgevics restored |
| | August | Trans-Siberian railway opened for through traffic |
| | 2 October | Russo-Austrian Murzsteg agreement on the Balkans |
| 1904 | 8 February | Japan attacks Russia |
| | 8 April | Anglo-French *entente* |
| | 28 July | Russo-German commercial treaty signed |
| | 15 October | Russo-Austrian neutrality treaty in the event of war with Britain or Italy |
| | 20 October | William II proposes Russo-German defensive alliance to Nicholas II; Russians stall |

| 1905 | 2 January | Fall of Port Arthur |
| | 22 January | 'Bloody Sunday'; troops fire on crowd in Petersburg |
| | 27 May | Battle of Tsushima |
| | 6 June | Delcassé falls from power |
| | 4 July | General A.F. Roediger appointed Minister of War |
| | 24 July | Treaty of Bjorkoe |
| | 5 September | Treaty of Portsmouth ends Japanese War |
| | 7 October | Nicholas II informs William II that Bjorkoe must be abandoned unless French agree to its terms |
| | 30 October | Imperial manifesto promises a constitution |
| | 30 October | S. Yu. Witte appointed Chairman of Council of Ministers |
| | 21 December | Moscow uprising begins; defeated by government |
| 1906 | 16 January | Algeciras Conference opens |
| | 7 April | Algeciras Act signed |
| | 17 April | Agreement on 2250 million franc loan to Russia signed in Paris |
| | 21 April | Protocol of meeting between Russian and French Chiefs of the General Staff signed; Russians agree that defeat of Germany the main aim in a European war; anti-British elements of previous military agreements dropped |
| | 6 May | New Fundamental Laws establish constitutional and representative institutions |
| | 7 May | I.L. Goremykin appointed Chairman of the Council of Ministers |
| | 9 May | V.N. Kokovtsov appointed Minister of Finance |
| | 10 May | First Duma's opening session |
| | 11 May | A.P. Izvol'sky appointed to head Ministry of Foreign Affairs |
| | 21 June | Council of State Defence established |

|  |  |  |
|---|---|---|
| | 23 July | P.A. Stolypin appointed Chairman of the Council of Ministers |
| 1907 | 15 April | Nicholas II confirms naval 'Small Programme' for Baltic battleship squadron |
| | 16 June | Electoral law illegally changed by Imperial decree to increase weight of propertied classes |
| | 28 July | Russo-Japanese fisheries convention |
| | 30 July | Russo-Japanese political agreement |
| | 3 August | Meeting of Russian and German Emperors at Swinemunde |
| | 31 August | Russo-British convention |
| | 29 October | Russo-German agreement on the Baltic |
| | 14 November | Third Duma's opening session; Octobrists the largest party with 154 of the 442 seats |
| 1908 | 27 January | Aehrenthal announces plans for railway-building in Sandjak of Novi Bazar |
| | 3 February | Izvol'sky warns ministerial conference about probable impending breakdown of status quo in the Balkans |
| | 12 June | Nicholas II and Edward VII meet at Reval |
| | 5 July | Young Turk revolution begins |
| | 16 September | Agreement at Buchlau between Izvol'sky and Aehrenthal |
| | 2 October | Council of Ministers protests to Nicholas II about agreement |
| | 5 October | Bulgaria declares itself independent |
| | 6 October | Austrians annex Bosnia and Hercegovina |
| | 9 October | Izvol'sky arrives in London; the British oppose his views on Straits |
| | 25 October | Council of Ministers, with Izvol'sky present, agrees to seek international conference to resolve annexation crisis |
| | 25 December | Izvol'sky addresses Duma on annexation crisis and foreign policy |
| 1909 | 8 February | Franco-German agreement on Morocco |

| | | |
|---|---|---|
| | 26 February | Turks agree to financial indemnity from Austria for annexation of Bosnia-Hercegovina |
| | 22 March | German ultimatum to Russia to accept annexation |
| | 24 March | General V. A. Sukhomlinov appointed Minister of War |
| | 31 March | Serbians formally accept annexation |
| | 8 May | Nicholas II vetoes Naval General Staff bill; Stolypin's government begins to move further to the right |
| | 30 June | Four battleships of Baltic fleet laid down |
| | 25 August | Abolition of Council of State Defence |
| | 7 November | Nationalist Party formed in Third Duma |
| 1910 | 21 January | Russia and Japan reject US proposals for 'open door' in Manchuria |
| | 4 July | Russo-Japanese agreement on Manchuria |
| | 9 July | New Russian plan for war in Europe requires troop concentration further in rear; mobilisation plan 19 introduced |
| | 27 September | S.D. Sazonov replaces A.P. Izvol'sky at Foreign Ministry |
| | 4–5 November | Nicholas II meets William II at Potsdam |
| 1911 | March | S.D. Sazonov falls ill; A.A. Neratov stands in |
| | 17 March–10 May | Western zemstvo crisis; Stolypin's position weakened |
| | 1 June | Bill passed for construction of battleship squadron in Black Sea |
| | 1 July | SMS *Panther* sent to Agadir |
| | 18 September | Death of P.A. Stolypin |
| | 24 September | V.N. Kokovtsov appointed Chairman of Council of Ministers |
| | 28 September | Outbreak of Italo-Turkish War |
| | 8 October | N.V. Charykov raises with Turks question of opening Straits for Russian warships |

|      |             |                                                                                                      |
|------|-------------|------------------------------------------------------------------------------------------------------|
|      | 4 November  | Franco-German agreement on Morocco                                                                   |
|      | 9 December  | Sazonov disavows Charykov's negotiations with Turks                                                  |
|      | 15 December | Sazonov resumes control of Foreign Ministry                                                          |
| 1912 | 14 January  | Poincaré becomes French Premier                                                                      |
|      | 13 March    | Serb-Bulgar alliance                                                                                 |
|      | 17 April    | Troops fire on workers on Lena goldfields. Wave of strikes begins                                   |
|      | 14 May      | Revised, more offensive Russian war plans for European theatre; Plans 'A' and 'G' formulated        |
|      | 29 May      | Greece joins Balkan League                                                                           |
|      | 4 July      | Nicholas II and William II meet at Baltic Port                                                       |
|      | 6 July      | 'Programme of Increased Ship Construction 1912–6' becomes law                                        |
|      | 18 July     | First conference of Russian and French Chiefs of Naval General Staff begins                          |
|      | 10 October  | Izvol'sky-Poincaré conversations reveal firm French support for Russia in the event of Austrian advance in Balkans |
|      | 18 October  | Outbreak of First Balkan War; Russia and Austria begin military preparations                         |
|      | 21 November | Conference of Chiefs of Staff of Kiev, Moscow and Kazan Military Districts decides that in future war Russian offensive must be fully developed before Austria crushes Serb army |
|      | 3 December  | Armistice between Turks and Balkan forces                                                            |
|      | 16 December | Ambassadorial conference opens in London                                                            |
| 1913 | 11 March    | Russia and Austria begin to release reservists from colours                                         |
|      | 4 May       | Montenegrins abandon Scutari                                                                         |
|      | 30 May      | Treaty of London ends First Balkan War                                                              |
|      | 29 June     | Outbreak of Second Balkan War                                                                       |
|      | 7 August    | French Army Bill ratified (3-year military service)                                                |

| | | |
|---|---|---|
| | 11 August | Treaty of Bucharest ends Second Balkan War |
| | 2 November | Petersburg informed of Liman von Sanders' appointment |
| | 4 November | Nicholas II approves army's 'Great Military Programme' |
| | 18 November | Kokovtsov discusses Liman's appointment with Bethmann-Hollweg |
| 1914 | 13 January | Special conference chaired by Kokovtsov to discuss Russian policy over Liman von Sanders affair |
| | 14 January | Liman von Sanders loses command of 1 Corps; appointed Inspector-General of Turkish army |
| | 12 February | V.N. Kokovtsov dismissed; I.L. Goremykin appointed Chairman of Council of Ministers; P.L. Bark to Ministry of Finance |
| | 21 February | Special Conference chaired by Sazonov discusses Russian policy at Straits |
| | 2 March | *Kölnische Zeitung* article starts Russo-German press war |
| | 18 March | General N.N. Yanushkevich appointed Chief of the General Staff |
| | 7 June | Start of Russo-British naval conversations |
| | 14 June | Nicholas II and Sazonov visit Rumania |
| | 28 June | Assassination of Archduke Francis Ferdinand |
| | 7 July | 'Great Military Programme' becomes law |
| | 20–2 July | Poincaré and Viviani in Petersburg |
| | 24 July | Council of Ministers decides to support any Serb rejection of parts of ultimatum impinging on national sovereignty |
| | 25 July | Conference of ministers and advisers chaired by Nicholas II confirms Council's decision<br>Austria severs relations with Serbia |
| | 26 July | Law of 2 March 1913 on Period Preparatory to War comes into force |
| | 28 July | Austria declares war on Serbia and bombards Belgrade; Mobilisation ordered |

|            | of Kiev, Odessa, Moscow and Kazan Military Districts, together with Baltic and Black Sea fleets |
|------------|---------------------------------------------------------|
| 29 July    | Nicholas II orders, then revokes, general mobilisation  |
| 30 July    | Russian and Austrian general mobilisation ordered for 31 July |
| 31 July    | German ultimatum to Russia                              |
| 1 August   | Germany declares war on Russia                          |
| 3 August   | Germany declares war on France                          |
| 4 August   | Britain declares war on Germany                         |

# Notes and References

NOTE: Where two dates are given, this refers to the 13-day difference between the Russian and European calendars. (Russian diplomats and statesmen often differed as regards which date they put first in their letter-headings).

1. RUSSIA AS A GREAT POWER

1. The manifesto is printed in *Novoye Vremya* (21 July/3 August 1914) p.1.

2. *KA*, vol.68 (1935) p. 36.

3. Information on the members of the State Council is contained in my article in the *Jahrbücher für Geschichte Osteuropas* xxix, (1982) 'The Russian Civil Service under Nicholas II: Some Variations on the Bureaucratic Theme'.

4. A.N. Naumov, *Iz utselevshikh vospominaniy*, vol.2 (1955) p. 224.

5. *SOGS*, Session 3, col.1711.

6. TsGIA, Fond 1044, Opis 1, Ed.Khr. 224, p. 4.

7. J.N. Westwood, *A History of Russian Railways* (1964) p. 304; A.M. Zayonchkovsky, *Podgotovka Rossii k mirovoy voyne. Ocherki voyennoy podgotovki i pervonachal'nykh planov*, (1926) p. 123. (henceforth *Podgotovka*).

8. S.Yu. Witte, 'An Economic Policy for the Empire', in T. Riha, *Readings in Russian Civilisation* (1964) pp. 428–41.

9. J.S. Keltie (ed.), *Statesman's Year Book* (1914) pp. 51–5.

10. A.N. Kulomzin, *Opytnyy podshchot sovremennogo sostoyaniya nashego narodnogo obrazovaniya* (1912) p.9; S.S. Oldenburg, *Last Tsar: Nicholas II; His Reign and His Russia* (1977) vol.3, pp. 146–7; *Statesman's Year Book*, pp. 12, 18, 33, 649, 651, 663, 667, 812, 816, 889, 895, 1016, 1023, 1051, 1229–30, 1237; C. Cipolla, *Literacy and Development in the West* (1969) gives figures for Germany in 1890 of 24 teachers per 10 000 population.

11. O. Crisp, 'Labour and Industrialisation in Russia', in *Cambridge Economic History of Modern Europe*, vol.7, part 2, p. 388.

12. K.F. Shatsillo, *Russkiy imperializm i razvitiye flota* (1968) p. 203; for statistics on the 1906 budget see G. Vernadsky (ed.), *A Source Book for Russian History from Early Times to 1917*, vol. 3 (1972) pp. 823–4; Zayonchkovsky, *Podgotovka*, p. 106.

13. MDSH, Carton 7N 1535, Matton to 2eme Bureau, 13/26 June 1909.

14. Princess Olga Trubetskaya, *Vospominaniya sestry* (1953) p. 67; *NV*, No. 11568, 27 May/9 June 1908, p. 3; no. 13221, 1/14 January 1913, p. 2; Yu.Ya.Solov'yov, *Vospominaniya diplomata* (1959) p. 208.

15. PRO, FO 371, 1468, no. 29844, O'Beirne to Grey, 8 July 1912, p. 452.

16. CUBA, MS. Kovalevsky, *Vospominaniya*, p. 94 writes that

whereas Struve and A.A. Makarov took this threat very seriously, he did not.

17. HHSA, PA X 140, Szapary to Berchtold, 23 February 1914 (private letter); Czernin to Berchtold, 23 May/5 June 1914, Report 26F; *NV*, for example, (22 February/7 March 1914) no. 13631, p. 13; (23 February/8 March 1914) p. 4; (31 March/13 April 1914) no. 13668, pp. 2–3.

18. *MY*, no. 48 (5 December 1909) (OS), pp. 1–7 on Russian nervous exaggeration of the Panislamic and Chinese threat; nos 34, 41 and 42, 1 September, 20 and 27 October 1907 contain articles entitled 'Panislamism' by MS which illustrate this exaggeration.

19. *LN*, vol.2, p. 352; PRO, FO 371, 727, no. 6057, Annual Review for 1908, pp. 474–5; 1471, no. 41779, Grey to Buchanan, 8 October 1912, pp. 109,119; FO 371, 978, no. 2551, pp. 91ff, contains interesting Foreign Office minutes and a report dated 24 January 1910 from Major G.E. Tyrrel, the Military Attaché in Constantinople, on the penetration of the Caucasus, Central Asia and Afghanistan by Ottoman officers in pursuit of the Young Turks' Panislamic policies.

20. D.W. Spring, 'Russian Imperialism in Asia in 1914', *Cahiers du monde russe et sovietique*, XX, 3–4 ( July/December 1979) pp. 305–22; A.F. Astaf 'yev, *Russko-Germanskiye diplomaticheskiye otnosheniya 1905–11* (1972) pp. 221–46, 265–82.

21. *MY*, no. 44 (7 November 1909) pp. 7–11.

22. P.R. Gregory, 'Russian National Income in 1913', *Quarterly Journal of Economics*, vol. XC, no. 3 (August 1976) p. 449.

23. A.P. Pogrebinsky, *Gosudarstvennye finansy tsarskoy Rossii v epokhu imperializma* (1968) p. 29.

24. Vernadsky, *Source Book*, pp. 823–4.

25. Vernadsky, *Source Book*, pp. 823–4, Pogrebinsky, *Finansy*, pp. 71–2, 74–5; defence budgets from *The Statesman's Year Book*, 1914; Pogrebinsky's statistics on national income should be regarded with caution.

26. P.A. Zayonchkovsky, *Samoderzhaviye i russkaya armiya na rubezhe* XIX–XX *stoletiy* (1973) pp. 275–9; PRO, FO 371, 727, no. 2213, Annual Report for 1908, p. 490.

27. PRO, FO 371, 1470, no. 27674, O'Beirne to Grey, 25 June 1912, p. 34.

28. L.N. Yasnopol'sky, 'Finansy Rossii i ikh podgotovlennost' k voyne' in P.P. Ryabushinsky, (ed.) *Velikaya Rossiya*, (1911) vol. 1, pp. 97, 99–102, 106, 110, 122; Pogrebinsky, *Finansy*, p. 126; E. Rosen-

*tal'*, *Diplomaticheskaya istoriya russko-frantsuzkogo soyuza v nachale xx veka* (1960) p. 95.

29. On the crucial importance and the vulnerability of grain exports see a useful report by O'Beirne; PRO, FO 371, 2094, no. 33826, 24 January 1914, pp. 69–70.

30. See G. Yaney, *The Systematisation of Russian Government* (1973) especially pp. 230–48, 319–99; N.B. Weissman, 'Rural Crime in Tsarist Russia', *Slavic Review*, XXXVII (1978) pp. 228ff; W. Santoni, 'P. N. Durnovo as Minister of Internal Affairs in the Witte Cabinet', Kansas University, Ph.D. Thesis, (1968) pp. 397 ff.

31. C. Read, *Religion, Revolution and the Russian Intelligentsia 1900 – 1912* (1979) pp. 6–7.

32. *MO*, 2nd Series, vol. 19ii, no. 415, Nostitz to Zhilinsky, 1 February/19 January 1912, pp. 74–5.

33. MDSH, Carton 7N 1535, 'Conference sur l'Armée Russe 1912–13; Langlois, p.15.

34. F. Venturi, *Roots of Revolution* (1960) p. 466, for the quotation from Lavrov; O.Radkey, *The Agrarian Foes of Bolshevism* (1958) p. 33 for the SR programme.

35. P. Kenez, 'A Profile of the Pre-Revolutionary Officer Corps', *California Slavic Studies* (1973) pp. 152–3.

36. See for example the series entitled 'Shkola patriotizma' by General E.V. Bogdanovich in many issues of *Grazhdanin* in April, May and June 1908.

37. Statistics on teachers cited in R. Pearson, *The Russian Moderates and the Crisis of Tsarism 1914–1917* p. 80.

38. B. Pares, *My Russian Memoirs* (1931) pp. 150–1.

39. Statistics on strikes from G.A. Arutyunov, *Rabocheye dvizheniye v Rossii v period novogo revolyutsionnogo pod'yoma 1910–1914* (1975) pp. 388–9; L. Haimson 'The Problem of Social Stability in Urban Russia', *Slavic Review*, XXIII, 1964, pp. 619–42.

40. Prince E.N. Trubetskoy, *Otechestvennaya voyna i yeya dukhovnyy symsl'* (1915) pp. 7–8.

41. *NV*, no. 13611 (1/14 February 1914) p. 13.

42. K.F. Shatsillo, *Rossiya pered pervoy mirovoy voynoy* (1974) p. 11.

43. In an interesting survey of Russian politics over the last half century presented to Nicholas II by Count K.I. Pahlen, O.B. Richter, A.N. Kulomzin, F.G. Terner, A.A. and P.A. Saburov and dated 5 May 1905; the survey is in *TsGIA*, Fond 1044, Opis 1, Ed.Khr. 233 and is discussed at some length in my 'Bureaucratic Liberalism in

Late Imperial Russia: The Personality, Career and Opinions of A.N. Kulomzin', *Slavonic and East European Review*, LX,3, (1982) 413–32.

44. Tikhomirov's letters are cited by A.Ya.Avrekh, *Stolypin i tret'ya Duma* (1968) pp. 213–27.

45. MDSH, Carton 7N 1485, Janin to Vignal, no. 23, 18 August 1911; on Nicholas' enthusiasm see the memoirs of the Minister of Education, A.N. Schwartz, RO,Fond 338, Opis 3, Delo 4, 'Moi Vospominaniya o Gosudare', p. 3.

46. Yu.N.Danilov, *Rossiya v mirovoy voyne 1914–1915* (1924) p. 36, *NV*, no. 13609, 30 January/12 February 1914, p. 5.

47. J. Connell, *Wavell: Soldier and Scholar* (1964) p. 67.

48. A.K. Wildman, *The End of the Russian Imperial Army*, (1980) pp. 101–5; Danilov, *Rossiya*, p. 112.

49. Wildman, *Army*, p. 77 quotes Oskin.

50. *NV*, no. 13778, 22 July/4 August 1914, p. 3.

51. Cited in D. Field, *The End of Serfdom* (1976), p. 55.

52. R. Byrnes, *Pobedonostsev* (1968) pp. 128–9.

53. RO, Fond 126, K.15, pp. 7, 21, 31, 35, 51, 72.

54. RO, Fond 126, K.13, p. 3.

55. RO, Fond 126, K.12, pp. 1, 18, 120, 255; K.14, pp. 158, 257; K.15, pp. 18, 20, 39.

56. RO, Fond 126, K.11, pp. 1, 3, 58, 82, 124, 179, 273, 315; K.12, pp. 1, 11, 33, 38, 60, 97, 135, 214, 250; K.13, pp. 17, 108, 188–9, 238; K.14, pp. 22, 79, 92, 153, 163, 284–5; K.15, pp. 2, 7, 41, 51.

57. P.A. Valuyev, *Dnevnik P.A. Valuyeva*, P.A. Zayonchkovsky (ed.) (1961) vol. 2, p. 324.

58. D. Geyer, *Der Russische Imperialismus* (1977) pp. 118–9, 131–3; A.Z. Manfred, *Obrazovaniye russko-frantsuzkogo soyuza* (1975) pp. 287–8, 332, 342, agrees that economic factors played a 'very small' role in the formation of the alliance.

59. V.N. Lambsdorff, *Dnevnik V.N. Lamzdorfa*, A.F. Rothstein (ed.), vol. 2 (1934) p. 214.

2. RUSSIAN FOREIGN POLICY 1905-1914

4 1. R. Girault, *Emprunts Russes et Investissements Français en Russie 1887–1914* (1973) pp. 414–43; J. Long, 'Franco-Russian Relations during the Russo-Japanese War', *SEER*, LII (1974) pp. 213–33.

2. Rozental', *Diplomaticheskaya*, pp. 216–28; MDSH, Carton 7N

1477, Moulin to 2eme Bureau, 10 December 1906.

3. Osten–Sacken to Izvol'sky, 14/27 May 1906, *Au Service de la Russie, Alexandre Iswolsky, Correspondence Diplomatique* (1937) vol. 1, pp. 41–2.

4. *KA*, vol. 5, 1924, pp. 14–15, 35–6.

5. *Correspondence Diplomatique*, vol. 1. Benckendorff to Izvol'sky, 18/31 October 1906, p. 390.

6. V.A. Marinov, *Rossiya i Yaponiya pered pervoy mirovoy voynoy* (1974) pp. 11–21.

7. *KA*, vol. 58 (1935) pp. 26, 36.

8. For example PRO, FO 371, 1743, no. 5856, p. 66, minutes by Grey, Nicolson and Mallet.

9. *KA*, vol. 60 (1933) pp. 55–9.

10. *KA*, vol. 69 (1935) p. 20.

11. See for example *Correspondence Diplomatique*, vol. 1, Izvol'sky to Poklevsky-Kozell, 18/31 October 1906, p. 390; PRO, FO 371, 517, no. 23176, Hardinge Memorandum, 12 June 1908, pp. 332–46.

12. PRO, FO 371, 514, no. 3643, Annual Report for 1907, pp. 17–18. M. Taube, *La Politique Russe d'avant-Guerre*, (1928) pp. 135–8.

13. *Correspondence Diplomatique*, vol. 1, pp. 69–70, 74–5, 78–80 letters between Izvol'sky and the Embassy in Berlin (November 1906).

14. PRO, FO 371, 514, no. 3643, Annual Report for 1907, p. 18.

15. *MY*, no. 1 (3 January 1909) (O.S.) p. 11.

16. E.A. Adamov, *Konstantinopol' i prolivy* (1925) p.9.

17. *Correspondence Diplomatique*, vol. 1, Izvol'sky to Sverbeyev, 12/25 October 1906, pp. 138–9.

18. Ibid., L.P. Urusov to Izvol'sky, 29 April/12 May 1907, pp. 156–8.

19. For example, B.M. Shaposhnikov *Mozg armii*, (1927) vol. 2, pp. 32, 64 for Conrad's views.

20. K.B. Vinogradov, *Bosniyskiy krizis 1908-9 gg*, (1964) pp. 71–4; PRO, FO 371, 514, no. 3643, Annual Report for 1907, p. 23; 727, no. 6057, Annual Report for 1908, p. 466.

21. *Istoricheskiy Arkhiv*, no. 5, 1962, L.P. Urusov to Charykov, 4/17 September 1908, pp. 121–2.

22. Ibid., Charykov to Izvol'sky, 6 September 1908 (OS) p. 125.

23. Ibid., pp. 121–2.

24. Ibid., Izvol'sky to Charykov, 3/16 and 11/24 September, pp. 122–4, 129.

25. Ibid., Charykov to Nicholas II, 29 September (OS), p. 135 for Izvol'sky's reaction to Aehrenthal's statement.

26. Ibid., pp. 133–4, 137–9; N.V. Charykov, 'Reminiscences of Nicholas II', *Contemporary Review*, vol. CXXXIV, 1928, pp. 448–9.

27. *Istoricheskiy Arkhiv*, No.5, 1962, pp. 137, 143–4.

28. *G.P.*, vol. 26 ii, no. 9460, Bulow to Pourtales, 8/21 March 1909.

29. *MO*, 3rd Series, vol. 5, no. 224, pp. 212–3.

30. For example, Lambsdorff, *Die Militarbevollmachtigen*, (Berlin, 1937) p. 342; also the comments of William II and Lichnowsky in July 1914, see Geiss, *July 1914* (1974) pp. 182–3.

31. *MO*, 2nd Series, vol. 18 i, no. 350, Izvol'sky to Neratov, (21/8 August 1911) pp. 358–61.

32. *MO*, 2nd Series, vol. 20 ii, no. 756, Kudashev to Neratov (24/11 September 1912) pp. 261–2.

33. N.de Basily, *Memoirs* (1973) pp. 163–5.

34. *KA*, vol. 6 (1924) pp. 57–9.

35. PRO, FO 371, 1472, no. 5026, Serbia: Annual Report for 1911, p. 179.

36. Ibid., 1748, no. 28340, Serbia: Annual Report for 1912, p. 55.

37. Ibid., 2099, no. 31367, p. 437.

38. *Materialy po istorii Franko-Russkikh otnosheniy za 1910–1914 gg* (1922) Izvol'sky to Sazonov, 17 February/2 March 1911, p. 37 and 8/21 November 1912, pp. 303–4.

39. N. Schebeko, *Souvenirs* (1936) p. 57.

40. *MO*, 3rd Series, vol. 5, Savinsky to Sazonov, 4 February/22 January 1914, pp. 442–3.

41. A.V. Neklyudov, *Diplomatic Reminiscences* (1920) pp. 49–50. *MO*, 2nd Series, vol. 19 ii, no. 535, Hartwig to Neklyudov, 24/11 February 1912, pp. 186–7; vol. 20 i, no. 365, Neklyudov to Sazonov, 26/13 July 1912, p. 370.

42. *MO*, 2nd Series, vol. 18 ii, no. 845, N. Giers to Neratov, 9 November/27 October 1911, pp. 343–5; vol. 19 ii, no. 646, N. Giers to Sazonov, 16/3 March 1912, p. 288.

43. *Correspondence Diplomatique*, vol. 1, Benckendorff to Izvol'sky, 27 July/9 August and 23 August/5 September 1906, pp. 345, 360.

44. *MO*, 2nd Series, vol. 18 ii, no. 801, Hartwig to Neratov, (4 November/22 October 1911) pp. 300–1.

45. *MO*, 3rd Series, vol. 5, Savinsky to Sazonov (4 February/22 January 1914) pp. 442–3.

46. PRO, FO 371, 1748, no. 21746, Paget to Grey, 9 May 1913, p. 31.

47. *MO*, 2nd Series, vol. 19 ii, no. 646, N. Giers to Sazonov, (16/3 March 1912) p. 288.

48. *MO*, 2nd Series, vol. 18 ii, no. 845, N. Giers to Neratov, (9 November/27 October 1911) pp. 343–5.

49. *SOGD*, 3rd Sozyv, 2 Sessiya, col. 2629.

50. *MO*, 2nd Series, vol. 18 ii, no. 512, Neklyudov to Neratov, (2 October/19 September 1911) pp. 63–4.

51. For example, vol. 19 ii no. 777, S. Urusov to Sazonov, 18/5 April 1912, pp. 421–4; vol. 20 i, no. 100, Neklyudov to Sazonov, 29/16 May 1912, pp. 187–8; no. 359, Neklyudov to Sazonov, 25/12 June 1912, p. 361 vol. 20 ii, no. 637, Neklyudov to Sazonov, 5 September/24 August 1912, pp. 163–6, for Neklyudov's fear of a European war.

52. For example, Kokovtsov's comment of July 1912 that 'Bulgaria . . . would never move without Russia's permission', PRO, FO 371, 1470, no. 31867, Buchanan to Grey (18 July 1912) p. 229.

53. *MO*, 2nd Series, vol. 19 ii, no. 777, S. Urusov to Sazonov, (18/5 April 1912) pp. 421–2.

54. *Materialy*, pp. 289–91, Izvol'sky to Sazonov (10/23 October 1912).

55. *Materialy*, p. 649, M.N. Giers to Sazonov (23 November 1913).

56. *MO*, vol. 20 ii, no. 640, Argyropoulo to Bronevsky (7 September/25 August 1912) p. 168.

57. Basily *Memoirs*, p. 154.

58. Adamov, *Konstantinopol'*, p. 71.

59. Quoted in F. Fischer, *War of Illusions*, (1975), pp. 334–6.

60. *MO*, vol. 18 i, no. 147, Benckendorff to Neratov (2 July/19 June 1911) pp. 160–1.

61. Ibid., no. 358, N. Vyazemsky to Neratov (24/11 August 1911) p. 369.

62. *MO*, vol. 20 i, no. 113, Bazarov to CGS (31/18 May 1912) p. 101.

63. *DDF*, 3rd Series, vol. VIII, no. 552, Maucorps to Ministry of War, (29 November 1913) pp. 691–7; PRO, FO 371, 1847, no. 55115, Tyrell to Mallet, 2 December 1913.

64. Ibid., no. 55197, Mallet to Grey, 2 December 1913, enclosing Tyrell's despatch of the same date; *DDF*, 3rd Series, vol. VIII, nos. 500, 550, 554, Bompard to Pichon, 19 November, 29 November and 30 November 1913, pp. 635–6, 689–90, 697–8; PRO, FO 371, 1847, no. 54955, Minutes by Grey and Nicolson of 7 December 1913.

65. *KA*, vol. 7, 1924, pp. 42–3.

66. Ibid., pp. 47–8; *MO*, 3rd Series, vol. 1, no. 122, Benckendorff to Sazonov (28/15 January 1914) pp. 137–40.

67. *MO*, 2nd Series, vol. 20 ii, no. 672, Izvol'sky to Sazonov, (12 September/30 August, 1912) pp. 198–200.

68. Ibid., no. 969, Izvol'sky to Sazonov (10 October/27 September 1912), pp. 414–5; *Materialy*, Izvol'sky to Sazonov (25 October/7 November 1912) p. 295–7.

69. *Materialy*, Izvol'sky to Sazonov (5/18 December 1912) pp. 311–3.

70. *KA*, vol. 7 (1924) p. 47.

71. PRO, FO 371, 1745, no. 22759, Buchanan to Grey, 15 May 1913, p. 280 for Kokovtsov's views; 2092, no. 15312, Buchanan to Grey, 3 April 1914, pp. 292–6 for those of Nicholas II.

72. *MO*, 3rd Series, vol. 1, no. 289, Sazonov to Benckendorff, (19/6 February 1914) pp. 360–1.

73. *KA*, vol. 62 (1934) Bazarov to QMG (10 March 1914) p. 126.

74. Ibid., Bruin de Saint-Hippolyte to Yanushkevich (26 May 1914) p. 127.

75. Ibid., Lomnovsky to Yanushkevich (8 February 1914) pp. 91–3.

76. PRO, FO 371, 2092, no. 15312, Buchanan to Grey (3 April 1914) pp. 292–6.

77. Russian military intelligence had for example supplied Charykov with the date for the annexation weeks before Izvol'sky's meeting at Buchlau but the Assistant Foreign Minister decided the information was 'scarcely probable', Vinogradov, *Bosniyskiy*, pp. 79–82.

3. WHO RULED IN PETERSBURG?

1. *SZ*, vol. 1, part 1 (1906) Art. 4; M. Szeftel, *The Russian Constitution of April 23 1906* (1976) provides an exhaustive study of the Fundamental Laws.

2. *SZ*, (1906), vol. I, part 1 Arts 13, 14, 96, 98–119; Szeftel, *Constitution*, pp. 127–8, 154, 223, 230, 326–7; P. Chasles, *Le Parlement Russe* (1909) also provides a useful survey of Russian constitutional law and practice.

3. Shatsillo, *Russkiy imperializm*, pp. 163–201; the texts of the original budgetary rules and of the August 1909 decree are given in F.I. Kalinychev, *Gosudarstvennaya Duma v Rossii v dokumentakh i materialakh* (1957) pp. 132–5, 404; PRO, FO 371, 512, no. 3630, p. 333; 514, no.

3642, p. 37; 513, no. 23188, p. 197; 976, no. 159, pp. 441–2 for British diplomatic and naval reports on this issue.

4. I.V. Bestuzher, *Bor'ba v Rossiy po voprosam vneshney politiki 1906–1910* (1961) p. 118; I.V. Bestuzhev, 'Bor'ba v Rossiy po voprosam vneshney politiki nakanune pervoy mirovoy voyny', *Istoricheskiye zapiski,* no. 75 (1965) pp. 68, 79; on the possible threat from the railway workers during mobilisation see MDSH, Carton 7N 1535, 'Notice statistique sur l' Armée Russe,' p. 50.

5. P.N. Durnovo led the fight to keep the Duma's influence in the armed forces to a minimum; *SOGS,* 3 sessiya, cols 2225–7; 4 sessiya, cols. 1345–50.

6. See A.P. Izvol'sky, *The Memoirs of Alexander Iswolsky* (trans. by C.L. Seeger) (n.d.) especially pp. 34–5, 110–11, 159, 188–9; S.D. Sazonov, *Fateful Years 1906–16* (1928) pp. 75, 277, 280–2; the memoir literature on both men is enormous; interesting comments in Western languages are to be found on Izvol'sky in for example. R.R. Rosen, *Forty Years of Diplomacy* (1922) vol. 1, pp. 172–3; vol. 2, pp. 19, 48, 81; V.N. Kokovtsov, *Out of My Past* (1935) pp. 142, 159–60, 173, A.D. Kalmykov, *Memoirs of a Russian Diplomat* (1971) pp. 176–7; M. Taube, *Politique Russe* pp. 104–115; on Sazonov see for example Taube *Politique russe,* pp. 248–252; N.V. Charykov, 'Sazonov', *Contemporary Review,* CXXXIII (1928) pp. 284–8; N.de Basily, *Memoirs,* p. 70.

7. A.A. Polivanov, *Iz dnevnikov i vospominaniy po dolzhnosti voyennogo ministra i yego pomoshchnika 1907–1916* (1924) p. 129; *PTR,* vol.7, pp. 63–6.

8. The Empress Marie said in February 1904, 'The Emperor sees no one, he ought to see more people', RO, Fond, 120, K.13, pp. 57, 303.

9. *SOGD* (1908) 3 Sozyv, 2 Sessiya, col. 2674.

10. MDSH, Carton 7N, 1535, Matton to 2eme Bureau, 16/29 May 1909.

11. PRO, FO 371, 1745, no. 27327, O'Beirne to Grey, 12 June 1913, p. 348.

12. PRO, FO 371, 1467, no. 8486, Buchanan to Grey, pp. 503ff. 24 February 1912; for Nicholas II's conversation with Hintze see Count G. von Lambsdorff, *Die Militarbevollmachtigen,* (1937) p. 319.

13. Naumov, *Iz utselevshikh,* vol. 2, p. 217.

14. The Emperor's Own Personal Chancellery should have played the role of a private office but in fact the First Section, the true personal secretariat, under the last three emperors was an organisation of very limited significance with virtually no influence on the overall

formulation of governmental policy; see V.N. Stroyev, *Stoletiye Sob-stvennoy Yego Imperatorskogo Velichestva Kantselyarii* (1912) pp. 203 ff; the memoirs of A.N. Schwartz, the Minister of Education from 1908–1910, provide a good picture of the very limited, though occasionally infuriating, involvement of the monarch in educational matters; see in particular *Moi vospominaniya o Gosudare*, RO, Fond 338, Opis 1, Delo 3/4, pp. 2–4.

15. RO, Fond 126, K.14, p.266; Taube, *Politique Russe*, pp. 167–8; Izvol'sky, *Memoirs*, p. 127; Oldenburg, *Last Tsar.*, vol. 1, p. 168; N.V. Charykov, 'Reminiscences of Nicholas II', *Contemporary Review*, CXXXIV (1928) p. 446.

16. M. Perrins, 'The Council of State Defence, 1905–1909: A Study in Russian Bureaucratic Politics', *SEER*, LVIII (1980) pp. 370–399; W.T. Wilfong, *Rebuilding the Russian Army 1905–1914* (Indiana University. Ph.D., 1977) pp. 43–5, 66, 93–4; I.I. Rostunov, *Russkiy front pervoy mirovoy voyny* (1976) pp. 28–34; Shatsillo, *Russkiy Imperializm*, pp. 54–66.

17. V. Sukhomlinov, *Vospominaniya* (1924) pp. 183, 297.

18. PRO, FO 371, 1743, 10175, Annual Report for 1912, p. 457.

19. *Grazhdanin* (13 March 1911) (OS) no. 10, p. 12; K.A. Krivoshein, *A.V. Krivoshein, Yego znacheniye v istorii Rossii nachala* xx *veka* (1973) pp. 154–220; V.N. Kokovtsov, *Out of my Past*, pp. 434ff.

20. *PSZ*, 3rd Series, vol xxv (1905) no. 26820; Kokovtsov, *Out of My Past*, pp. 215–217; PRO, FO 371, 729, no. 17571, p. 144; Taube, *Politique*, p. 304.

21. *LN*, vol.2, pp. 385–6; Kokovtsov, *Out of My Past*, p. 359; Sukhomlinov, *Vospominaniya*, p. 183; Taube, *Politique Russe*, p. 335; RO, Fond 126, K.11, p. 233.

22. Rosen, *Forty Years*, vol.1, pp. 19, 65; Solov'yov, *Vospominaniya*, pp. 27, 30–32; P.S. Botkin, *Kartinki diplomaticheskoy zhizni* (1930) pp. 26, 29–31; D.I. Abrikossow, *Revelations of a Russian Diplomat* (1964) pp. 85, 93–4, 140–2; Bestuzhev, *Bor'ba . . . 1906–1910*, pp. 60–1; on the Civil Service Regulations see Lieven, *The Russian Establishment*, part 3, ch. x; the service regulations for diplomatic, consular and Foreign Ministry officials are collected in *Svod rasporyazheniy Ministerstva Inostrannykh del po Departamentu Lichnogo Sostava i Khozyaystvennykh Del, (1912)*; the interesting answers to a long questionnaire about the diplomatic service sent by the Ministry to heads of mission abroad are contained in 'Ministerstvo Inostrannykh Del: Kommissiya po reorganizatsii zagranichnoy sluzhby', *Svod otchetov zagranychnykh ustanovleniy ministerstva na voprosnik kasatel' no organizatsii zagranichnoy sluzhby*

(n.d.); for consuls' complaints about their inferior status in the Ministry see for example pp. 7, 12–13, 165–6, 417–8; for criticism of the irregular promotion system see pp. 416–7; many heads of mission, especially the ambassadors in the major capitals, stressed the need for a diplomat to have a private income (pp. 148–53) though there was strong opposition to making this a statutory requirement.

23. Ministerstvo Inostrannykh Del, *Svod*, pp. 158–68 on the problems of gerontocracy, retirement and pensions which were discussed in detail and with a heat which suggests this was a major problem; Shebeko, *Souvenirs* pp. 7, 94, 95, 99.

24. Taube, *Politique Russe*, p. 163; Abrikossow, *Revelations*, p. 103 writes 'Our foreign office could be very indulgent'; PRO, FO 371, 729, no. 17571, FO Minute, p. 144.

25. Lieven, *The Russian Establishment*, part 3, ch. x; Basily, *Memoirs*, p. 24.

26. Abrikossow, *Revelations*, p. 213, on lack of discipline among Russian diplomats; Rosen, *Forty Years*, vol. 1 pp. 107–8, 116–7, 128–9.

27. On Neratov, see E. de Schelking, *Suicide of a Monarch* (1918) pp. 229–30; Taube, *Politique Russe*, p. 209 on Charykov, whom Nicolson called 'an intelligent and hard-working man. He is, I think, a little too loquacious, and I have not much confidence in his judgement'; PRO, FO 371, 730, no. 21128, p. 710; on Vlangali and Shishkin see for example Lambsdorff, *Dnevnik*, vol. 1, pp. 56, 361; vol. 2, pp. 58, 73, 244, 332.

28. For example *MO*, 3rd Series, vol. 1, no. 122, Benckendorff to Sazonov (28/15 January 1914) pp. 137–40; 2nd Series, vol. 19 ii, no. 747, Izvol'sky to Sazonov (10 April/28 March 1912) pp. 390–1.

29. For example *MO*, 2nd Series, vol. 18 i, no. 423, Benckendorff to Neratov 12 September /30 August 1911) pp. 427–30; *Materialy*, Izvol'sky to Neratov (18/31 August 1911) pp. 112–3; (24 November/7 December 1911) pp. 138–41.

30. On the Neratov-Charykov muddle see E.C. Thaden, *Russia and the Balkan Alliance of 1912* (1965) pp. 42–57 and the attack on Charykov in *Novoye Vremya* (18 March 1912) which drew comments both from London and from Buchanan in Petersburg: PRO, FO 371, 1468, no. 12852, p. 216; on Hartwig see Chapter 2, footnotes 35–48.

31. Sukhomlinov, *Vospominaniya*, p. 297.

32. Kokovtsov, *Out of My Past*, pp. 345–6; the Russian army in fact carried out a number of large-scale trial mobilisations in the years before 1914.

4. ACTORS AND OPINIONS

1. CUBA, Bark MS., ch. 1 provides a very full and fair appreciation of Nicholas II; for Nicholas' reaction to the humiliation of 1905
and 1909 see Kireyev's diary, RO, Fond 126, K. 14, p. 320; K.15,
p. 39; Lambsdorff, *Die Militarbevollmachtigen*, p. 345. *DDF*, 3rd series,
vol. 9, no. 189.

2. For example PRO, FO 371, 2092, no. 10412, p.49 (4 March
1914) Annual Report for 1913, on the 'Emperor's determination to
maintain peace at any price'. HHSA, P.A.X.140, Report 8F, Czernin
to Berchtold (13 February/31 January 1914) on the 'peaceful direction of the Emperor'; on Nicholas II's 'extreme loathing' for war in
July 1914 see Schilling's diary, *MO* 3rd Series, vol. 5, no. 284,
pp. 256ff.

3. On Bjorkoe see *KA*, vol. 5 (1924) pp. 5–49; Lambsdorff to
Nelidov, (23 September 1905 (OS)) quotes Nicholas II's views.

4. V.N. Kokovtsov, *Out of My Past*, p. 349; Taube, *Politique*,
p. 365.

5. CUBA, Bark MS., ch. 6, pp. 3–5.

6. On Nicholas' great interest in Russian Asia see Oldenburg,
*Last Tsar*, especially vol.1, ch.5; on the navy see above ch.3 note 3.

7. PRO, FO 371, 729, no. 15520, Nicolson to Grey, 14 April
1909, p. 197 on Nicholas II's belief that firm solidarity within the
Entente camp was needed to stand up to the united Dual Alliance;
this belief did not waver and had grown stronger by 1914; PRO, FO
371, 980, no. 29448, Nicolson to Grey, August 6 1910, p. 237; 1217, no.
29095, Minute by Nicolson: 'H.M. is determined to stand by us and
would like the Entente developed into something stronger', 31 July
1911, p. 437; 2092, no. 15312, Buchanan to Grey, April 3 1914, pp.
292–6; *MO*, 3rd Series, vol. 4, Benckendorff to Sazonov (28/15 June
1914) p. 3; Nicholas II to Marie Fyodorovna (18–19 March 1909) pp.
240–1 in Bing, *Letters*.

8. PRO, FO 371, 1467, no 8486, Buchanan to Grey, Febuary 24
1912, p. 504.

9. RO, Fond 126, K. 14, p. 320; PRO, FO 371, 976, no. 159,
Annual Report for 1909, p. 423; Austrian support for the Ukrainian
movement for example was intended to show Petersburg that it governed a vulnerable multi-national state; HHSA, P.A.X. 140, Private
Letter, Szapary to Berchtold, 23/10 February 1914; MO, 2nd Series,
vol. 19ii, no. 749, N. Giers to Sazonov (10 April/28 March 1912)

p. 393; 3rd Series, vol. 3, no. 39, Shebeko to Sazonov (19/6 May 1914) pp. 39–40; for Nicholas II's anti-Austrian comments in 1914 see 3rd series, vol. 2, no. 321, Shebeko to Sazonov (29/16 April) pp. 412–3; no. 331, Shebeko to Sazonov (30/17 April) p. 429; vol. 3, no. 293, Shebeko to Sazonov (17/4 June 1914) pp. 346–7.

10. PRO, FO 371, 2092, no 15087, Buchanan to Grey, 31 March 1914, pp. 215–6.

11. PRO, FO 371, 1467, no. 8486, Buchanan to Grey, 24 February 1912, p. 504.

12. See for example his comment to Bulow in 1899 quoted by Oldenburg, *Last Tsar* vol. 1, p. 131.

13. Witte, *Vospominaniya*, vol. 2, pp. 101–4; Rosen, *Forty Years*, vol. 1, p. 128. *KA*, 1922, vol. 1, pp. 156–162.

14. PRO, FO 371, 1467, no. 8486, February 24 1912, Buchanan to Grey, p. 504.

15. For Nicholas' comments and views see: PRO, FO 371, 2092, no. 15312, Buchanan to Grey, 3 April 1914, pp. 292–6 and no. 10412, Annual Report for 1913, p. 53; also *DDF*, 3rd Series, vol. 9, no. 189.

16. A. A. Mossolov, *At the Court of the Last Tsar* (1935) is a good source on Nicholas II's household; see especially pp. 108–10, 119–23, 146, 163; Mossolov's comments are echoed in an intelligent letter from the British Counsellor in St Petersburg, PRO, FO 371, 1469, no. 29840, O'Beirne to Grey, 5 July 1912, pp. 444–5; Lambsdorff, *Die Militarbevollmachtigen*, pp. 258, 335–9, 340, 343–5.

17. Bing, *Letters*, provides examples of Marie Fyodorovna's views on Germany and Izvol'sky, for example pp. 241–2; Isvol'sky, *Memoirs*, pp. 22, 31; N. F. Grant (ed.), *The Kaiser's Letters to the Tsar* (n.d.) pp. 157–9, 15 January 1905.

18. MDSH, Carton 7N 1478, Laguiche to Ministry of War, 24 March/6 April 1913 and 24 June/7 July 1914.

19. Sukhomlinov, *Vospominaniya*, pp. 180–1, 216, 278–9, 289, 303–14, Yu.N. Danilov, *Velikiy Knyaz' Nikolay Nikolayevich* (1930) pp. 80–4.

20. MDSH, Carton 7N 1477, Moulin to Ministry of War, 20 November 1906.

21. Danilov, *Velikiy Knyaz'*, pp. 9, 54; Witte, *Vospominaniya*, vol. 2. p. 479.

22. Danilov, *Velikiy Knyaz'*, pp. 11–12, 83; PRO, FO 371, 519, no. 28444, O'Beirne to Grey, August 13 1908; p. 1.

23. PRO, FO 371, 1743, Annual Report for 1912, p. 457.

24. CUBA, Bark MS., chapter 7, p. 22; Sukhomlinov, *Vospomina-*

*niya*, pp. 284–5; on p. 288 Sukhomlinov states that 'in those days before the war the Tsar was fully under his uncle's influence' but Sukhomlinov's desire to absolve himself of responsibility for the outbreak of war added to his loathing for Nicholas Nikolayevich weakens the value of this comment.

25. Danilov, *Velikiy Knyaz'*, pp. 38, 71–9; MDSH, Carton 7N 1478, Laguiche to Ministry of War, 1/14 December 1912.

26. Danilov, *Velikiy Knyaz'*, p. 84; MDSH, Carton 7N 1478, Laguiche to Vignal, 30 March/12 April 1913.

27. MDSH, Carton 7N 1478, Laguiche to Ministry of War, 12/25 November 1912; Laguiche to Vignal, 10/22 November 1912.

28. British reports in particular stressed Nicholas Nikolayevich's arrogance; PRO, FO 371, 519, no. 28444, O'Beirne to Grey, August 13 1908, p. 1; 1746, no. 41222, Knox to Buchanan, 27 August 1913, pp. 214, 228.

29. RO, Fond 126, K. 14, pp. 78, 106, 193, 231, 303.

30. Taube, *Politique*, pp. 296–300.

31. H.W. Williams, *Russia of the Russians* (1914) p. 114.

32. For example, *Grazhdanin*, nos. 37–8, (25 May 1908 [OS]) p. 10; no. 25; (3 July 1911 [OS]), p.11; *NV*, no. 13616 (6/19 February 1914) p. 4.

33. For example, *Grazhdanin*, no. 8 (31 January 1908 [OS]) pp. 1–2; no. 9 (6 March 1911 [OS]) p. 16; no. 12 (27 March 1911 [OS]) p. 13; no. 14 (17 April 1911 [OS]) p. 18; no. 19 (30 May 1910 [OS]) pp. 15–18; no. 23 (27 June 1910 [OS]) pp.1, 2, 9.

34. *NV*, no. 13616 (6/19 February 1914) p. 4; *Grazhdanin*, no. 28 (24 July 1911 [OS]) p. 13; no. 44 (10 November 1913 [OS]) p. 3; no. 49 (15 December 1913 [OS]) pp. 11–12; the references from *Grazhdanin* could be multiplied one-hundred-fold.

35. TsGIA, Fond 1200, Opis 16/2, Ed.Khr. 1 and 2, p. 125; MDSH, Carton 7N 1535, Conference sur l'Armée Russe 1912–3, Captain Langlois, p. 39; Lambsdorff, *Die Militarbevollmachtigen*, p. 402, Report of von Hintze, 19 August 1910.

36. RO, Fond 126, K. 11, pp. 19, 57, 274; K. 13, p.1.

37. For Kireyev's changing attitude see: RO, Fond 126, K. 12, p. 83; K. 13, pp. 3–4, 25, 126.

38. RO, Fond 126, K. 15, pp. 15, 18, 20–1, 31, 51, 72.

39. HHSA, P.A.X.138, Report 7A, Thurn to Berchtold, 2 March/18 February 1912.

40. HHSA, P.A.X., 135, Report 2D, Berchtold to Aehrenthal, 17/4

January 1910; P.A.X., 138, Report 7A, Thurn to Berchtold, 2 March/ 18 February 1912; P.A.X., 139, Report 43D, Czernin to Berchtold, 21/8 November 1913.

41. Taube, *Politique Russe*, pp. 331–9 provides useful information on the pro-Germans' attitudes and actions in 1914; Yu.Ya. Solv'yov, the Counsellor in Madrid in 1914, was a 'pro-German' liberal; see his *Vospominaniya diplomata* for example p. 209; for Baron R.R. Rosen, another diplomatic liberal, see the following section of this chapter.

42. In March 1907 Nicholas II told Prince A.A. Shirinsky-Shikhmatov that he would never again appoint Witte to any position; RO, Fond 126, K.14, p. 213; Durnovo commented about being ignored to A.A. Polovtsov see KA, 1923, vol. 4, p. 124; for Durnovo and Witte's views on Nicholas II see respectively, S.E. Kryzhanovsky,*Vospominaniya*, (n.d.) p. 75 and Witte, *Vospominaniya*, vol. 2, p.6.

43. For Witte's views see his memoirs, *Vospominaniya*, vol. 2, pp. 121–3, 457–81; vol. 3, pp. 226, 235, 246, 457, 536; Baron R.R. Rosen, *Forty Years*, vol. 1, pp. 191, 209, 291, 302–3; Witte expressed his views twice incognito in *Novoye Vremya* in March 1914, no. 13643, (6/19 March 1914) p. 3. and no. 13648 (11/24 March 1914) p. 3; for Nicholas II's comments on Witte's ideas see PRO, FO 371, 2092, no. 15312, pp. 292–6; for Witte's wartime activities see G. Katkov, *Russia 1917, The February Revolution* (1967) p. 65.

44. On Durnovo see M. Aldanov, 'P.N. Durnovo, Prophet of War and Revolution' *Russian Review*, vol. 2 (1942) pp. 31–45; also my own 'Bureaucratic Authoritarianism in Late Imperial Russia: The Personality, Career and Opinions of P.N. Durnovo', *Historical Journal*, 1983; of the memoirists V.I. Gurko, *Features and Figures of the Past* (1939), pp. 178–83, 404–15, 438–58 gives probably the fullest summary of Durnovo's views and character; the memorandum is in F. Golder *Documents on Russian History, 1914–1917* (1927) pp. 3–24.

45. K.H. Jarausch, *The Enigmatic Chancellor* (1973) pp. 162–3.

46. *NV*, no. 13029 (21 June/4 July 1912) p.3.

47. J. Joll, '1914: The Unspoken Assumptions' in H.W. Koch (ed.), *The Origins of the First World War* (1972) pp. 309–16.

48. The best history of the Lycée in the first seven decades of its existence is by N.I. Kareyev, 'Kratkiy ocherk istorii Litseya, sostavlenniy professorom N.I. Kareyevym' in *Pamyatnaya knizhka Imperatorskogo Aleksandrovskogo Litseya* (1886) pp. 1–277. The *Pamyatnaya knizhka* for 1898–9, pp. 3ff takes the story on to the end of the century; there is another useful survey in CUBA, MS. Fliege, *Istoricheskiy ocherk Impera-*

*torskogo Aleksandrovskogo Litseya* (1936). A.A. Rubetz, *Kratkaya istoricheskaya pamyatka Imperatorskogo Aleksandrovskogo, byvshego Tsarskosel's-kogo Litseya* (1911) though short, is, in parts, revealing; there is also a very interesting article by A. Sinel on the Lycée and its first cousin, the Imperial School of Law in *Russian History*, vol. 3, p 1 (1976) p. 1–33 entitled 'The Socialisation of the Russian Bureaucratic Elite 1811–1917'.

49. The *Pamyatnaya knizhka Litseyistov* (1907) provides lists of former students and their present occupations; the *Pamyatnaya knizhka* for 1898–9 provides statistics for the distribution of Lyceists in government departments; 86 were in the Foreign Ministry, 96 in the Ministry of Finance, 121 in the Ministry of Justice and 156 in the Ministry of the Interior; the small overall size of the Foreign Ministry and the key positions occupied there by Lyceists made them far more conspicuous in this department than elsewhere; for lists of Russian Foreign Ministry and diplomatic personnel see *Adres kalendar' Rossiyskoy Imperii* (1914).

50. T. Darlington, *Board of Education: Special Reports on Educational Subjects, Vol. 23, Education in Russia* (1909) p. 233; Darlington's very thorough work is still the outstanding book in English on education in Imperial Russia; Kareyev, *Pamyatnaya*, pp. 177–257. CUBA, MS. V.N. Kokovtsov, *Vospominaniya detstva i litseyskoy pory grafa V.N. Kokovtsova*, pp. 218–9, 254–5; P. Popov (P. Knyazhnin), *Shest' let v Imperatorskom Aleksandrovskom Litseye* (1911) pp. 72–3.

51. XXXI *kurs Imperatorskogo Aleksandrovskogo Litseya cherez 25 let posle vypuska 1871–1896* (1896) pp. 16–17.

52. Popov, *Shest' let*, pp. 38–9.

53. See for example CUBA, Fliege, *Istoricheskiy ocherk*, pp. 136–8, 149; CUBA, Kokovtsov, *Vospominaniya*, pp. 174–5, 285; Popov, *Shest' let*, pp. 105ff; XXXI *Kurs*, pp. 21–3 for Yu.Yu.Beketov's comments which completely contradict those of L.S. Birkin; Sinel, 'Socialisation', pp. 4–6.

54. See in particular Rubetz, *Kratkaya*, pp. 16–17; also the same author's account of the Lycée's centenary celebrations in A.A. Rubetz, *Stoletniy yubiley Imperatorskogo Aleksandrovskogo byvshego Tsarskosel'skogo Litseya* (1912) passim.

55. See *Imperatorskiy Aleksandrovskiy Litsey: xl Kurs* (1909) pp. 9, 32. N.V. Tcharykow, *Glimpses of High Politics* (1931) pp. 270–1.

56. Baron F.F. Wrangel, 'Ob'yasnitel'naya zapiska k instruktsii gg vospitatelyam Imp. Aleksandrovskogo Litseya', in *Pamyatnaya*

*knizhka* (1886) pp. 263–6; for Grot's comments see *Pamyatnaya knizhka Imperatorskogo Aleksandrovskogo Litseya, 1856–7*, (1856) pp. 33–47.

57. N.de Basily, *Memoirs*, p. 90; *Pamyatnaya knizhka* (1886) p. 265. *xl Kurs* (1909) pp. 7, 11, 15; Popov, *Shest'let*, pp. 23, 32–4, 105ff; CUBA, MS. Fliege, *Istoricheskiy*, pp. 73, 104–5, 136–8, 146; CUBA, MS. Kokovtsov, *Vospominaniya*, pp. 161–70, 174–5, 236–244.

58. *Svod rasporyazhenii Ministerstva Inostrannykh Del po Departamentu Lichnogo Sostava i Khozyaystvennykh Del, (1912)*, p. 4, Art. 5.

59. F. Martens, *Sovremennoye mezhdunarodnoye pravo tsivilizovannykh narodov*, 2 vols. (1895) vol. 1, pp. 182–4, 235, 303, 309, 354; vol. 2, p. 211.

60. Ibid., vol. 1, pp. 5–6, 18–19, 201–2; vol. 2, pp. 138–9, 211, 476, 478–9; Lambsdorff, *Dnevnik*, for example vol. 1, p. 212; vol. 2, p. 209.

61. Martens, *Sovremennoye*, vol. 1, pp. 296–7, 307; vol. 2, pp. 474–93.

62. E. Bourgeois, *Manuel Historique de Politique Etrangère*, 3 vols (1898); vol. 2, pp. 6–8, 13–15; vol. 3, pp. 178–9, 184–5, 818–25.

63. Witte, *Vospominaniya*, vol. 2, pp. 279, 403; Rosen, *Forty Years*, vol. 2, pp. 84–6; for Rosen's background, family and his service record, TsGIA, Fond 1162, Opis 6, Ed.Khr.461, pp. 23ff is very useful.

64. The memorandum is in TsGIA, Fond 543, Opis 1, delo 672 but unfortunately I have not been able to read it; large extracts are, however, cited by Rosen in his memoirs and by B.I. Bovykin, *Iz istorii vozniknoveniya pervoy mirovoy voyny: otnosheniya Rossii i Frantsii v 1912–1914 gg* (1961) pp. 116–7.

65. Rosen, *Forty Years*, vol. 1, pp. 106–22; vol. 2, pp. 88–99.

66. Ibid, vol. 2, pp. 100–4.

67. Ibid, vol. 2, p. 107.

68. Ibid, vol. 2, pp. 105–8; *SOGS*, 9 sessiya, cols. 864–8.

69. *SOGD*, 3 sozyv, 5 sessiya, col. 2170.

70. RO Fond 126, K. 13, p. 4.

71. P.B. Struve, (ed.), *Pamyati knyaz'ya G.N. Trubetskogo* (1930) pp. 12–13.

72. On Trubetskoy's links with liberal imperialist and Slavophil circles see Struve, *Pamyati*, pp. 12, 23, 28–30, 157; J.L. West, *The Moscow Progressists: Russian Industrialists in Liberal Politics 1905–1914* (Princetown, Ph.D., 1975) pp. 223–40; P. Vysny, *Neoslavism and the Czechs* (1977) pp. 76, 167.

73. On Trubetskoy's background, family and childhood see the memoirs of his brother and sister, Prince E.N. Trubetskoy, *Vospomina-*

*niya* (1922) pp.22–5, and *Iz proshlogo* (n.d.) pp. 7, 11, 22, 31–36, 70; Princess Olga Trubetskaya, *Vospominaniya sestry* (1953) p.7.

74. *MY*, no. 50 (18 December 1907) pp. 31, 39; no. 31 (21 October 1906) p. 29; no. 40 (23 December 1906) pp. 9–25; no. 43 (1 November 1908) p. 5. All *MY* dates are Old Style.

75. *MY*, no. 43 (1 November 1908) pp. 4–5; no. 50 (19 December 1908) p. 18; no. 49 (12 December 1909) p. 11.

76. *MY*, no. 45 (15 November 1908) pp. 25, 27.

77. *MY*, no. 1 (3 January 1909) p. 14; no. 9 (28 February 1909) pp. 1–2, 4.

78. *MY*, no. 17 (15 July 1906) pp. 29–30; nos. 26–7 (14 July 1907) p. 11; no. 1 (3 January 1909) p. 13; no. 44 (7 November 1909) pp. 10–11; *MY*, no. 9 (28 February 1909) p. 6; Ryabushinsky, *Velikaya*, vol. 1, p. 23; *MY*, no. 45 (15 November 1908) p. 18; no. 20 (23 May 1909) p. 48; no. 25 (26 June 1910) p. 36.

79. G.N. Trubetskoy, 'Rossiya v Evrope', *Polyarnaya zvezda* (3 February 1906) quoted in Struve, *Pamyati*, p. 67; *MY*, nos. 26–7, (14 July 1907) p. 15; no. 29 (7 October 1906) pp. 29–30.

80. *MY*, no. 29 (7 October 1906) pp. 34–5; no.1 (6 January 1907) p. 19.

81. Ryabushinsky, *Velikaya*, vol. 1, pp. 97–8; *MY*, no. 45 (15 November 1908) p.27.

82. Trubetskoy, *Polyarnaya zvezda*, quoted in Struve *Pamyati*, pp. 65–8.

83. *MY*, no. 1 (6 January 1907) p. 22; no. 13 (27 March 1910) pp. 11–20; no. 45 (15 November 1908) p. 27.

84. *MY*, no. 13 (27 March 1910) p. 19; no. 25 (27 March 1909) pp. 59, 64; no. 18 (9 May 1909) pp. 49–51; no. 48 (4 December 1907) p.10; no. 9 (28 February 1909) p.6.

85. Ryabushinsky, *Velikaya*, vol. 1, p. 104; *MY*, no. 1 (6 January 1907) pp. 22–3; no. 1 (3 January 1908) pp. 36–45.

86. *MY*, no.1 (6 January 1907) p. 24; no. 1 (3 January 1908) pp. 44–5; no. 45 (15 November 1908) pp. 18, 20–1; no. 12 (21 March 1909) pp. 55–6 (on Russian generals' unworthy panic at the very thought of war with Germany); no. 25 (27 June 1909) pp. 61–4; no. 18 (9 May 1909) p. 52; no. 9 (27 February 1910) pp. 13–18; Ryabushinsky, *Velikaya*, vol. 1, pp. 39, 105; E.N. Trubetskoy, *MY*, no. 12 (21 March 1909) pp. 1–6.

87. *LN*, vol. 2, pp. 373–6; Baron B.E. Nolde establishes Trubeskoy's authorship in Struve (ed.), *Pamyati*, p. 14.

88. *MY*, no. 1 (6 January 1907) pp. 20–1; nos. 26–7 (14 July 1907) pp. 11–16; no. 3 (15 January 1908) pp. 22–3; Ryabushinsky, *Velikaya*, vol. 2, p. 334.

89. G.N. Trubetskoy, 'Rossiya v Azii', *Polyarnaya zvezda* (27 January 1906) quoted in Struve (ed.), *Pamyati*, pp. 54–62; *MY*, no. 39 (6 October 1907) pp. 54–9; no. 40 (13 October 1907) pp. 45–53; Ryabushinsky, *Velikaya*, vol. 2, pp. 344–53.

90. *MY*, no. 28 (30 September 1906) pp. 20–1; no. 43 (3 November 1907) pp. 49–51; nos. 26–7 (14 July 1907) pp. 16–17; no. 3 (15 January 1908) p. 24; Ryabushinsky, *Velikaya*, vol. 1, pp. 117–133; vol. 2, pp. 365–7.

91. *MY*, no. 29 (7 October 1906) pp. 35–6; nos 26–7 (14 July 1907) pp. 16–17 for Trubetskoy's comment that relations with Germany were very good despite the Franco-Russian alliance and that if agreement were achieved with London 'Russia would have no one and nothing to fear'; no. 1 (3 January 1909) p. 11; Ryabushinsky *Velikaya*, vol. 1, pp. 83, 94–6, 100–101.

92. Ryabushinsky, ibid., vol. 1, pp. 31, 104; *MY*, no. 13 (27 March 1910) pp. 17–18; no. 49 (12 December 1909) p. 17; no. 45 (15 November 1908) p. 27.

93. *MY*, no. 45 (15 November 1908) pp. 16–17, 21–24; no. 1 (3 January 1909) pp. 10–13; no. 48 (5 December 1908) pp. 9–14; no. 49 (12 December 1909) pp. 15–18; Ryabushinsky, *Velikaya*, vol. 2, pp. 324–5.

94. *MY*, no. 44, (7 November 1909), pp. 7–11; no. 49 (12 December 1909) p. 15; Struve (ed.), *Pamyati*, pp. 154–7 quoting from Trubetskoy's letters from 1910 to his friend Professor M.E. Edzekowski.

95. A.M. Zayonchkovsky, *Podgotovka*, pp. 31–46, 66–7, 68–78, 183–257; Rostunov, *Russkiy front*, pp. 63–95; A. Kersnovsky, *Istoriya Russkoy Armii*, 4 vols (1935) vol. 3, pp. 619–24.

96. Rostunov, *Russkiy front*, pp. 77–81; Kersnovsky, *Istoriya*, p. 620; MDSH, Carton 7N 1485, 'Rapport sur un Séjour à Varsovie', October 1902, Capt Mahon, pp. 36–7 for a discussion between a French officer and the staff of the Warsaw District about an offensive from the Western Vistula area; Zayonchkovsky, *Podgotovka*, pp. 39, 46, 73–5.

97. Zayonchkovsky, *Podgotovka*, pp. 66, 164; *LN*, vol. 2, Protocols des Conférences militaires Franco-Russes, Huitième Conférence, pp. 427–8; MDSH, Carton 7N 1485, 'Rapport', Capt. Mahon, pp. 42–3; Russian respect for the Austrian forces grew somewhat in the period

immediately before the war; even so, in comparison to Germany's troops they were despised; MDSH, Carton 7N 1485, 'Rapport Sommaire de Lieut, Colonel d'Infanterie breveté Janin à l'issue de sa mission à l'Academie de Guerre Nicolas à St Petersburg 1910–1911', p. 3: 'the true enemy, hated and detested in Austria'; MDSH, Carton 7N 1535, 'Conference sur l'Armée Russe 1912–1913', Capt Langlois, p. 39 for French fears that Russian feelings about Austria and Germany were distorting good strategy.

98.  MDSH, for example Carton 7N 1535, 'Note sur l'Action Militaire de la Russie en Europe', 2eme Bureau, August 1912, for French fears of a German spoiling offensive in the east; in May 1912 Zhilinsky, the Russian CGS, told Knox that 'though a passive attitude on the part of the German army corps was possible, Russia could not count on it', PRO, FO 371, 1470, no. 26329, Knox to War Office, 28 May 1912, pp. 76–8; for examples of French thinking on a Russian offensive see, MDSH, Carton 7N 1535, 'Note sur le Stationnement de l' Armée Russe en temps de Paix et sur sa Concentration', 2eme Bureau, December 1909, pp. 4–5; 'Note sur l' Action Militaire de la Russie en Europe', August 1912, 3eme Bureau, pp. 3–5; 'Note pour le General Chef d' Etat', July 1913, 3eme Bureau, p.9.

99.  Rozental', *Diplomaticheskaya*, pp. 217–226; MDSH, Carton 7N 1477, Moulin to 2eme Bureau, 27 January 1906; Laguiche to Dupont, 12 February 1914. The General Staff appreciation, not dated but written in December 1913 or January 1914, is to be found without a page number among press extracts at the back of Carton 7N 1478.

100.  MDSH, Carton 7N 1535, 'Note sur l'Action Militaire de la Russie en Europe', August 1912, 3eme Bureau, p. 6; Rostunov, *Russkiy front*, pp. 75–7; Kokovtsov, the Minister of Finance, for instance had already stated in February 1910 that, in view of the rapid improvement in the financial situation, 'it was time for Russia to rest from borrowing', PRO, FO 371, 978, no. 7611, p. 431. Pogrebinsky, *Finansy*, pp. 73–5, 81–84.

101.  PRO, FO 371, 979, no. 12149, Nicolson to Grey, 7 April 1910, p. 210; no. 32998, O'Beirne to Grey, 8 September 1910, p. 432. FO 371, 1746, no. 41222, Knox to Buchanan, 27 August 1913, p. 212; MDSH, Carton 7N 1535, 'Conférence sur l'Armée Russe 1912–1913', Capt Langlois, p.40; Carton 7N 1485, Janin to Vignal, no. 16, 9 May 1911; 'Rapport Sommaire de Lieut Colonel Janin . . . 1910–1911' pp. 2–3; carton 7N 1478, Laguiche to 2eme Bureau, 26 June/9 July 1914 quoting Sukhomilinov's comments about how good Franco–Russian

relations were. *M O* 3rd Series, vol. 2, Ignat'yev to Yanushkevich, (27 March/9 April 1914) pp. 266–7.

102. MDSH, Carton 7N 1535, Laguiche to 2eme Bureau 16/29 March 1913; *MO*, 3rd Series, vol. 1, no. 77, Ignat'yev to Danilov (22–29 January 1914) p. 86.

103. MDSH, Carton 7N 1535, 'Conférence sur l' Armée Russe', Langlois, p. 40; Carton 7N 1485, Janin to Vignal, no. 1, 14/27 October 1910; Carton 7N 1478, Laguiche to 2eme Bureau, 1/14 December 1912; PRO, FO 371, 981, no. 45701, Buchanan to Grey, 15 December 1910, p. 361.

104. MDSH, Carton 7N 1485, Janin to Vignal, no. 4, 27 November/10 December 1910.

105. MDSH, Carton 7N 1478, Laguiche to Vignal, 6/19 December 1912; Carton 7N 1535, 'Observations sur l' Armée Russe', Capt Buchenschuth, 2eme Parti, 3eme Chapitre, p. 261.

106. Yu.N.Danilov, *Rossiya*, pp. 87–9. *MO*, 3rd Series, vol.2, no. 366, Nakashidze to Danilov (23 April/6 May 1914) pp. 475–8 on the extreme likelihood of the German initial offensive's violation of Belgian neutrality.

107. *MO*, 2nd Series, vol. 20ii, Ignat'yev to Zhilinsky (15/28 April 1912) pp. 108–110.

108. Zayonchkovsky, *Podgotovka*, pp. 279, 311–14. *LN*, vol. 2, p. 423; Kersnovsky *Istoriya*, pp. 624–5.

109. Kersnovsky, *Istoriya*, pp. 622–3. Zayonchkovsky, *Podgotovka* p. 311. N. Stone, *The Eastern Front 1914–1917* (1975) pp. 33–6.

110. The best work on the Russian navy in the pre-war era is K.F. Shatsillo, *Russkiy Imperialism i razvitiye flota* (1968); PRO, FO 371, 1470, no. 27674, O'Beirne to Grey, 25 June 1912, p. 34; no. 27675, Grenfell to O'Beirne, 22 June 1912, pp. 40–2.

111. Shatsillo *Imperializm* pp. 44–160; *KA*, 'Konstantinopol' i Prolivy', vol. 6, 1924, pp. 48–76; vol. 7 (1924) pp. 32–54; *MO*, 2nd Series, vol. 20i, no. 299, Draft of the Franco-Russian Naval Convention, pp. 295–6; no. 301 (3/16 June 1912) Minutes of the Conference between the Russian and French Chiefs of the Naval General Staff, pp. 298–302, *MO*, 3rd Series, vol. 1, no. 295, Journal of Special Conference (8/21 February 1914) pp. 663–91; no. 325 Sazonov to Stein (12/25 February 1914) pp. 432–5; vol 2, no. 384 (25 April/8 May 1914) Sazonov to Benckendorff, pp. 510–11; K. Robbins, *Sir Edward Grey* (1971) pp. 283–5; PRO, FO 371, 1745, no. 51200, Bagge to Grey, 5 November 1913, p. 58 on the rapid progress of the shipyards in

Southern Russia; A.J. Marder, *From the Dreadnought to Scapa Flow* (1965) vol 2, pp. 20–41.

112.  PRO, FO 371, 1470, no. 35876, Grenfell to Buchanan, August 21, 1912, p. 382; 1743, no. 1685, Buchanan to Grey, 9 January 1913, pp. 219ff; 1746, no. 41224, Grenfell to Buchanan, 10 July 1913, p. 165; no. 41225, O'Beirne to Grey, 4 September 1913, p. 167. A.A. Lieven, *Dukh i ditsiplina nashego flota* (1914) pp. 23–8, 34, 41, 48–60, 86–9.

113.  On the army between 1906 and 1914 see for example Zayonchkovsky, *Padgotovka*, pp. 83–154; Rostunov, *Russkiy front*, pp. 35–41, 42–59; Kersnovsky, *Istoriya* pp. 594–617; W.T. Wilfong, *Rebuilding the Russian Army*. The British Embassy's annual reports on Russia often contained useful information on the army: see in particular PRO, FO 371, 1214, no. 11045, 22 March 1911, pp. 393–8; 727, no. 6057, pp. 488–90; Knox's fullest reports are in PRO, FO 371, 1744, no. 10994, Buchanan to Grey, 6 March 1913, pp. 327–8 and 1746, no.41222, Knox to Buchanan, 27 August 1913, pp. 212–47; the two best French surveys on the Russian Army, both in MDSH, Carton 7N 1535, are 'Conférence sur l'Armée Russe 1912–13' by Captain Langlois and the anonymous 'Notice Statistique sur l' Armée Russe'.

114.  Rostunov, *Russkiy front*, pp. 58–9; Zayonchkovsky, *Podgotovka*, pp. 93–4. MDSH, Carton 7N 1535, 'Note sur les Projets de Renforcement de l' Armée Russe', 6 July 1914; Carton 7N 1478, Laguiche to 2eme Bureau, 16/29 March 1913.

115.  MDSH, Carton 7N 1485, Matton to 2eme Bureau, 11/24 January 1910.

116.  PRO, FO 371, 727, no. 6057, Annual Report for 1909, pp. 488–9. Rostunov, *Russkiy front*, pp. 38,40.

117.  PRO, FO 371, 1467, no. 8229, Knox to Buchanan, February 22 1912, p. 489.

118.  For example the activities of A.A. Polivanov, Sukhomlinov's deputy; Polivanov combined great ability with a considerable taste for intrigue.

119.  On the failings of Russian generals and, in particular, the faults of the General Staff Academy see: MDSH, Carton 7N 1535, 'Conférence sur l' Armée Russe 1907; Colonel Pierre, pp. 27–9, 52–3; 'Conférence sur l'Arme Russe 1912–1913', Capt Langlois, pp. 5, 14, 24–6; 'Notice Statistique sur l' Armée Russe, 1913', anon. p.36; Carton 7N, 1485, Janin to Vignal, no. 1, 14/27 October 1910; Zayonchkovsky, pp. 96–7; Kersnovsky, *Istoriya*, pp. 611–14.

120. Sukhomlinov's statement is quoted in Zayonchkovsky, *Podgotovka*, p. 87; Polivanov's Commission for the supply of artillery shells planned for a war lasting from 2–6 months, Rostunov, *Russkiy front*, pp. 96–100; Zayonchkovsky, *Podgotovka*, p. 287 editor's note. On German views on the length of a future war see B.M. Shaposhnikov, *Mozg Armii*, vol. 1, pp. 236–40.

121. Kenez, 'A Profile of the Prerevolutionary Officer Corps', p. 146; N.N. Golovin, *Voyenniya usiliya Rossii v mirovoy voyne*, 2 vols (1939) vol. 1, pp. 10, 15–19, 37, 45–7.

122. MDSH, Carton 7N 1486, 'Rapport du Capitaine d' Infanterie Jacquinot sur un Stage de Six Mois accompli dans l' Armée Russe' (1913).

123. MDSH, Carton 7N 1535, 'Conférence sur l' Armée Russe', Langlois, pp. 23–4; 'Notice Statistique', anon., pp. 14, 25–7; Carton 7N 1486, 'Rapport du Capitaine Lelong detaché a la Brigade de Chasseurs de Suwalki sur les premiers impressions receuillies au Cours de son Stage', pp. 5–7.

124. A.A. Brusilov, *Moi vospominaniya* (1963) pp. 51–2; A.I. Denikin, *The Career of a Tsarist Officer* (1975) pp. 209–10; PRO, FO 371, 516, no. 10737, pp. 79–80 contains Kuropatkin's interview with Hamilton and Wyndham, the British Military Attaché, which is an interesting document; MDSH, Carton 7N 1478, Letter of a Russian officer to Captain Engasser, 27 January/9 February 1913 about the officers' attempts to explain to their men the significance of events in the Balkans.

125. For Grigorovich's comment see General Dobrorol'sky, 'La Mobilisation de l' Armée Russe en 1914', *Revue d'Histoire de la Guerre Mondiale* (1923) p. 147 ('Our fleet isn't in a state to measure up to the German Fleet . . . Kronstadt will not save the capital from bombardment'); for Sukhomlinov, see Basily, *Memoirs*, pp. 90–1.

126. P.V. Petrov (ed.), *Vöyennyy Sobesednik* (1910) is an excellent source on the ideology instilled through the Cadet Corps, especially pp. 1–55; there is a good general servey of military education up to 1880 in Maj. General Lalayev, *Istoricheskiy ocherk voyenno–uchebnykh zavedeniy* (1880) though it concentrates more on the academic than the moral aspects of education; D.N. Lyovshin, *Pazheyskiy Yego Imperatorskogo Velichestva Korpus za sto let* (1902) is of great interest, as is M. Maksimovsky, *Istoricheskiy ocherk razvitiya Glavnogo Inzhenernogo Uchilishcha* (1869); Lyovshin and Maksimovsky's works complement each other, the first covering the education of the social élite of the

army at the Pages' Corps and the latter the education of its intellectual élite in the Engineering School, most generals coming from one or other of these two groups; CUBA, MS von Dreyer, *Memoirs*, pp. 1–16 is interesting about his education in the military virtues in the 2nd Orenburg Cadet Corps.

127. Lieven, *Dukh i ditsiplina*, pp. 13–18, 34, 51, 72.

128. P. Kenez, 'The Ideology of the White Movement', *Soviet Studies* (1980) no. 1, pp. 58–82; CUBA, MS. A. Levitsky, *Lichniye vospominaniya o russko-yaponskoy voyne*', pp. 130–4.

129. MDSH, Carton 7N 1478, Wehrlin to 2eme Bureau, 8/21 November 1912. Laguiche to 2eme Bureau, 30 November/13 December 1912; Danilov, *Rossiya v mirovoy voyne*, p. 25; *NV*, no. 13303 (25 March/7 April 1913) pp. 2–4. No. 13304 (26 March/8 April 1913) pp. 2–4

130. MDSH, Carton 7N 1535, 'Conférence sur l'Armée', Capt Langlois, pp. 38–9; 'Notice Statistique', 1913, anon., p. 22; Carton 7N 1485, Janin to Vignal, no. 6, 5 January 1911 and no. 12, 4/17 March 1911; Carton 7N 1478, Laguiche to 2eme Bureau, 15/28 November and 28 November/11 December 1912, records, however, that some generals now believed Francis Ferdinand to be less bellicose towards Russia than they had previously imagined.

131. MDSH, Carton 7N 1485, Janin to Vignal, no. 2, 30 October/ 12 November 1910.

132. MDSH, Carton 7N 1535, 'Obeservations sur l' Armée Russe', Buchenschuth 2eme Parti, 3 eme Chapitre, pp. 257–8; 'Notice Statistique', 1913, anon., pp. 22–3; Lambsdorff, *Die Militarbevollmachtigen*, p. 402.

133. MDSH, Carton 7N 1535, 'Conférence sur l' Armée Russe', Langlois, p. 39; 'Observations sur l' Armée Russe', Buchenschuth, p. 266; 'Notice Statistique 1913', p. 55; Carton 7N 1478, Laguiche to 2eme Bureau, 27 March/9 April 1914.

134. MDSH, Carton 7N 1477, Moulin to 2eme Bureau, 10 December 1906; Carton 7N 1478, Laguiche to 2eme Bureau, 1/14 February 1913; Wehrlin to 2eme Bureau, 16 February/1 March 1913; see Carton 7N 1535, Matton to 2eme Bureau, 13/26 June 1909 and Lambsdorff *Die Militarbevollmachtigen*, p. 272 for military suspicion of England.

135. Sukhomlinov in fact dedicated his memoirs to the German Emperor.

136. MDSH, 7N 1477, Moulin to 2eme Bureau, 1 December 1906,

speaks of Sukhomlinov as an old friend with whom he had an enthusiastic discussion about war with Germany in 1902; 'Notice Statistique 1913', pp. 30, 53; in contrast to most French sources Laguiche
was not impressed by Sukhomlinov though he never doubted his
loyalty to France; Carton 7N 1478, Laguiche to Dupont, 30 January/
12 February 1914; Sukhomlinov, *Vospominaniya*, pp. 53, 91, 103.

137.  Sukhomlinov, *Vospominaniya*, pp. 200–1; PRO, FO 371, 2092,
no. 11456, Buchanan to Grey, 15 March 1914, p. 15.

138.  MDSH, Carton 7N 1485, Janin to Vignal, no. 1, 14/27 October 1910.

139.  MDSH, Carton 7N 1478, Laguiche to 2eme Bureau, 26 June/
9 July 1914.

140.  On the Duma see G. Hosking, *The Russian Constitutional Experiment* (1973). On the press H.W. Williams, *Russia of the Russians*,
pp. 99–125 provides a useful survey.

141.  On the Duma Right see H. Rogger, 'The Formation of the
Russian Right 1900–6', *California Slavic Studies*, vol. 3 (1964) pp. 66–
94; 'Was there a Russian Fascism? The Union of the Russian People',
*Journal of Modern History*, vol. 36 (1964) pp. 398–415; for the Right's
views on foreign policy see Bestuzhev, *Bor'ba*, pp. 71, 276, 297–8, 306,
314, 318–20; *Istoricheskiye Zapiski*, no. 75, pp. 50, 64, 80; *SOGD*, 3
Sozyv, 2 Sessiya, cols 1273–41 and 2652–8 for Purishkevich's fury at
blows to Russian pride, desire for peace but belief in the inevitability
of a future war of the Austrian succession; cols 2670–1 for G.A. Shech-
kov's assertion of Russia's role in the Balkans; N.E. Markov's speech
of 6 June 1914 (OS) *SOGD*, 4 Sozyv, 2 Sessiya, cols 420–31 is reprinted in part in Golder, *Documents*, pp. 24–8.

142.  The Social Democrats spoke in most debates on foreign policy. See I.P. Pokrovsky's speeches in *SOGD*, 3 Sozyv, 2 Sessiya, cols
2632–4; 3 Sessiya, cols 2813–22; 4 Sessiya, cols. 3337–43 and those of
A.I. Chkenkheli, *SOGD*, 4 Sozyv, 1 Sessiya, cols 1058–79; 2 Sessiya,
cols 393–411, 472–5; K. Chkheidze's speech in a defence debate,
*SOGD*, 3 Sozyv, 2 Sessiya, cols 1257–60 ('we will always be against
the army') is also interesting.

143.  *Grazhdanin*, no.2, (10 January 1910 [OS]) p. 13.

144.  PRO, FO 371, 1743, no. 10175, Annual Report for 1912, p.
463; MDSH, Carton 7N 1478, Laguiche to Vignal, 18/31 January
1913 and 30 March/12 April 1913; informed French military circles
were much more scared (and realistic) about the dangers of revolution should war occur than was the ambassador, Paleologue; MDSH,

Carton 7N 1478, Laguiche to 2eme Bureau, 21 April/4 May 1914; Carton 7N 1485, Janin to Vignal, no. 13, 18/31 March 1911; no. 21, 20 July 1911; DDF, 3rd Series, vol. X, no. 267.

145. HHSA, P.A.X. 139, Czernin to Berchtold, Report 40c, 24/11 October 1913.

146. HHSA, P.A.X. 138, Szapary to Berchtold, Report 19A, 1 May/18 April 1912; 140, Czernin to Berchtold, Report 8A, 13 February/31 January 1914; Basily, *Memoirs*, p. 90.

147. The essential basis for generalisations about the parties' attitudes is study of the speeches of their representatives in the foreign policy debates in the Duma; Hosking, *Constitutional Experiment*, pp. 215–42 provides a survey of Duma attitudes to foreign policy as do Bestuzhev's two works; on the Kadets see, U. Liszkowski, *Zwischen Liberalismus und Imperialismus* (1974) and P.N. Milyukov, *Political Memoirs* (1967); on the Octobrists, J.F. Hutchinson, 'The Octobrists and the Future of Imperial Russia as a Great Power', *SEER*, vol. 50, 1972, pp. 220–37; L. Menashe, 'A Liberal with Spurs: Alexander Guchkov, A Russian Bourgeois in Politics', *RR*, vol. 26 (1967) pp. 38–53; B.C. Pinchuk, *The Octobrists in the Third Duma* (1974) Ch.3; on the Nationalists see R. Edelman, *Gentry Politics on the eve of the Revolution* (1980); Bernard Pares wrote a number of useful reports for the British Foreign Office on the parties' views on foreign policy, see PRO, FO 371, 512, no. 30901, 4 September 1908, pp. 532ff; 979, no. 30814, 22 August 1910, pp. 402ff; 2090, no. 3312, 13 January 1914, pp. 201ff.

148. See Prince E.N. Trubetskoy's comments on this in *MY*, no. 15 (1 July 1906 [OS]) pp. 6–9 and G.N. Trubetskoy's in no. 44 (7 November 1909 [OS]) p.7.

149. *SOGD*, 4 Sozyv, 2 Sessiya, cols 351–65.

150. See G.N. Trubetskoy's comments on Russian nervousness in *MY*, no. 48, (5 December 1909 [OS]) pp. 1–8 which are borne out by the exaggerated fears expressed in a series of anonymous articles entitled 'Pan-Islamism' in *MY*, nos 34, 41 and 42 (1 September, 20, 27 October 1907) pp. 13–24, 15–29, 28–37 respectively.

151. PRO, FO 371, 976, no. 159, Annual Report for 1909, p. 415; *MO*, 3rd Series, vol. 1, No. 144, Izvol'sky to Sazonov (30/17 January 1914) p. 167.

152. PRO, FO 371, 512, no. 30901, 4 September 1908, p.8 of Pares' memorandum.

153. Liszkowski, *Liberalismus*, pp. 13–37; W.G. Rosenberg, *Liberals in the Russian Revolution* (1974) pp. 11–38.

154. Liszkowski, *Liberalismus,* pp. 38–9, 50–6.

155. Ibid., pp., 240–54; Milyukov, *Memoirs,* pp. 189–91.

156. Liszkowski, *Liberalismus,* pp. 38–9, 45, 86, 94, 97, 151; Dr S. Galai was kind enough to show me a collection of private letters of I.I. Petrunkevich, the Kadet Party's Chairman, some of which are published in *Jahrbücher fur Gechichte Osteuropas,* vol. 29i (1981) pp. 1–29; these bring out Petrunkevich's humanity, loathing of nationalism and fear of the consequences of war.

157. Ibid., pp. 53, 86–92, 111–22, 157–9, 190–201, 232–8; Milyukov, *Memoirs,* pp. 166–90, 238–89; Milyukov sharply attacked Sazonov in March 1911, above all because of suspicion that Potsdam symbolised a return to secret 'dynastic' and pro-German diplomacy; *SOGD*, 3 Sozyv, 4 Sessiya, cols. 3300–30.

158. *SOGD*, 4 Sozyv, 3 Sessiya, col. 1019 for Milyukov's comment that the nationalists and the Kadet opposition had changed roles'.

159. *Rech's* editorials of no. 162 (17/30 June 1914) and from no. 185, (12/25 July) to no. 193 (22 July/4 August) provide the best day-to-day guide to Milyukov's views during the crisis.

160. *Rech,* no. 181 (6/19 July 1914) p.1; Milyukov, *Memoirs* p.352 ('the war occurred as a result of Serbian megalomania'); Hosking, *Constitutional Experiment* p.237.

161. Liszkowski, *Liberalismus,* pp. 186–9; for a Progressist and Right Kadet view on Balkan affairs in 1913 see, *Interesy na Balkanakh i pravitel' stvennoye soobshcheniye* (1913) A.N. Bryanchaninov (ed.).

162. *MY*, no. 43 (1 November 1908) pp. 6–13 published a talk by V.A. Maklakov entitled 'Serbiya i Slavyanskiy vopros'; PRO, FO 371, 733, no. 5128, Whitehead to Grey (4 February 1909) p. 316 records that when in Belgrade at a banquet Maklakov proposed a toast to Greater Serbia and encouraged Serb territorial ambitions; *NV*, no. 13369 (1/14 April 1914) p. 4 for Maklakov's views on Austrian persecution of Ruthenes.

163. R. Pipes, *Struve: Liberal on the Right 1905-1944* (1980) pp. 72, 87.

164. P.B. Struve, 'Velikaya Rossiya: Iz razmyshleniy o probleme russkogo moguchestva', *Russkaya Mysl'* (January 1908) 2, pp. 143–57; 'Otrykvi o gosudarstve i natsii,' *Russkaya Mysl'* (May 1908) 2, pp. 187–93; 'Unizheniye Rossii', *MY*, no. 12, (21 March 1909 [OS]) pp.5–8.

165. P.B. Struve, 'Velikaya Rossiya i Svyataya Rus', *Russkaya Mysl'*, (December 1914) pp. 176–80.

166. See especially P.B. Struve, 'Intelligentsiya i revolyutsiya', pp.

156–75 in *Vekhi* (1909).

167. Edelman, *Gentry Politics*, pp.7–10, 37–9, 144–6, 191–6.

168. Edelman, *Gentry Politics*, pp. 44, 79, 191–2, 216–24; M.C. Brainerd, 'The Octobrists and the Gentry, 1905–1907: Leaders and Followers' pp. 67–94 in L.H. Haimson (ed.), *The Politics of Rural Russia, 1905–1914* (1979).

169. *SOGD*, 3 Sozyv, 2 Sessiya, col. 2674.

170. Menashe, 'Guchkov', pp. 43,52; Hutchinson, 'Octobrists', pp. 220–37. Pinchuk, *Octobrists*, pp. 12–15, 65.

171. PRO, FO 371, 1496, no. 23436, Knox to O'Beirne, 27 May 1912, p. 301.

172. Quoted by Hutchinson, 'Octobrists', p. 225.

173. *MO*, 2nd series, vol. 20ii, no.631, Artamonov to Danilov (5 September/23 August 1912) p.158.

174. CUBA, MS. Shebeko, contains Berchtold's reflections on Sazonov's memoirs, see p. 10.

175. PRO, FO 371, 512, no. 30901, p. 4 of Pares' report of 4 September 1908; no. 28438, Bayley to O'Beirne, 8 December 1908, on Dmowski.

176. PRO, FO 371, 517 no. 23176, Memorandum by Hardinge, pp. 345–6.

177. PRO, FO 371, 517, no. 19622, O'Beirne to Grey, 2 June 1908, p. 412.

178. PRO, FO 371, 514, no. 3643, p.17 of the Annual Report for 1907.

179. PRO, FO 371, 979, no. 32998, O'Beirne to Grey, 8 September 1910, p. 48.

180. PRO, FO 371, 981, no. 40354, O'Beirne to Grey, 28 October 1910, p. 188.

181. Lambsdorff, *Die Militarbevollmachtigen*, p. 317.

182. *DDF*, 3rd Series, vol. 5, no. 105.

183. Williams, *Russia*, p. 107.

184. For *Novoye Vremya's* editorial policy, readership and views on internal policy see D.R. Costello, 'Novoe Vremia and the Conservative Dilemma 1911–1914', *RR*, vol. 37i, January 1978, pp. 30–50; typical of the confusion caused to diplomats were the British statements that *Novoye Vremya* was the leading pro-Entente paper and its chief columnist, M.O. Menshikov, 'the most eminent publicist' for a Russo-German *entente*: see PRO, FO 371, 1469, no. 29840, O'Beirne to Grey, 5 July 1912, p. 444; in fact the British exaggerated the consistency of

Menshikov's pro-German views.

185. *NV*, no. 13580 (1/14 January 1914) p.2.

186. *NV*, no. 11573 (1/14 June 1908) p.3.

187. Bestuzhev, *Bor'ba*, pp. 183–4.

188. *NV*, no. 11784 (1/14 January 1909) p. 2.

189. *NV*, no. 11857 (16/29 March 1909) p. 2

190. *NV*, no. 11859 (18/31 March 1909) p. 4.

191. PRO, FO 371, 979, no. 8691, Nicolson to Grey, 5 March 1909; p. 31 reporting the words of Wesselitsky, *Novoye Vremya's* influential correspondent in London.

192. For example *NV*, no. 12997 (20 May/2 June 1912) p. 4; no. 13221 (1/14 January 1913) p. 2.

193. For example *NV*, no. 13580 (1/14 January 1914) p.4; no. 13585 (6/19 January 1914) pp. 2–3; no. 13694 (28 April/11 May 1914) p. 3.

194. *NV*, no. 13742 (16/29 June 1914) p. 2.

195. *NV*, no. 13638 (1/14 March 1914) p. 4.

196. B. Bonwetsch, 'Handelspolitik und Industrialisierung' in D. Geyer (ed.), *Wirtschaft und Gesellschaft im vorrevolutionaren Russland* (1975) pp. 288–93; Bestuzhev, *Bor'ba*, pp. 65–7; P.A. Buryshkin, *Moskva kupecheskaya*, (1954) pp. 77–8, 184, 267; J.L. West, *The Moscow Progressists*; pp. 139–40, 170–1, 351; R.A. Roosa, 'The Association of Industry and Trade 1906–1914'. (Ph.D., Columbia University, 1967) pp. 178–197, 548–623.

197. West, *Progressists*, pp. 223–40.

198. Ibid, pp. 312–35.

199. Buryshkin, *Moskva*, pp. 280–1.

200. For the views of Bethmann-Hollweg, Jagow and Tschirschsky see: K.H. Jarausch, *The Enigmatic Chancellor* (1973) p. 163. Jagow to Lichnowsky, 18 July 1914 in I. Geiss, *July 1914 (1974)* p. 123; F. Fischer, *War of Illusions* (1975) p. 437.

201. West, *Progressists*, pp. 305, 325; Buryshkin, *Moskva*, pp. 294–5; R.A. Roosa, 'The Association' pp. 186, 581–623.

202. PRO, FO, 371, 726, no. 30738, O'Beirne to Grey, 12 August 1909 contains the record of an interesting interview with Kokovtsov on these lines.

203. *MY*, no. 44 (7 November 1909) pp. 7–11; P.B. Struve, *Pamyati*, pp. 154–7.

204. CUBA, MS. M.M. Kovalevsky, *Vospominaniya*, pp. 79–80.

205. Danilov, *Rossiya v mirovoy voyne*, p. 112.

5. THE JULY CRISIS

4   1. L. Albertini, *The Origins of the War of 1914* (1952) vol. 2, pp. 82–6

2. *MO*, 3rd Series, vol. 3, nos 280, 281, Hartwig to Sazonov (16/3 June 1914) pp. 327–30; vol. 5, Artamonov to QMG, 17/4 June 1914, pp. 453–8.

3. *MO*, 3rd Series, vol. 3, no. 284, Artamonov to QMG (16/3 June 1914) pp. 335–6; vol. 5, no. 9, Strandtmann to Sazonov (23/10 July 1914) pp. 8–10; vol. 1, no. 7, Hartwig to Sazonov (14/1 January 1914) pp. 8–9.

4. *Pièces diplomatiques relatives aux Antecedents de la Guerre de 1914*, translated by C. Jordan (1922) vol. 2, no. 73, Szapary to Berchtold, 27 July 1914, pp. 162–6; on the assassination see V. Dedijer, *The Road to Sarajevo* (1966) especially Ch XVII.

5. L. Albertini, *Origins*, vol. 2, p. 82.

6. *Pièces Diplomatiques*, vol. 3, no. 6, Szapary to Berchtold, 29 July 1914, pp. 17–19.

7. *MO*, 3rd Series, vol. 4, no. 248, Shebeko to Sazonov (16/3 July 1914) pp. 299–311; *British Documents on the Origins of the War*, G.P. Gooch and H. Temperley (eds), 11 vols (London 1927–38) vol. XI, no. 60, Buchanan to Grey (18 July 1914) p. 47.

8. Shebeko, *Souvenirs*, p. 218; *MO*, 3rd Series, vol. 4, no. 132, Shebeko to Sazonov (8 July/25 June 1914) p. 175; no. 235, Shebeko to Sazonov, (15/2 July 1914) pp. 283–4; no. 272, Daily Record (18/5 July 1914) p. 329; *BD*, vol. XI, no. 676, Bunsen to Grey, (1 September 1914) pp. 356ff.

9. CUBA, MS. Bark, 7, pp. 1–6.

10. *BD*, vol. XI, no. 101, Buchanan to Grey, 24 July 1914, pp.80–1. For French activity in St Petersburg during the crisis see Albertini, *Origins*, vol. 2, pp. 182, 192–7, 294, 536–7, 583–610.

11. The source for the following pages are the memoirs of Peter Bark, Imperial Russia's last Minister of Finance; Bark, a reliable source, recounts the conversations in the Council in such detail that either he must have kept a very full diary or he had access to the Council's minutes when writing his memoirs.

12. CUBA, MS. Bark, 7, pp. 7–13.

13. Ibid, Ch 6, p. 13; Ch 7, pp. 7,17, HHSA, P.A.X., 135, Report 2D, Berchtold to Aehrenthal, 17/4 January 1910 on Krivoshein's skill and influence.

14. CUBA, MS. Bark, 7, pp. 13–16.

15. CUBA, MS. Bark, 7, pp. 17–22; *MO*, 3rd Series, vol. 5, no. 19, Special Journal of the Council of Ministers, 24/11 July 1914, pp. 38ff.

16. *MO*, 3rd Series, vol. 5. nos 35 and 37, Strandtmann to Sazonov, (24/11 July 1914) pp. 53–5; no. 75, Strandtmann to Sazonov (25/12 July 1914) pp. 92–3.

17. Albertini, *Origins*, vol. 2, pp. 352–62.

18. *MO*, 3rd Series, vol. 5, no. 97, Yanushkevich to Sazonov (25/12 July 1914) pp. 98–113.

19. *MO*, 3rd Series, vol. 5, no. 79, Journal of the Committee of the General Staff (25/12 July 1914) pp. 95ff.

20. *Pièces Diplomatiques*, vol. 2, no. 93, Szapary to Berchtold, 28 July 1914, pp. 193–4.

21. *BD*, vol. xi, no. 105, Grey to Buchanan, 25 July 1914, p. 84.

22. *Documents Allemands relatifs à l' Origine de la Guerre* (1922) vol. 1, no. 238, Pourtales to Jagow, 26 July 1914, pp. 295–6.

23. *MO*, 3rd Series, vol. 5, no. 224, Daily Record, pp. 212–4.

24. Ibid, p. 213; *Documents Allemands*, vol. 2, no. 342, Bethmann-Hollweg to Pourtales (29 July 1914) p. 76.

25. Rosen, *Forty Years*, vol. 2, pp. 163–4, 170, 188.

26. *MO*, 3rd Series, vol. 5, no. 251, Savinsky to Sazonov (29/16 July 1914) p. 234.

27. Ibid, no. 154, M.N. Giers to Sazonov (27/14 July 1914) pp. 168–70.

28. L.C.F. Turner, 'The Russian Mobilisation in 1914', *Journal of Contemporary History*, 3, I (1968).

29. PRO, FO 371, 2092, no. 10412, Annual Report for 1913, p. 53.

30. See MDSH, Carton 7N 1535, Matton to 2eme Bureau, 13/26 June 1909 for Sukhomlinov's comment on this in June 1909.

31. Zayonchkovsky, *Podgotovka*, pp. 271ff.

32. Ibid.

33. MDSH, Carton 7N 1535, 'Les caractèristiques de l'armée Russe', Wehrlin, pp. 20–1; 'Conférence sur l' Armée Russe', Langlois, pp. 33–4; 'Notice Statistique', pp. 47–50.

34. MDSH, Carton 7N 1478, Wehrlin to 2eme Bureau, 23 November/6 December 1912; Laguiche to 2 eme Bureau, 30 November/13 December 1912.

35. MDSH, Carton 7N 1535, 'Conférence sur l'Armée Russe', Langlois, pp. 10–11; 'Conférence sur l'Armée Russe', 1907, Capt Pierre, p. 8; 'Conférence sur l'Armée Russe', 1911, Capt Gros, p. 12; 'Notice Statistique', p. 11; Danilov, *Rossiya v mirovoy voyne*, pp. 14–15;

Rostunov, *Russkiy front*, pp. 46–8.

36. Kcrsnovsky, vol. 3, pp. 631ff; Dobrorol'sky, 'Mobilisation' pp. 65–7; A.I. Denikin, *The Career of a Tsarist Officer*, pp. 221–3.

37. MDSH, Carton 7N 1535, 'Les caractèristiques de l' Armée Russe', Wehrlin, pp. 16, 21; the French were, in 1914, concerned above all at the inadequacy of the lines into the Warsaw District; Carton 7N 1478, Wehrlin to 2eme Bureau, 15/28 March 1914.

38. *MO*, 3rd Series, vol. 5, no. 243, Shebeko to Sazonov (29/16 July 1914) p. 229; no. 99 (26/13 July 1914) Berens to Rusin, pp. 128–30 felt that even by 26 July Berlin had gone too far to draw back, though he believed that if the Germans were able to retreat without undermining their ally they might well be pleased to do so.

39. Geiss, *July 1914*, pp. 317–22.

40. Albertini, *Origins*, vol. 3, pp. 28–31.

CONCLUSION

1. *NV*, no. 13777 (21 July/3 August 1914) p. 3.

# Select Bibliography

ARCHIVAL SOURCES

*Columbia University. Bakhmetev Archive (New York)*
P.A. BARK, unpublished memoirs and private papers.
V. N. KOKOVTSOV, unpublished first volume of memoirs.
M.M. KOVALEVSKY, unpublished memoirs.
*Haus-Hof-und-Staatsarchiv* (Vienna)
Politisches Archiv x,
Russland, Kartons 134–140, correspondence of the Austrian Embassy in Petersburg 1909–14.
*Ministère de Defense. Service Historique* (Vincennes)
Cartons 7N 1477, 1478, 1485, 1486, 1535, correspondence of France's military attachés in Petersburg 1905–14; correspondence and reports of French officers visiting or seconded to the Russian army 1903–14; French General Staff appreciations of the nature, strengths, weaknesses and readiness for war of the Russian army 1907–14.
*Public Record Office* (London)
PRO FO 371, correspondence of the British Embassy in Petersburg 1906–14; of the British Foreign Office and of other British missions overseas.
*Otdel rukopisey biblioteki imeni Lenina* (Moscow)
GENERAL A.A. KIREYEV, unpublished diaries.
A.N. SCHWARTZ, unpublished memoirs and correspondence.
*Tsentral'nyy gosudarstvennyy istoricheskiy arkhiv Okt'yabrskoy Revolyutsii* (Moscow)
P.A. SABUROV, private correspondence.
COUNT V.N. LAMBSDORFF, private correspondence.
*Tsentral'nyy gosudarstvennyy istoricheskiy arkhiv* (Leningrad)
P.A. SABUROV, official memoranda.

PRIMARY SOURCES

D.I. ABRIKOSSOW, *Revelations of a Russian Diplomat* (Seattle, 1964).

E.A. ADAMOV, *Konstantinopol' i prolivy* (Moscow, 1925).

*Adres kalendar' Rossiyskoy Imperii* (Petersburg, 1914).

*Almanach de Saint Petersbourg: cour, monde et ville* (Petersburg, 1914).

N. DE BASILY *Memoirs* (Stanford, 1973).

COUNT L. BERCHTOLD, 'Russia, Austria and the World War', *Contemporary Review*, CXXXIII (1928).

I.V. BESTUZHEV, 'Bor'ba v pravyashchikh krugakh Rossii po voprosam vneshney politiki vo vremya Bosniyskogo krizisa', *Istoricheskiy Arkhiv*, V (1962).

E.J. BING (ed.), *The Letters of Tsar Nicholas and the Empress Marie* (London, 1937).

M. BOGITSHEVICH, *The Causes of the War* (London, 1920).

P.S BOTKIN, *Kartinki diplomaticheskoy zhizni* (Paris, 1930).

E. BOURGEOIS, *Manuel Historique de Politique Etrangère*, vols 2, 3 (Paris, 1898 and 1906)

*British Documents on the Origins of the War*, G.P. Gooch and H. Temperley (eds), II vols (London, 1927–38).

A.A. BRUSILOV, *Moi vospominaniya* (Moscow, 1963).

A.N. BRYANCHANINOV (ed.), *Interesy na Balkanakh i pravitel'stvennoye soobshcheniye* (Petersburg, 1913).

N.V. CHARYKOV, *Glimpses of High Politics* (London, 1931).

N.V. CHARYKOV, 'Reminiscences of Nicholas II', *Contemporary Review*, CXXXIV (1928).

N.V. CHARYKOV, 'Sazonoff', *Contemporary Review*, CXXXIII (1928).

YU N. DANILOV, *Rossiya v mirovoy voyne* (Berlin, 1924).

A.I. DENIKIN, *The Career of a Tsarist Officer* (Minneapolis, 1975).

*Die Grosse Politik der Europäischen Kabinette 1871–1914* (Berlin, 1922).

S. DOBROROL'SKY, 'La Mobilisation de L' Armée Russe en 1914', *Revue d' Histoire de la Guerre Mondiale*, I, 1923.

*Documents Allemands Relatiefs à l'Origine de la Guerre*, (trans. C. Jordan) (Paris, 1922).

*Documents Diplomatiques Francais*, 2^e Serie (Paris, 1930–5); 3^e Serie (Paris, 1929–36).

I. GEISS, *July 1914* (New York, 1974).

N.K. GIERS, *The Education of a Russian Statesman*, C. and B. Jelavich (eds) (California, 1962).

F. GOLDER, *Documents on Russian History 1914–1917* (New York, 1927).

N.F. GRANT (ed.), *The Kaiser's Letters to the Tsar* (London, n.d.).

*Grazhdanin*, (Petersburg, 1908–13).

*Imperatorskiy Aleksandrovskiy Litsey: XL Kurs* (Petersburg, 1909).

A.P. IZVOL'SKY, *Au Service de la Russie, Alexandre Iswolsky, Correspondence Diplomatique*, 2 vols (Paris, 1937 and 1939).

A.P. IZVOL'SKY, *The Memoirs of Alexander Iswolski* (London).

F.I. KALINYCHEV, *Gosudarstvennaya Duma v dokumentakh i materialakh* (Moscow, 1957).

A.D. KALMYKOV, *Memoirs of a Russian Diplomat* (Yale, 1971).

J.S. KELTIE (ed.), *The Statesman's Year-Book* (London, 1912, 1913, 1914).

P. KNYAZHNIN (P. POPOV pseud.) *Shest' let v Imperatorskom Aleksandrovskom Litseye* (Petersburg, 1911).

V.N. KOKOVTSOV, *Out of My Past* (Stanford, 1935).

*Krasnyy Arkhiv*, 'Russko-germanskiye otnosheniya', I (1922).

'Russko-germanskiy dogovor 1905 goda', v (1924).

'Konstantinopol' i prolivy', VI and VII (1924).

'Rossiya i Alzhesiraskaya konferentsiya' XLI, (1930).

'Novye dokumenty ob Alzhesiraskoy konferentsii i zayme 1906 g', XLIV (1931).

'Proyekt zakhvata Bosfora v 1896 g', XLVII (1931).

'Anglo-russkoye sopernichestvo v Persii v 1890–1906 gg', LVI (1933).

'K istorii Potsdamskogo soglasheniya 1911 g', LVIII (1933).

'Iz zapisok A.F. Redigera', LX (1933).

'K voprosu o podgotovke mirovoy voyny', LXIV (1934).

'K istorii anglo-russkogo soglasheniya 1907 g', LXIX (1935).

S.E. KRYZHANOVSKY, *Vospominaniya* (Berlin, n.d.)

COUNT G. VON LAMBSDORFF, *Die Militarbevollmachtigen Kaiser Wilhelms II am Zarenhofe 1904–1914* (Berlin, 1937).

COUNT V.N. LAMBSDORFF, *Dnevnik V.N. Lamzdorfa*, A.F. Rothstein (ed). (Moscow, 1926 and 1934).

PRINCE A.A. LIEVEN, *Dukh i ditsiplina nashego flota* (Petersburg, 1914).

F. MARTENS, *Sovremennoye mezhdunarodnoye pravo tsivilizovannykh narodov*, 2 vols (Petersburg, 1895).

*Materialy po istorii franko-russkikh otnosheniy za 1910–1914 gg* (Moscow, 1922).

*Mezhdunarodnye Otnosheniya v Epokhu Imperializma*, 2nd and 3rd series (Moscow, 1931–40).

P.N. MILYUKOV, *Vospominaniya*, 2 vols (New York, 1955).

MINISTERSTVO INOSTRANNYKH DEL, *Kommissiya po reorganizatsii zagranichnoy sluzhby, svod otchotov zagranichnykh ustanovleniy ministerstva na voprosnik kasatel'no reorganizatsii zagranichnoy sluzhby* (Petersburg, n.d.)

MINISTERSTVO INOSTRANNYKH DEL, *Svod rasporyazheniy ministerstva inostrannykh del po departamentu lichnogo sostava i khozyaystvennykh del (Petersburg, 1912).*

*Moskovskiy Yezhenedel'nik* (Moscow, 1906–10).

A.A. MOSSOLOV, *At the Court of the Last Tsar* (London, 1935).

A.N. NAUMOV, *Iz utselevshikh vospominaniy,* 2 vols (New York, 1955).

A.V. NEKLYUDOV, *Diplomatic Reminiscences* (London, 1920).

*Novoye Vremya* (Petersburg, 1906–14).

P.V. PETROV (ed.), *Voyennyy sobesednik* (Petersburg, 1910).

*Pièces Diplomatiques Relatives aux Antecedents de la Guerre de 1914,* trans. by C. Jordan (Paris, 1922).

R. PIPES (ed.), *P.B. Struve: Collected Works in Fifteen Volumes* (Ann Arbor, 1970).

M. POKROWSKI, *Drei Konferenzen (zur Vorgeschichte des Krieges)* (1920).

A.A. POLIVANOV, *Iz dnevnikov i vospominaniy po dolzhnosti voyennogo ministra i yego pomoshchnika 1907–1916* (Moscow, 1924).

*Pol'noye Sobraniye Zakonov Rossiyskoy Imperii,* 3rd Series, vol. XXXV (Petersburg, 1908).

*Rech'* (Petersburg, 1908–14).

T. RIHA, *Readings in Russian Civilisation* (Chicago, 1964).

BARON R.R. ROSEN, *Forty Years of Diplomacy,* 2 vols (London, 1922).

P.P. RYABUSHINSKY (ed.), *Velikaya Rossiya,* 2 vols (Moscow, 1910-11).

S.D. SAZONOV, *Fateful Years 1909–16* (London, 1928).

N. SCHEBEKO, *Souvenirs* (Paris, 1936).

YU. YA. SOLOV'YOV, *Vospominaniya diplomata* (Moscow, 1959).

*Stenograficheskiy otchot Gosudarstvennogo Soveta* (Petersburg, 1906–17).

*Stenograficheskiy otchot Gosudarstvennoy Dumy* (Petersburg, 1906–17).

G. STOKES, 'The Serbian Documents from 1914: A Preview', *Journal of Modern History,* XLVIII (1976) Supplement.

P.B. STRUVE (*et al.*), *Vekhi. Sbornik stat'ey o russkoi intelligentsii* (Moscow, 1909).

V. SUKHOMLINOV, *Vospominaniya* (Berlin, 1924).

BARON M. TAUBE, *La Politique Russe d' avant-Guerre* (Paris, 1928).

N.V. TCHARYKOW (see under N.V. CHARYKOV).

XXXI *Kurs Imperatorskogo Aleksandrovskogo Litseya cherez 25 let posle vypuska 1871–1896* (Petersburg, 1896).

PRINCESS O. TRUBETSKAYA, *Vospominaniya sestry* (New York, 1953).

PRINCE E.N. TRUBETSKOY, *Otechestvennaya voyna i yeya dukhovnyy smysl' (Moscow, 1915).*

PRINCE E.N. TRUBETSKOY, *Vospominaniya* (Sofia, 1922).

PRINCE G.N. TRUBETSKOY, *Pamyati knyaz'ya Gr. N. Trubetskogo: Sbornik stat'ey* (Paris, 1930).

*Un Livre Noir: Diplomatie d' Avant-Guerre d'après Les Documents des Archives Russes,* preface by R. Marchand, 2 vols (Paris, n.d.)

P.A. VALUYEV, *Dnevnik P.A. Valuyeva,* P.A. Zayonchkovsky (ed.) 2 vols (Moscow, 1961)

G. VERNADSKY (ed.), *A Source Book for Russian History from Early Times to 1917,* Vol.3 (Yale, 1972).

S. YU. WITTE, *Vospominaniya,* 3 vols (Moscow, 1960).

SECONDARY WORKS

L. ALBERTINI, *The Origins of the War of 1914,* 3 vols (London, 1952).

M. ALDANOV, 'P.N. Durnovo, Prophet of War and Revolution', *Russian Review,* II (1942).

W.E.D. ALLEN, *The Ukraine* (Cambridge, 1940).

R.H. ALLSHOUSE, *Alexander Izvolskii and Russian Foreign Policy 1910–1914* (Case Western Reserve University Ph.D., 1976).

G.A. ARUTYUNOV, *Rabocheye dvizheniye v Rossii v period novogo revolyutsionnogo pod'yoma 1910–1914* (Moscow, 1975).

I.I. ASTAF'YEV, *Russko-germanskiye diplomaticheskiye otnosheniya 1905–1911 gg* (Moscow, 1972).

A. YA AVREKH, *Stolypin i tret'ya Duma* (Moscow, 1968).

S.A. BELOKUROV, *Ocherk istorii Ministerstva Inostrannykh Del, 1802–1902* (Petersburg, 1902).

V.R. BERGHAHN, *Germany and the Approach of War in 1914* (London, 1973).

I.V. BESTUZHEV, *Bor'ba v Rossii po voprosam vneshney politiki 1906–1910* (Moscow, 1961).

B. BONWETSCH, 'Handelspolitik und Industrialisierung' in D. Geyer (ed.) *Wirtschaft und Gesellschaft in vorrevolutionaren Russland* (1975).

B.I. BOVYKIN, *Iz istorii vozniknoveniya pervoy mirovoy voyny: otnosheniya Rossii i Frantsii v 1912–1914 gg* (Moscow, 1961).

J.F.N. BRADLEY, 'Czech Pan-Slavism before the First World War', *Slavonic and East European Review,* XL (1961).

F.R. BRIDGE, *From Sadowa to Sarajevo* (London, 1972).

P.A. BURYSHKIN, *Moskva kupecheskaya* (New York, 1954).

P. CHASLES, *Le Parlement Russe* (Paris, 1909).

M. CHERNIAVSKY, *Tsar and People* (New Haven, 1960).

D.R. COSTELLO, 'Novoe Vremia and the Conservative Dilemma

1911–1914', *Russian Review*, XXXVII (1978).

R.J. CRAMPTON, 'The Decline of the Concert of Europe in the Balkans 1913–1914', *Slavonic and East European Review*, LII (1974).

O. CRISP, *Studies in the Russian Economy before 1914* (London, 1976).

O. CRISP, 'The Russian Liberals and the 1906 Anglo-French Loan to Russia', *Slavonic and East European Review*, XXXIX (1961).

YU N. DANILOV, *Velikiy Knyaz' Nikolay Nikolayevich* (Paris, 1930).

T. DARLINGTON, *Board of Education: Special Reports on Educational Subjects*, Vol.23, *Education in Russia* (London, 1909).

R. EDELMAN, *Gentry Politics on the Eve of the Russian Revolution* (Rutgers, 1980).

F. FISCHER, *War of Illusions* (London, 1975).

D. GEYER, *Der Russische Imperialismus* (Gottingen, 1977).

R. GIRAULT, *Emprunts Russes et Investissements Francqis en Russie, 1887–1914* (Paris, 1973).

N.N. GOLOVIN, *Voyenniya usiliya Rossii v mirovoy voyne*, 2 vols (Paris, 1939).

M.R. GORDON, 'Domestic Conflict and the Origins of the First World War: the British and the German Cases', *Journal of Modern History*, XLVI (1974).

P.R. GREGORY, 'Russian National Income in 1913: Some Insights into Russian Economic Development', *Quarterly Journal of Economics*, XC (1976).

L.H. HAIMSON (ed.), *The Politics of Rural Russia, 1905–1914* (Indiana, 1979).

L.H. HAIMSON, 'The Problem of Social Stability in Urban Russia', *Slavic Review*, XXIII, XXIV (1964 and 1965).

E.C. HELMREICH, *The Diplomacy of the Balkan Wars* (Harvard, 1938).

G. HOSKING, *The Russian Constitutional Experiment* (Cambridge, 1973).

J.F. HUTCHINSON, 'The Octobrists and the Future of Russia as a Great Power', *Slavonic and East European Review*, L (1972).

A.V. IGNAT'YEV, *Russko-angliyskiye otnosheniya nakanune pervoy mirovoy voyny* (Moscow, 1962).

K.H. JARAUSCH, *The Enigmatic Chancellor* (Yale, 1973).

J. JOLL, '1914: The Unspoken Assumptions' in H.W. Koch (ed.), *The Origins of the First World War* (London, 1972).

R.A. KANN, *The Multinational Empire*, 2 vols (New York, 1950).

F. KAZEMZADEH, *Russia and Britain in Persia 1864–1914: A Study in Imperialism* (Newhaven, 1968).

P. KENEZ, 'A Profile of the Pre-Revolutionary Officer Corps',

*California Slavic Studies*, VII (1973).

P. KENEZ, 'The Ideology of the White Movement', *Soviet Studies*, XXXII (1980).

G.F. KENNAN, *The Decline of Bismarck's European Order: Franco-Russian Relations, 1875–1890* (Princeton, 1979).

P. KENNEDY (ed.), *The Warplans of the Great Powers 1880–1914* (London, 1979).

A. KERSNOVSKY, *Istoriya Russkoy armii, chast'3, 1881–1917* (Belgrade, 1935).

H. KOHN, *Panslavism* (New York, 1960).

K.A. KROVOSHEIN, *A.V. Krivoshein, yego znacheniye v istorii Rossii nachala xx veka* (Paris, 1973).

A.N. KULOMZIN, *Opytnyy podshchot sovremennogo sostoyaniya nashego narodnogo obrazovaniya* (Petersburg, 1912).

LALAYEV, *Istoricheskiy ocherk voyenno-uchebnykh zavedeniy* (Petersburg, 1880).

W.L. LANGER, *The Franco-Russian Alliance* (Harvard, 1929).

D.C.B. LIEVEN, 'Bureaucratic Authoritarianism in Late Imperial Russia: The Personality, Career and Opinions of P. N. Durnovo', *Historical Journal*, XXVI (1983).

D.C.B. LIEVEN, 'Bureaucratic Liberalism in Late Imperial Russia: The Personality, Career and Opinions of A.N. Kulomzin', *Slavonic and East European Review*, LX (1982).

D.C.B. LIEVEN, 'Pro-Germans and Russian Foreign Policy 1890–1914', *International History Review*, 11 (1980).

D.C.B. LIEVEN, 'The Russian Civil Service under Nicholas II: Some Variations on the Bureaucratic theme', *Jahrbücher für Geschichte Osteuropas*, XXIX (1982).

U. LISZKOWSKI, *Zwischen Liberalismus und Imperialismus* (Stuttgart, 1974).

J. LONG, 'Franco-Russian Relations during the Russo-Japanese War', *Slavonic and East European Review*, LII (1974).

M. MAKSIMOVSKY, *Istoricheskiy ocherk razvitiya glavnogo inzhenernego uchilishcha 1819–1869* (Petersburg, 1869).

A.Z. MANFRED, *Obrazovaniye russko-frantsuzkogo soyuza* (Moscow, 1975).

A.J. MARDER, *From the Dreadnought to Scapa Flow. The Royal Navy in the Fisher era*, vol.1 *The Road to War 1904–1914* (London, 1961); vol.2 *The war years: to the eve of Jutland* (London, 1965).

V.A. MARINOV, *Rossiya i Yaponiya pered pervoy mirovoy voynoy* (Moscow, 1974).

D.R. MATHIEU, *The Role of Russia in French Foreign Policy, 1908–1914* (Stanford University, Ph.D.,1969).

A.J. MAYER, 'Internal Causes and Purposes of War in Europe, 1870–1956: A Research Assignment', *Journal of Modern History*, XXXXI (1969).

L. MENASHE, ' "A Liberal with Spurs": Alexander Guchkov, a Russian Bourgeois in Politics', *Russian Review*, XXVI (1967).

G. MICHON, *The Franco-Russian Alliance* (London, 1929).

W.E. MOSSE, 'Imperial favourite: V.P. Meshchersky and the Grazhdanin' *Slavonic and East European Review*, LIX (1981).

BARON B. NOLDE, *L'Alliance Franco-Russe* (Paris, 1936).

S.S. OLDENBURG, *Last Tsar: Nicholas II: His Reign and His Russia*, 4 vols (Gulf Breeze, 1975).

*Pamyatnaya knizhka Imperatorskogo Aleksandrovskogo Litseya*, (Petersburg, 1856, 1886 and 1899).

*Pamyatnaya knizhka litseyistov*, (Petersburg, 1907).

M. PERRINS, 'The Council for State Defence, 1905–1909: A Study in Russian Bureaucratic Politics', *Slavonic and East European Review*, LVIII (1980).

M.B. PETROVICH, *A History of Modern Serbia*, 2 vols (New York, 1976).

B.C. PINCHUK, *The Octobrists in the Third Duma 1907–1912* (Seattle, 1974).

R. PIPES, *Struve: Liberal on the Right, 1905–1944* (Harvard, 1980).

R. PIPES, 'Russian Conservatism in the Second Half of the Nineteenth Century', *Slavic Review*, XXX (1971).

A.P. POGREBINSKY, *Gosudarstvennye finansy tsarskoy Rossii v epokhu imperializma* (Moscow, 1968).

J.G. PURVES and D.A. WEST, *War and Society in the Nineteenth Century Russian Empire* (Toronto, 1972).

C. READ, *Religion, Revolution and the Russian Intelligentsia 1900–1912* (London, 1979).

H. ROGGER, *National Consciousness in Eighteenth Century Russia (Harvard, 1960)*.

H. ROGGER, 'Reflections on Russian Conservatism 1861–1905', *Jahrbücher für Geschichte Osteuropas*, XIV (1966).

H. ROGGER, 'The Formation of the Russian Right 1900–6', *California Slavic Studies*, III (1964).

H. ROGGER, 'The Skobelev Phenomenon', *Oxford Slavonic Papers*, IX (1976)

H. ROGGER, 'Was there a Russian Fascism? The Union of the Russian People', *Journal of Modern History*, XXXVI (1964).

R.A. ROOSA, *The Association of Industry and Trade 1906–1914*, (Columbia University Ph.D., 1967).

W.G. ROSENBERG, *Liberals in the Russian Revolution* (Princeton, 1974).

A. ROSSOS, *Russia and the Balkans 1909–14* (Stanford University, PhD., 1971).

I.I. ROSTUNOV, *Russkiy front pervoy mirovoy voyny* (Moscow, 1976).

E. ROZENTAL', *Diplomaticheskaya istoriya russko-frantsuzkogo soyuza v nachale xx veka* (Moscow, 1960).

A.A. RUBETZ, *Kratkaya istoricheskaya pamyatka Imperatorskogo Aleksandrovskogo, byvshego Tsarskosel'skogo Litseya* (Petersburg, 1911).

B.E. SCHMITT, *The Annexation of Bosnia 1908–9* (Cambridge, 1937).

H. SETON-WATSON, *The Russian Empire 1801–1917* (Oxford, 1967).

B.M. SHAPOSHNIKOV, *Mozg armii*, 3 vols (Moscow, 1927).

K.F. SHATSILLO, *Rossiya pered pervoy mirovoy voynoy* (Moscow, 1974).

K.F. SHATSILLO, *Russkiy imperializm i razvitiye flota* (Moscow, 1968).

A. SINEL, 'The Socialisation of the Russian Bureaucratic Elite, 1811–1917', *Russian History*, III (1976).

D.W. SPRING, 'Russian Imperialism in Asia in 1914', *Cahiers du Monde Russe et Sovietique*, XX (1979).

D.W. SPRING, 'The Trans-Persian Project and Anglo-Russian Relations 1909–1914', *Slavonic and East European Review*, LIV (1976).

Z.S. STEINER, *Britain and the Origins of the First World War* (London, 1977).

N. STONE, *The Eastern Front 1914–1917* (London, 1975).

V.N. STROYEV, *Stoletiye Sobstvennoy Yego Imperatorskogo Velichestva kantselyarii* (Petersburg, 1912).

M. SZEFTEL, *The Russian Constitution of April 23 1906* (Brussels, 1976).

E.C. THADEN, *Conservative Nationalism in Nineteenth Century Russia* (Seattle, 1964).

E.C. THADEN, *Russia and the Balkan Alliance of 1912* (Pennsylvania, 1965).

R.O. TOMPKINS, *Anglo-Russian Diplomatic Relations* (North Texas State University, Ph. D., 1975).

L.C.F. TURNER, *Origins of the First World War* (London, 1970).

L.C.F. TURNER, 'The Russian Mobilisation in 1914' *Journal of Contemporary History*, III (1968).

K.B. VINOGRADOV, *Bosniyskiy krizis 1908–9 gg* (Leningrad, 1964).

P. VYSNY, *Neo-slavism and the Czechs* (Cambridge, 1977).

A. WALICKI, *The Slavophile Controversy* (Oxford, 1975).

J.L. WEST, *The Moscow Progressists: Russian Industrialists in Liberal*

*Politics 1905–1914* (Princeton University, Ph.D., 1975).

J.N. WESTWOOD, *A History of Russian Railways* (London, 1964).

J.A. WHITE, *The Diplomacy of the Russo-Japanese War* (Princeton, 1974).

A.K. WILDMAN, *The End of the Russian Imperial Army* (Princeton, 1980).

W.T. WILFONG, *Rebuilding the Russian Army 1905–1914* (Indiana University, Ph.D., 1977).

H.W. WILLIAMS, *Russia of the Russians* (London, 1914).

P.N. YEFREMOV, *Vneshnyaya politika Rossii 1907–1914* (Moscow, 1961).

A.S. YERUSALIMSKY, *Vneshnyaya politika i diplomatiya germanskogo imperializma v kontse* XIXv (Moscow, 1951).

A.M. ZAYONCHKOVSKY, *Podgotovka Rossii k imperialisticheskoy voyne. Ocherki voyennoy podgotovki i pervonachal'nykh planov* (Moscow, 1926).

A.M. ZAYONCHKOVSKY, *Podgotovka Rossii k mirovoy voyne v mezhdunarodnom otnoshenii* (Moscow, 1926).

P.A. ZAYONCHKOVSKY, *Samoderzhaviye i russkaya armiya na rubezhe* XIX–XX *stoletiy* (Moscow, 1973).

# Index